The Beatles and Beyond

For my loving wife Wendy
and
for my talented and inspirational granddaughters Daisy and Alice, who not only coerced me into writing my memoirs, but also researched and assembled the book to share with their cousins James, Laura, Jonathan, Henry, Lotte and
Olivia, as a record of the social fabric that existed in the time of my generation.

The Beatles and Beyond

The Memoirs of Don Short

WYMER
PUBLISHING
Bedford, England

First published in Great Britain in 2020
by Wymer Publishing
www.wymerpublishing.co.uk
Tel: 01234 326691
Wymer Publishing is a trading name of Wymer (UK) Ltd

ISBN: 978-1-912782-34-5

Typeset by Andy Bishop / 1016 Sarpsborg.
Printed by CMP, Dorset, England.

A catalogue record for this book is available from the British Library.

'I remember Don's story about the break-up [of The Beatles] because I was a news sub on The Sun at the time. When the first edition of the Mirror arrived, the newsdesk was unable to verify whether it was true.

'While we were dithering over what to do, wondering if we should follow the Mirror or not, the deputy editor (and former Mirror executive), Bernard Shrimsley, arrived on the floor to say: "If Don Short says it's true then it is." There cannot be a better tribute to a journalist than that. And he was, of course, bang on the money.'

[from Roy Greenslade, 'Down Memory Lane with the Reporter who Coined the Term Beatlemania'. Roy Greenslade's Media blog, Guardian online. 26 March 2014.]

CHAPTER ONE

NOT THE FIFTH BEATLE —
BUT CLOSE ENOUGH

It was the night I was never going to forget. That momentous night of 9th April 1970.

My world exclusive was splashed, in banner headlines, on the Daily Mirror's front page: 'Paul Quits The Beatles.'

Unimaginable drama was to unfold. While Fleet Street rivals were left trailing in a daze, greater shockwaves of despair and consternation reverberated across the world. It was a world left asking "Where will we be without the Beatles?"

There could be no other interpretation. Those four fateful words of the headline signalled the irretrievable end to a tumultuous, exuberant era that had changed the lives of millions.

At the time, I was the Daily Mirror's Showbusiness columnist and I would always have cause to remember the events of that night.

I had been at my desk for most of the day. As evening approached, the newsroom was in full throttle. Noise levels were at their peak. The metallic rattle of typewriter keys tapped out by reporters desperate to meet the first edition deadline resounded interminably across the floor. Copy boys darted through the aisles, while editors gathered in a huddle at the Picture Desk to sift through the day's crop of photographs.

It was a familiar scene as I prepared to go home. I had just put on my coat and locked down my attaché case when my office phone rang. I was halted in my tracks and felt a little annoyed that I was being potentially delayed. It would have been easy just to let the wretched thing ring out. But, knowing I could easily miss a story by ignoring the call, I reluctantly picked it up.

Instantly, I recognised the voice of one of my Beatles' contacts. From the quiver in his tone, I knew that he had something serious to impart.

"What is it?" I asked him, as he kept repeating that I would not believe the news he was about to give me.

Finally, quelling his emotion, he stuttered out: "Paul is quitting Don. It's definite. It's all over. The Beatles are breaking up. Can you believe that?"

I could. My other sources had been hinting at a break-up for some months. Rumours had already reached me that John Lennon and Paul McCartney were at loggerheads over the band's future direction, while George and Ringo were staying neutral on the side-lines. But no journalist had been able to break the story. It was clearly the scoop of a lifetime.

I slammed down the phone and called the home of a Beatles aide who was an executive of their Apple company. There was some reluctance on his part to elaborate on the situation, but, vitally, he confirmed the story.

It was close to 8:00pm. The Night Editor and his backbench team were frantically searching for a front-page story — nothing was coming out of the political scene from Westminster and things were unusually quiet from my chums on the crime beat at Scotland Yard. The deadline hour was rapidly approaching. The Beatles breaking up was like a gift waiting to be unwrapped for those of us still in the office.

I alerted the News Desk of the story I was about to deliver. The whole room was on tenterhooks. Was it as good as I had described? My faithful Imperial typewriter went into overdrive with a copy boy collecting each page as I thrashed out the story.

There could be no fear of rejection. My copy streamed through the sub's desk and, in a bold typeface normally reserved for earthquakes, plane crashes and other dreadful disasters, the Mirror's front page first edition broke the news: 'Paul is Quitting the Beatles' and then in later editions, simply: 'Paul Quits The Beatles.'

When the early editions hit the streets, our rivals could only poach my copy to catch up on the story. It was also relayed internationally by Reuters and the Press Association on their wire services. Into the early hours, the Mirror's switchboard was swamped with calls from global newspapers wishing to confirm and expand the story. I was hauled onto the news desk to help and spoke with several radio stations across the world, including CBS in New York.

By morning the pandemonium had grown. Distraught fans continued to block our switchboard and many teenagers assembled outside the Mirror's offices in Holborn Circus, sobbing in sheer disbelief. Paul McCartney issued a statement saying he had split because of personal, business and musical differences, adding later: "I have a better time with my family."

In the cold light of the morning, it dawned on me that this could very well be my last major story on The Beatles as a group.

It had been a long and incredible journey. Wearily, as I drove home, I had time to reflect on how it all began. My mind flashed back to June 1963 — the year when I wrote the very first national newspaper story on the Beatles.

It did not reflect too well on John Lennon, who, inebriated at a party in Liverpool to celebrate Paul's 21st birthday, had got into an altercation with local DJ Bob Wooler. Lennon had lashed out at him when he had apparently suggested that the Beatle was gay as he had just returned from a holiday in Spain with the group's homosexual manager Brian Epstein. A hungover Lennon apologised the next morning for his actions and Wooler decided not to go to his lawyers, but was left with a black eye, bruised ribs and torn knuckles.

John told me: "Why did I have to go and punch my best friend? I was so high I didn't realise what I was doing."

It was time to investigate things on the ground. Who exactly were The Beatles?

I travelled north and before I descended the steps of the dark Liverpool Cavern, there was another club I had to visit. Known as the Blue Angel, its owner was none other than Allan Williams, a man who found fame for all the wrong reasons. He had been the Beatles manager but then handed the group over to Brian Epstein, whose family ran a record store in the City. Allan told him: "You can have them — but if I were you, I wouldn't touch them with a barge pole. They'll never make it."

Allan appeared a sorrowful figure as he thought over his decision. "I know. I know. It was the biggest mistake of my life" — which was the understatement of the decade. But Allan Williams was not the only player in the field who turned the Beatles down. Dick Rowe of the mighty Decca record company also suffered prolonged ridicule for similarly turning the Beatles away.

Fortunately for Rowe, there was a reprieve that probably saved his standing. He signed the Rolling Stones and all was forgiven by the hierarchy.

In the meantime, The Beatles were snapped up by George Martin, a shrewd and brilliant producer for EMI. It was the beginning of a long and fruitful association.

My own relationship with the Beatles flourished paving the way for many exclusives down the line.

I toured with them for their first major concert tour. Chaos broke out from hysterical fans all the way, from Cheltenham to Leeds and London, and every stop on the tour.

By sheer chance, I may have spawned a strand of their fame when I was credited with coining the term 'Beatlemania.' For the Daily Mirror it was a banner headline blazed across its pages and cribbed without credit by rival papers in the days to follow. It was the only term that seemed to fit the scenes I witnessed at one of the earliest Beatles concerts; the cacophony of hysterical fans as they mobbed the stage; the electric energy in the room. The atmosphere was absolutely manic. Beatlemania became a live rhizome in the press and it was here to stay.

"Do you see what you have started?" remarked the sub who had projected my copy.

From that day on, the Mirror gave me carte blanche to pursue the Fab Four. Every move, every activity involving John, Paul, George and Ringo became essential information. It was necessary to unearth their roots in Liverpool, their foundation as a group as well as trace their busy, unreported days playing gigs in Hamburg before chasing the trail back to the Cavern.

I flew to Hamburg and within a day or two stumbled upon The Beatles' former landlady Frau Rosa Hoffman who charged them fifty shillings a week to kip down on her lakeside houseboat. She also worked cleaning at the Top Ten Club where the Beatles and other British rock 'n' roll wannabes played their first gigs. Peter Eckhorn, who ran the club, disclosed that he paid the Beatles £3-10s a night.

The night time delights of Hamburg certainly made their impression on the Beatles. John Lennon was to tell me in later times that their hit record 'Ticket To Ride' had been inspired by the German city's red light district where girls of the night had to have medical certificates before they could peddle their wares. It was a believable theory.

The Mirror, anxious to retain its position as the world's biggest daily newspaper (with a circulation in excess of 5,000,000 copies recorded in 1969) recognised the advantages in giving maximum space to the adventures of these new mop heads on the block. That penetrating focus by the Mirror added another 100,000 copies of the paper a day at the height of The Beatles fame and their ultimate recognition as the world's greatest band.

With their charisma and emotive music, The Beatles reshaped the world. They wove exhilaration through sound into the fabric of society, influencing fashions and challenging the status quo. I felt privileged to have a ringside seat monitoring their lives and careers. I toured with them across many parts of the world and formed a strong bond with them. But each side knew its boundaries.

I had to ensure that my friendship with them did not compromise my aspirations as a journalist, while for their part John, Paul, George and Ringo were urged by their advisers to guard their innermost secrets. Their tenacious road managers, Neil Aspinall and Mal Evans were a tight-lipped duo, all too aware of the consequences of talking to the Press. To some degree, it became a cat and mouse game, particularly in the early days of our association. Gradually, through reporting accurately on their evolution as a band, I earned the respect of the foursome's inner circle.

That said, the group was curious about my sources. An internal probe was conducted within the Beatles empire when I revealed that John was the only member of the group who was married. He had married his girlfriend from art school, Cynthia Powell, in 1962. Epstein was furious that the news had leaked out. It was an era when agents and managers mistakenly believed that music fans invariably flocked to unmarried stars but would shun any who were married.

George Harrison was often convinced I had a mole somewhere in the organisation. Realising too many 'leaks' were occurring, the band changed their strategy and decided to get me 'on side'. I happily occupied a role that my rivals on other papers envied: access to the Beatles' home phone numbers was something of a trump card.

Going to ground was all part of the Beatles formula when they were off duty, especially early on.

One morning in March 1964, I got a call from one of my contacts who said that John Lennon and George Harrison were taking a break from the mayhem of their concert schedule and were heading for Ireland. John and George had chartered a private plane from Biggin Hill with their respective partners, John's wife Cynthia and fashion model Pattie Boyd, soon-to-be George's bride.

The Beatles and Beyond

Once more, I thumbed the pages of my well-sullied contacts book, a priceless tool that I relied on frequently throughout my career as it contained a list of ex-directory numbers. Who would be able to help me in Ireland? I made a shoal of calls and early one morning I got a crucial lead from Shannon in County Clare. Two suites had been booked at the luxurious Dromoland Castle hotel for a party under the name of Spencer, but the four young guests did not fit that identity. My source recognised John Lennon and George Harrison: "There are two girls with them but I couldn't say who they are..." my contact obliged.

I flew out to the town of Shannon that night and checked into Dromoland Castle. There was no sign of the Beatles and the hotel staff denied their presence, having been well tipped to ensure secrecy. The bellboy and other staff eyed me with suspicion. From their mannerisms — nervous, jaunty — I could tell that the Beatles were safely installed somewhere within the castle walls.

I hired a car and drove off. I found a village inn less than a mile down the road: the kind of pub in which locals would surely congregate and among them, I figured, might be the odd worker from the big hotel I had just left. Sure enough, I was quickly in conversation with two off duty porters with an admirable capacity for Guinness. "Not much happens in these parts" said one. "Who would have thought the Beatles would come to Dromoland Castle?"

Very soon, I had a roughly drawn map of the hotel's layout and the location of the adjoining suites now occupied by the 'Spencer' party. I bought a bottle of Scotch and returned to my room in the hotel. I identified from the drawing that I would be seen if I took the main staircase up to the Beatles' suites. But outside my room was a small patio, the other side of which was a parapet just below one of the suites. Putting aside my fears of an attack of vertigo, I climbed out through my window, crossed the patio and trod warily onto the parapet vaguely lit by the hotel's floodlights below. I clambered to some masonry above the parapet and carefully inched along to a turreted window and peered through. I felt cheered to see the Beatles spread out on the floor playing cards, poker or three-card brag. John and George looked up at me in astonishment. I showed them the bottle of Scotch indicating that I had brought them a present and John opened the window and leaned forward: "You had better come in," he laughed. George joked: "Yeah, just pass in the Scotch just in case you fall. We wouldn't want to waste a bottle of Scotch, would we John?" Pattie and Cynthia were smiling as I scrambled into the safety of the room. We spent the evening chatting over Scotch and cokes, the Beatles' drink of the day, and played cards, pontoon for pennies.

I called the news desk the next morning. We had an exclusive break on the story and I suggested that we fly a photographer out. I visualised it on the pages of the paper as a happy foursome appearing for a nice holiday snap. But an hour or two before the photographer was due to arrive, the Beatles had a change of tactic. During the night Brian Epstein had called. He did not want them to appear in any photographs with Cynthia and Pattie, again fearing that fans would be lost if they found out about the band's existing romantic attachments.

So, following Epstein's advice, the Beatles decided to move out of the hotel and left me stranded. I ran to every perceptible exit of the imposing stone hotel building, but I never caught sight of them. I dashed through the kitchens to the courtyard. One large wicker laundry basket steered by a kitchen hand whooshed past me followed by another, which were then wheeled into the back of a waiting laundry van. I doubled back into the hotel, well-versed in the building's layout, still searching for the missing party. But there was no sign of them. One of the porters whose acquaintance I had made in the village pub was on duty in the hallway, now an imperious looking figure in his green livery, shook his head and whispered to me: "They've gone..."

I later learned how the Beatles had escaped. I had been cleverly duped. Those two laundry baskets that had swept so innocently past me in the kitchen were the means of their escape. John and George had occupied one of the two laundry baskets and Pattie and Cynthia the other. I was speechless. The Beatles in a basket. Who would have thought it? Imagine the headline!

Pattie told me afterwards: "It was our only ruse to escape. One of the waiters suggested it to us and we just went along with it. We got to the airport in the back of that laundry van."

Beatlemania was now erupting all over the world. The big band sound was toppling, obliterated by Ringo's drums and the electric guitars of John, George and Paul. This was the Mersey Sound; raw but pulsating and blasting the airwaves, with songs like 'Love Me Do' and 'Twist and Shout.'

It was in November 1963 when the Beatles claimed their most significant triumph. They headed the cast at the Royal Variety show at the London Palladium. John won over the bow-tied audience and millions of viewers when he bawled into the microphone before the band sang 'Twist and Shout': "The people in the cheaper seats clap your hands. And the rest of you, just rattle your jewellery." It was to become an iconic quote. Even the Queen Mother in the Royal box was seen to laugh amid the wild cheers of the audience.

My friendship with the Beatles grew in mutual trust over the months ahead. Things got social. Paul, George and Pattie came around to dinner one night at my home and it was a relaxed fun-filled and off-the-record evening. My six-year-old daughter Amanda couldn't sleep so Paul settled her back in bed and sang a lullaby to her. A few days later a disbelieving school headmistress telephoned and asked: "Can it be true as I hear from your daughter that some of The Beatles were with you earlier this week?" My wife confirmed the unbelievable and said that they had in fact visited us.

"Oh," said the headmistress, seizing an opportunity she could not resist. "In that case could you please ask Paul McCartney to come and open our school fete on Saturday?"

When John and Cynthia moved house to a mansion on the St George's Hill estate in Weybridge, I arrived on the scene before the removal vans drew onto the drive. John was unperturbed. He had become accustomed to my presence in odd places. "I knew that when I bought a new house I would find you in the kitchen," he laughed.

Back on the road, I joined the group for another series of gigs in the North. We were booked into a hotel just outside Leeds for a couple of nights. In spare moments, John had been working on something new. He was writing a book titled 'A Spaniard In The Works' and one morning, emerging from the bathroom, he had produced the first chapter, scrawled on the remnants of an old envelope and two sanitary disposal bags.

"Here Don," he said handing me one of the scrawled drafts, "They're yours. Flog 'em if you ever go broke, or buy yourself a new kitchen."

I duly followed Lennon's instructions and I did precisely that a few years later! The book eventually appeared and he wove my name into the satirical texts. It was a well-meaning name-check.

Back at work in the newsroom, I was able to reveal bigger plans for the Beatles. Two tours to the States were scheduled and tours to Australia and the Far East were also planned.

First though was an invasion of Europe. I travelled with them for most of the way, standing in the wings of concert stages, occupying hotel rooms on the same floor, often dining with them and even getting a seat in their limo. The Beatles' entourage party with their huge pieces of sound and lighting equipment and mountains of suitcases, resembled a travelling circus on the international stage. My own suitcase thankfully travelled safely with them.

The Beatles always took their meals in one of the larger rooms of their multiple suites. Usually, for sheer expediency, they would prefer simple meals like toast and beans or scrambled eggs and bacon. But hotel chefs were always ready to please them with specially prepared dishes.

Over dinner one night in Milan, the sensitive Ringo bequeathed his meal to me to eat. It was a rather large sea bream and the chef had not cut away its head. Ringo looked disdainfully at the fish and pushed it away. "I cannot stand those eyes staring up at me," he complained. I happily obliged and polished off the delicious dish.

While the Beatles' best performances were for the public on stage, I was lucky enough to witness their well-rehearsed routines backstage in their dressing room, a cave of intrigue from which all other visitors were barred and always protected by a security guard. The boys would tune their guitars and John and Paul, sometimes with the input of George and Ringo, would decide on the running order of their hits for the night. The room always held a spellbinding atmosphere. Laughter and jokes interspersed the loose notes that were plucked from their guitars as a warm-up to some of their songs. My eyes often fell on road manager Neil Aspinall who, with a variety of pens, would sometimes be squat in the corner as he forged the band's signatures on postcard photographs to be sent out to fans. I have often wondered how many hundreds of forged autographs of the Fab Four are still in circulation in the global market. Even top experts have failed to detect the difference. John Lennon confessed to me that Neil's version of his signature was pretty well identical to his own. I mused: "So it's a good job that you trust Neil implicitly, otherwise he could clean out all your bank accounts in one sweep!" John laughed, dismissively: "That will be the day."

There was an unexpected hitch at the starting gate in Europe in 1964. Without warning, Ringo was taken ill with tonsillitis, creating a huge dilemma. But Brian Epstein decreed that the tour should go ahead and a replacement drummer found. A frantic behind-the-scenes search went out and an experienced drummer named Jimmy Nicol was found. Jimmy had played in the past with Georgie Fame's band and he stepped into Ringo's role perfectly — but not before another candidate was rehearsed and dismissed. "Stick to the day job, Don," said Paul as I climbed out of Ringo's drum kit. Ringo quickly recovered and re-joined the group within a matter of days.

When the tour hit Rome, I bumped into the great composer Noël Coward, who was staying in the same hotel as the Beatles party. He asked me politely if I could introduce him to the Beatles. Mistakenly I assured him that I could. But when I led Noël up to the band's floor the boys were having none of it. There was a brief handshake at the door of George's suite, a quick "Nice to meet you" and a swift exchange of pleasantries. Downstairs Noël shook his head sadly and asked, "Is that how they always behave?" Upstairs the Beatles were in a rare truculent mood and complaining: "Who's Noël Coward?" and lightly brushing off his legendary contribution to the music and theatrical world.

Life became a little more relaxed on the Cote d'Azur. I strolled down the Cannes promenade with John Lennon who suddenly darted into a men's store on the front. His eyes were on a peaked cap which he tried on and bought, starting a new fashion craze around the world. Paying a visit to the same shop just a year later he joked with the manager: "I've called for my commission."

John was a man of extreme temperaments. But when he was in good humour he was priceless. Such humour was on the agenda in Spain.

I could tell John was in a mischievous mood when he invited me to join him for drinks in his hotel suite prior to the night's big concert. It was a scheme he must have dreamed up only minutes before. He asked me to call room service and order the drinks. A few minutes later the waiter arrived with a tray full of beverages. I opened the door and waved him through. The waiter looked quickly around the room but could see no clear surface to put down his tray, as we had deliberately piled luggage and bric-a-brac all over the coffee table and the flanking sideboard. There was absolutely no clear space in the room other than the floor. It was at this point that the waiter looked up to consider the situation. Only then was he aware of another presence. A contorted expression filled his face and the bizarre sight that confronted him would surely stay with him for the rest of his life.

John Lennon was sitting in an armchair in the far corner of the suite completely encased in a plastic bag. He had found the oversized bag, seemingly used for the delivery of a new mattress, folded up in a blanket box at the end of the bed. Before I called room service,

John had blithely climbed into it and instructed me to zip him in. With infectious zeal, Lennon was all set to study, if not challenge, the ingenuity of the hotel service.

Now John's hand was extended within the confines of the transparent bag ready to take one of the drinks from the waiter's tray. The awe-struck waiter moved forward believing there was a gap through which he could serve his drinks, but there was none. John, the master of trickery and chicanery, deliberately gave him the impression that he might be able to deliver his drink and moved his hand to the right, then the left, and then higher and lower within the lining as the waiter, with the deftness of an acrobat, floated the laden tray in all directions without the slightest spill. Still no aperture appeared. Lennon kept a straight, deadpan face not allowing a trace of the humour that must have been bursting from his lips, but by now our patient waiter was frowning. Suddenly his frustration erupted into a forlorn cry and he surrendered the battle, depositing the tray on my lap as he took his exit.

"Pity that," said John, climbing out of the bag with my aid, "He didn't stay for his tip." The next tray of drinks we ordered was left outside the door!

I later wondered whether, in that very bizarre escapade, the seeds of 'bagism' had formed in John's inventive mind. Climbing into a bag became a theme that he developed with his second wife Yoko Ono. They liked the idea of camping out in a bag which they claimed would obliterate prejudice and racism. Together they climbed into a huge white bag at an underground artists' event at the Royal Albert Hall in 1968 to monitor audience reaction, prompting one teenage girl to strip off and dance in delight. Others were inspired to do the same. John also went on to form a new public relations company he named Bag Productions Ltd. Bagism would become a symbolic strand of his life.

While we were in Spain, there was the usual round of Press conferences. John was asked by a local newsman whether he knew who Shakespeare was and John replied in measured, sarcastic tones: "Of course. But he didn't sell records did he?"

But unseen trouble loomed in Madrid for John. An embassy official's daughter fell head over in heels in love with him. Two months later she telephoned me to say she was expecting his baby.

"I'm ready to have an abortion," she said. "But I need a hundred dollars."

When I told John, he scowled and bluntly denied the girl's

claims. "What will they try next?" he muttered in exasperation. We didn't hear from her again.

Another girl also came on my line to claim that Paul was the father of her daughter Bettina. She spoke of having had an affair with Paul at a time when the Beatles had been performing in Hamburg. She went to court and Paul had to pay costs although ultimately a blood test proved that he could not have been the girl's father.

It was an ongoing problem for the Beatles. My office was inundated with calls from many other teenage girls claiming they were pregnant by one Beatle or another. We could only advise them to seek help from their parents or consult with a solicitor.

The Beatles were in high demand, holding many fans in a total trance. I remember a countess once grounded a Beatle by using her pearl necklace as a lasso.

In early 1967, back in London, Brian Epstein invited me to his Belgravia home to hear an acetate of a new Australian group called the Bee Gees. It was their very first record and Brian and the Aussies' manager Robert Stigwood were considering an alliance. I looked at both Stiggy and Eppy, as they were generally nicknamed.

"Maybe the Bee Gees are going to give us a lot to think about. Beatles beware..." I suggested in good humour to the delight of the two managers.

Eppy introduced me to his associate as someone who might become known as the fifth Beatle. He is so close to the boys, Eppy told him. I shook my head. "I am afraid I am a diehard reporter," I responded. They laughed.

Epstein liked to keep in touch, but there was a surprise element when he called me one day to enquire whether I knew the whereabouts of John Lennon. On this occasion I could not help him as John often went missing.

It transpired that in an off-beat moment, John had given the notion to Eppy that he was ready to extend his cultural interests.

"What John needs," Eppy decided, "is an oil painting. An old master to hang in his home." Epstein had spent several months trying to find the right picture and finally traced a Modigliani for sale in Paris.

He persuaded the art dealers to bring the $100,000 painting to London and managed to get a special license to import it.

A caviar and champagne party was organised at Claridge's Hotel for the transaction to be completed. The painting was mounted on an easel and a sheet tossed over it, so that it could be unveiled by

Not The Fifth Beatle — But Close Enough

John Lennon when he arrived. The hours ticked by and the French dealers grew more and more agitated when John did not appear. Finally, their patience was exhausted. Epstein took all the flak as the dealers repacked the painting and left the hotel in a huff to catch the evening flight back to Paris.

John Lennon did not surface until the next morning saying he must have overslept and did not hear his phone ringing. "What is all the fuss about? A painting? What painting?" he asked painfully.

Confronted by Eppy, and told of the whole farcical episode, he offered the only excuse left to him: "Sorry. I was only joking. Why would I need a painting?"

I was often privy to the band's personal, familial matters. John and his father Freddie were locked in a life-long feud, and the story of how it came to be defused I relate in the forthcoming chapter.

By comparison, Paul was close to his father Jim. Paul called me one night to join him in the trendy West End nightclub Tramp. His father had come down from Liverpool for the night and Paul wanted me to meet him. They had real veneration and complete trust in each other. Apparently, Jim had once had ambitions as a singer. He told me he had called his group Jim Mac's Jazz Band and they had played at local gigs. He laughed: "My son has done a lot better!" Later, Paul gave his father a racehorse as a birthday gift but warned me "Don't tell your readers to back it. Tell them to save their money!"

Having lunch one day with Brian Epstein at his Belgravia home, I was discussing the managerial problems of running a group like the Beatles, when Eppy suddenly asked me the question: "Which one of them do you think is the most difficult to handle?"

I opted for John Lennon knowing just how feisty he can get when in a tight corner.

"Wrong," said Eppy, beaming at my mistake. "It's Paul. Yes, really."

Frustratingly though there wasn't time to elaborate, as Brian's secretary Joanne appeared at the door asking him to take an urgent call. I caught a cab back to my office trying to fathom out the reasons for Brian's thinking. Could that be true? John had always appeared the most outspoken member of the group and never less than blunt. But Ringo for one saw him differently as he was keen to clarify: "He's given as being a hard and calculating cynic always putting people down. But John is like a teddy bear, kind and considerate and helpful always to those in need."

The Beatles and Beyond

The Beatles' second tour of the States in 1965 provided me with one of the most spectacular highlights in their global travels. As never before Beatlemania gripped 56,000 fans packed into the mighty Shea Stadium baseball ground in New York. Helicopters whirring above cast cool beams of searchlights over the airless arena, flash-bulbs like shooting stars popped from every vantage point and the noise was deafening as I stood alongside the podium built like a boxing ring on which the Beatles performed.

Similar hysterical scenes erupted at all the other remaining concerts across the States, but near disaster came when many young fans were badly crushed as they attempted to lay siege to the stage at San Francisco's Cow Palace. I reported that there were over 300 casualties. A police chief later told me it was lucky there were no fatalities.

Wherever the Beatles travelled, there were always lurking in the background the temptations of drugs offered by those pushers who saw music groups as easy targets to off-load their narcotics. Few parties ended without someone producing a pocketful of joints. But in Los Angeles, the Beatles were being introduced to something very different.

Peter Fonda, the well-known actor son of Hollywood star Henry Fonda, came up with several friends to a hillside house overlooking one of the canyons on Beverly Hills where the Beatles were holding court. One of the guests brought packets of LSD — and for the first time the Beatles were worried by my presence as they had been talked into experimenting with it.

As the party was gathering pace, I was invited to play a game of pool by Neil Aspinall. I didn't suspect at the time that he had an ulterior motive. Nor could I have guessed that Neil was acting as a decoy to distract my attention. I followed Neil down to the base-ment below where the pool table was installed. He played a blinder and I marvelled at every shot he made. He won three games in a row before I managed to sink a single ball. After the game I was told the party was breaking up and someone had ordered a taxi for me to take me back to my hotel. I left and thought nothing of it. Later, however, the truth became clear. While some of the Beatles had taken LSD, Paul had given his share to Neil doubling his intake of the drug. He said afterwards: "When I played Don Short pool I saw every ball on the table the size of a football. I was that high". No wonder he won! John Lennon said apologetically: "Sorry Don. We had to get rid of you. We didn't want to get you into bad habits!"

Not The Fifth Beatle — But Close Enough

More invitingly, the Beatles were in touch with Elvis Presley who had arranged a party for them at another mansion in Beverley Hills. It was to be the first meeting of these pop giants. Neither side knew what to expect. My vain attempts to access this momentous summit were truly thwarted at the door by a security guard and I was shown a red card for my troubles. I had no option but to return to my hotel.

The Beatles at this period in their careers routinely refused to recognise the appeal of such Hollywood greats as Elizabeth Taylor, Cary Grant, James Stewart, Robert Mitchum, Ava Gardner — or Frank Sinatra for that matter.

The Beatles' sage would cast them aside "Who they?" and in this list of dismissals was Elvis Presley who had got the damp downpour of John's scorn. "Who he?" he asked. "It's only the Beatles now Don. You'll see." Of course, I was well aware of John's scornful rhetoric remembering his blunt dismissal of Noël Coward in Rome.

But the following morning, I got a first-hand account of how their meeting went. John's attitude was conciliatory: "Elvis was great," John intimated. "It's taken four of us to do it — but he made it on his own."

Paul agreed it had been a relaxed party: "It wasn't staged for publicity — that was the best thing. It was just an informal domestic affair. Elvis? Great man."

I asked what else had been discussed between the five of them. The Beatles said Elvis got out a bass guitar that he had just started learning to play. Suddenly, Paul and John and George produced their guitars for an unrehearsed singing session. If a disc had been cut, it would probably have been a world best-seller. They compared notes on their experiences with fans. Elvis told them: "It got so bad one time that I decided to learn karate." To which Paul replied: "Well, that's not happened to us. Maybe they don't like taking on four at a time!"

A week later I was able to talk to Elvis myself. He was working on a film set but he broke off to tell me: "They're wonderful fellows. They are just as zany as I imagined them." Wasn't there a clash of egos? I asked him. Elvis shook his head. "Believe me. There is no competition between us. They do their thing and I do mine. There is plenty of room for us all."

The Beatles travelled across America in their own chartered plane. John came up with a game just to pass the time. Sat next to me on one stage of our journey, John grabbed my pen and notepad to make a list of potentially fateful events that could affect his future. Between us, we must have conjured a score of bizarre happenings, far beyond the realms of crystal-ball gazing.

Lennon, to whose black humour this macabre game appealed, loved every moment of it. "What are the permutations left on my life?" he asked. "What else can happen to me that you haven't already written about?"

"Other than…" I stopped.

"Death? Don't be daft Don. Beatles don't die," he chuckled.

Ironically, on the very next flight, all our lives were in danger as one of the plane's engines caught fire as we were coming into land at Portland, Oregon. Paul McCartney, sitting at the back of the plane, suddenly yelled: "We're on fire!" John, in the seat next to me, spotted a thick cloud of black smoke pouring from the engine and nudged me, repeating Paul's words. "We're on fire! Start writing, Don, this could be your last Beatles story."

I hastily produced an empty film spool from my bag and John snatched it from me saying, "Let's write our last messages down and put them into the cartridge. If the plane goes down someone will find it," John scribbled his message on a sheet of my notepaper.

All I saw him write was: "Goodbye friends and…" — the rest was tantalisingly illegible as he rolled his scrawled message into the spool. With the plane descending, we could see fire engines and ambulances lining the tarmac. There were strained faces but strangely no panic. Thankfully the plane landed safely amid cheers and applause from all on board. As everyone hurried to the exits John yelled out: "Beatles, women and children off first!" His humour rarely deserted him. My only regret is losing that cartridge in the rush to get off the plane. What else had he written on that message?

One summer in 1968, I took a two-week break with my family and the editor of The Mirror asked me if I could get two star guests to take over my column. I managed to persuade both Mick Jagger and Ringo Starr to step into the breach. Mick Jagger reviewed a new album from the American group The Byrds saying: "It is the best thing I've heard them do." He concluded his piece with a rather pithy line: "All of the other records I played, which took two hours, were awful." A week later, Ringo urged readers to go out that day and buy a copy of Simon and Garfunkel's new single 'Mrs Robinson' taken from their soundtrack to the chart-topping film The Graduate. Ringo also reviewed other discs by José Feliciano, Louis Armstrong and Roy Orbison. Ringo decided to keep the discs for himself — or those he really liked. He joked at the foot of the column: "I'm going to keep all the records I gave reasonable marks to. The rest can go to Don Short on holiday in case it's raining in Ramsgate." How did he guess?

A few months earlier, however, another Beatles mission was upon me.

Some way back, George had woven elements of Indian music into the Beatles' sound. He had discovered the world of Hari Krishna and been introduced to its obscure doctrine by a new friend, the sitar-playing Ravi Shankar.

George had also found a mentor, the spiritual guru Maharishi Mahesh Yogi who lived reclusively with his sect in the Himalayas. The Beatles, pronouncing themselves physically and mentally exhausted and in need of a break, were persuaded that transcendental meditation would restore their wellbeing. Their concerts, their travels and the unrelenting demands of their fans had reduced them to a near state of breakdown. It was time to convalesce. They would no longer be tempted by drugs or the wider perils of the universe. Their troubled souls would be healed.

Their arrival in India in February 1968 brought a warm reception. I flew to be with them in time for their initiation ceremony, conducted in a spartan wooden ashram lying at Rishikesh in the shadow of the vast mountain range, where the Maharishi's followers congregated.

The Maharishi cloaked in a flowing white robe, his grey beard neatly combed and his hands outstretched in greeting, beamed down on his new quartet of would-be disciples.

They were four of the most famous people on the planet, but they were now meekly squatting cross legged before the Maharishi, listening intently to his exultations. Each had to settle on just one word known as a mantra, which they were instructed to recite to themselves repeatedly, until all the turmoil of the past dissipated from their minds and they found inner peace.

I had gate-crashed many Beatles parties before — but I had not anticipated a time when I would be infiltrating a spiritual coming in their lives of this kind.

One of the Maharishi's aides unmasked my identity but George Harrison — the motivator of this expedition — came to my rescue and confided to the guru: "His name is Don Short. We know him well."

The Maharishi giggled and in a forgiving gesture allowed me to photograph him. I managed to wire the picture to London to make the Mirror's pages. In the coming days, I found the Maharishi seemed to laugh at most things but perhaps it was disingenuous of me to suspect that by enrolling the Beatles into his spiritual cult, he had scored a major commercial coup. Multitudes of Beatles fans would flock to become worshippers — and so it proved in so many distant lands.

In the meantime, the Beatles were already being joined in Rishikesh by other curious stars — Hollywood actress Mia Farrow, Mike Love of the Beach Boys and others. John Lennon's wife Cynthia had travelled with the party too along with George's wife Pattie Boyd, who had urged her husband to listen to the Maharishi's teachings earlier in London. Paul's actress girlfriend of the time Jane Asher was with the party and so too Ringo's wife Maureen.

George told me his view on the place: "I believe I have already extended my life by twenty years. I believe there are bods up here in the Himalayas who have lived for centuries." John added: "The way George is going he will be flying on a magic carpet by the time he is forty."

There was music and banter and happiness and lots of delicious vegetarian dishes at mealtimes. Under the blue skies of Rishikesh, the Maharishi surveyed his new followers and in an aside remarked to me: "I am much pleased."

It was difficult to question the Maharishi's preachings. Solemn in nature, but studded with his words of wisdom on the paths of our lives. Puritanical messages of love, peace and devotion. At the end of each lesson his blue eyes would twinkle and the smile returned to his lips, which clearly brought more joy to his devout followers.

I left the Beatles deep in their meditations believing that all was well in this new kingdom.

It was something of a shock to learn only a week later that the peaceful chantings had struck a discord. Apparently rumours had swept the ashram that the Maharishi had groped Mia Farrow during one of his lectures. True or otherwise, it had a catastrophic effect on the gathering of the young worshippers. One by one, the Beatles discreetly made their exit and returned to London where both Paul and John rubbished the Maharishi's teachings.

But things were not as they seemed. One of the Maharishi's resident disciples dismissed the claims which had been falsely circulated by one of the Beatles' hitherto admirers. The aide also explained that the Beatles' sudden departure were due to suspicions that they had smoked cannabis in the evenings which had displeased the Maharishi.

Through their connections and taking stock of the situation on their return home, the Beatles conveyed their apologies to the Maharishi. The worldly philosophical Maharishi was not angered by Paul and John's earlier assaults on his beliefs and integrity. He said of them: "I could never be upset by angels." Harmony was once more restored.

When he was home, George Harrison presented me with a copy of a book on yoga which he inscribed: "To Don. Hoping you come through too.' A sentiment I hoped would prevail.

It had little to do with any of the Biblical commandments, but the Beatles made a secret, sacred pact never to covet the others' wives or girlfriends.

"That," said John Lennon, "would be far worse than just making out with your best friend's lady. The Beatles are a family. It would be incest."

Whatever happened on tour the Beatles were still jealous of their loved ones at home. When John heard rumours that George had formed a friendship with Ringo's wife Maureen he blew up into a frenzy. He called George and told him it was against the rules. John recalled: "Someone had to say something." At the time I doubted if George would easily accept John's condemnation but whatever was said between them it did not impair their friendship.

I could not help but feel that John was not in a position to call the kettle black. He had his own problems to resolve. His long-term marriage to Cynthia was crumbling. By chance, he had looked in on an art exhibition in London being staged by a Japanese sculptress and artist who would change his life forever. Her name was Yoko Ono.

She had a hypnotic effect on him. The Beatle could not dismiss Yoko from his mind. He sent her secret missives. John told me later that if he did not fall in love with Yoko that very first day then it was not long after.

Cynthia sensed his unhappiness in their marriage and asked him if he was in love with someone else. John stalled her but finally gave his answer to Cyn in a letter delivered by an aide when she was on vacation in Italy.

"It was quite a shock," Cynthia confided to me later, "and I can't tell you the turmoil I have gone through. The thought of divorce was so desperate, so alien to me. But what could I do? It would have been impossible to talk things out with John. When he does something, he is totally committed. He can never reverse."

Sympathetic fans felt for her. Many Beatles admirers thought that John had lost his way.

Yoko, already twice married, seemed to live in a Bohemian style which appealed to John's imagination. Her artwork was controversial. She had produced a film in America starring 365 bare bottoms and her art exhibition was a bewildering array of floating balloons and blank canvases.

John, having dropped in on the exhibition through sheer curiosity, was not recognised by Yoko who asked him if he would hammer a nail into one of the canvases.

"John wasn't one of those who asked why," Yoko said afterwards. "He understood why, if only using an imaginary hammer."

I was to see John just a few days later. "What else can I do? I thought my marriage to Cyn would last forever," he told me wistfully. "She was so loyal, so well-meaning and understanding. But everything has changed. I have never met anyone like Yoko. I have got to halt my marriage to Cyn. We were not unhappy but we were in a terrible rut, nothing was happening and you can only sustain that until you meet someone who sets you alight. Yoko did just that."

Close friends tried to bring about a last minute reconciliation between John and Cynthia but their efforts all failed. I asked John about the effect the breakup would have on their son Julian but his attitude by then was pretty hardened.

"Julian won't suffer," he said tersely. "I'll see to that. Look Don these things happen. Isn't it better to avoid rearing children in a strained atmosphere? Are they going to thank you when they are eighteen for remaining together? I doubt it."

There was no other remedy now but for Cynthia to file for a divorce. Yoko also filed for divorce from her husband American film producer Anthony Cox by whom she had a five-year-old daughter Kyoko. Yoko told me: "I was in the same trap as John. I wasn't in love either. But my marriage was showing the trace of not going anywhere, we were leaving one another and going back to leave again. I am sure many people blame me for John leaving Cynthia. There are those, I'm sure, who see me as the most evil woman on earth. I just wish they would look at things differently. John made his own decision to leave Cynthia without any encouragement from me. I am going to marry John. He is the most compelling man in the world."

Soon after the divorce proceedings went through John and Yoko made an album together, 'Two Virgins' and posed in the nude for the sleeve picture. To many it was a scandalous act and many stores banned the record or sold it wrapped in brown paper bags. But John had a different explanation.

"We did the picture to show that we were not just a couple of demented freaks, that we were not deformed in any way and that our minds were healthy," explained the Beatle.

The couple complained when the album did not get the kind of acclaim they expected. John accused his own Apple company, along with EMI the main global distributers of blocking its release. I also received a postcard from them on holiday in Spain headed 'A Letter from Two Nudes.' It was intended to draw my attention to the fact that the Mirror had omitted mentioning the 'famous, controversial, history making' album from its pages.

"I mean it's just not on Don. What have they got against us?" John wrote. The controversy was never resolved.

Tragic news devastated the Beatles when Brian Epstein was found dead in his country home after taking an accidental overdose of drugs in August 1967. He was only 32. It was no secret to me that Brian was going through a managerial crisis with the group at the time despite the fact he had guided them through to international fame. He had moulded the Beatles like a sculptor might an effigy. He was cool, calm and collected, always able to take on the big decisions. But in the months before his death he appeared to have lost his grip. The Beatles were big boys now. They were millionaires and self-assured. They were no longer four young men seeking Epstein's guidance. Crucially, they had begun to reverse his decisions and that embarrassed him. His pride may have been hurt, but he was philosophical about the way things were deteriorating for him.

"They are four incredible individuals and I can't keep them in harness forever," he told me on the last occasion that I was to see him alive.

Without Epstein at the helm, the Beatles were now plunged into a major crisis of their own. Who could lead them? All four had different ideas for the future, but nonetheless, they were committed to their studio recordings in Abbey Road in which Yoko was to make her presence felt by sitting in the producer's chair while the recordings were being made. A bold move for the band's most recent companion.

John told me at the time: 'When the others get to know Yoko they will appreciate her ideas. She's not trying to interfere but she is aiming to project things in a new dimension. We can either accept it or reject it." Yoko knew she was unpopular — not only with the rest of the Beatles — but with the fans. She was accused of cashing in on John's fame and of being a disruptive influence on him.

"I haven't split the Beatles or enticed John away from them," she said. "But John is anxious about his future and we must think about that."

It seemed it was wedding season for the band. Paul McCartney invited me to attend his wedding to the American photographer Linda Eastman at Marylebone Register Office on 12th March 1969. It was an unexpected honour. After many months of courtship Paul had finally popped the question.

But there was a hitch at the wedding. A big and worrying hitch. The best man, Paul's brother Mike McGear (of The Scaffold pop group) was missing. Where was he? And what about the wedding ring in his pocket? The Registrar became agitated as he kept glancing at the clock. The bridal couple put a brave face on the delay and I tried to break the tension by recounting some anecdotes from early Beatles days.

Some light relief was provided by little Heather — Linda's six-year-old daughter by her first marriage to American geologist Melville See. Heather had taken the day off from school and as a charade she pretended to organise her own wedding. Then she flopped on a settee. Everyone laughed. Paul plucked a bloom from the spray of freesias she was carrying — and I provided a paper clip to fasten one of the flowers to her hair. "Now that will make you look pretty," said Paul.

Time was dragging. Besides Paul, Linda, Heather and myself, there were only Beatle aides Mal Evans and Peter Brown and photographer John Kelly in the room. To kill time Paul, the last bachelor Beatle, began to sing the 'Stars and Stripes' using a registrar's notice on the wall as the lyrics.

Then, suddenly, and to the relief of the party, the door burst open and there was Mike McGear crawling in on his hands and knees muttering: "Forgive me. It wasn't my fault. The train broke down."

Paul quipped: "That's British Rail for you. Good old British Railways!" He turned to me and suggested: "Here's your Mirror headline Don. 'It wasn't the bride or bridegroom who were late — it was the best man.'" Of course, those words were reproduced verbatim in the Mirror the next morning on our centre page spread.

The Registrar, with greater relief than others, now sped ahead with the ceremony. Linda looked beautiful in a bright yellow maxi-coat over a simple beige dress and brown buckle shoes. "You look wonderful," Paul told her affectionately.

Minutes later, the happy bridal couple took their first steps as man and wife outside the Register office to face jubilant fans and the world's Press. The couple moved on to St. John's Wood parish church for a blessing from the Vicar, the Rev. Noel Perry-Gore.

Pausing only to change his yellow kipper tie for a more subdued brown one, Paul joked: "If there are any blessings going, I'm not missing out on them." After that, there was a cosy lunch at the Ritz. The honeymoon, they explained, would be taken later. Paul left in the evening and explained: "I have got a recording session tonight." I responded: "Besides, who could think of a honeymoon in Abbey Road?"

John and Yoko flew out to Gibraltar and got married in 1969 a week later. They went to Paris for the first stage of their honeymoon and dined with Salvador Dali before heading for Amsterdam where they announced, "a special event."

They wanted the world to share their honeymoon with a "love-in" at the Amsterdam Hilton hotel. For them it was a unique way of expressing a protest against war and violence throughout the world. I was the first caller at their suite — the hotel's Presidential suite which had been reserved especially for them to stage their surreal seven-day bed-in.

John, in a pair of striped pyjamas, was sitting up in bed next to Yoko, who wore a white, high necked, old fashioned nightie. Both were clutching white tulips as a symbol of peace. John grasping a flower was somehow contrary to his accepted mercurial image. I had been around on 200 or more Beatle concerts when his fingers darted over the strings of his guitar. The Beatle was now in repose. At the crossroads of his life, he inferred.

"We've got to tell the world that we are with them," he said.

Yoko nodded. "People must be moved to protest against the conflicts of the world," she said. "We can't leave it to the politicians."

Instinctively, I knew a string of amusing situations would evolve. Such was the awkward moment each morning when a housemaid appeared specifically to tidy the room and to change the sheets on the makeshift floor-bed that the couple occupied. You could see her thinking: what is the correct etiquette to employ here? Should she ask the pyjama-clad couple clutching their white tulips to climb out of the bed so she could change the sheets? The nervous girl shook her head not knowing what to do. But John told her: "Just get on with it, love. We will just hop in and out when you're ready." And so they did — behind closed doors before allowing in each day's fresh pack of journalists, radio and television commentators. John and Yoko wanted to re-stage the whole thing in New York but were advised that their drug convictions could prohibit them from going there. The couple decided to restage the event in Montreal instead where once more they created a huge reaction. Anti-war, anti-violence was the repetitive protest and with wall-hung posters and pamphlets their message was clear: peace, ad infinitum. Many journalists pronounced the whole movement as a publicity stunt but John Lennon was already too famous and didn't need publicity at that stage of his life. "When will the world wake up and find peace?" he asked me.

John and Yoko's drug convictions had occurred in earlier months in London. From a contact at Scotland Yard, I learned that the couple's home was going to be raided. Ethically, I knew it was the wrong thing to do, but John was a friend and I could not let him down. I warned him that he was about to be busted. They were then living in a flat in Montague Square which had been occupied in the past by other rock stars including Jimi Hendrix.

Three weeks later, a squad of eight police officers descended on the house just after dawn. John and Yoko, who was pregnant at the time, were still in bed and pretty well naked. Constant knocking on the door and loud voices woke John who scrambled into his trousers to confront a policeman at one of the windows. As a delaying tactic, he insisted on the policeman reading out the search warrant before allowing the squad into the house. He yelled for Yoko to get their lawyer on the phone.

John and Yoko believed the house was entirely clear of any incriminating drugs, but police dogs sniffed out marijuana and quantities of hashish stashed in the most obscure places, even in a binocular case on the mantelpiece. They were arrested on the spot and in a state of bewilderment were marched out to a police van to be charged with the possession of drugs. John fearing that Yoko might be deported as a result of the case, pleaded guilty in court and was fined £150. John told his Apple colleagues: "Don Short had told us 'they're coming to get you' three weeks before. So believe me I'd cleaned the house out because Jimi Hendrix had lived there. I'm not stupid. I went through the whole damn house." There was one small detail that John had overlooked. He had not counted on police sniffer dogs uncovering the evidence.

Happier news came for the couple a few years later. After two miscarriages, Yoko gave birth to their son Sean — a half-brother to Julian and to Yoko's daughter Kyoto. As a family they decided to take refuge from the public gaze in New York after lawyers persuaded the authorities to issue them with residency permits. The couple settled in an apartment in The Dakota building.

They were content to lead a quiet, reclusive life. John felt he had paid his dues to society and that he didn't owe anything to anyone.

"Why should I go on?" he questioned when I told him that a genius shouldn't shelve his talents.

"I am not a genius," John responded in a self-deprecating manner. "I'm just a guy who wrote a lot of music that I thought mattered at the time."

Over time, the restless Beatle complained of feeling "suffocated." He asked himself questions that he could find no logical answers to. He went to spend a few days in the sunshine in Los Angeles to get over his blues. Yoko encouraged John's secretary May Pang to go with him. But they did not return. They were together for almost two years.

During that time John stayed silent. When I telephoned him he said, "I don't want to say anything that is going to upset Yoko. Everything is delicate."

I got the impression that John was suffering from feelings of guilt, if not remorse. Yoko was still very much in his mind and finally they were reconciled in New York after an Elton John concert. Yoko was concerned about John. He was overweight and seemed to be drinking more than in the past. She preached discipline to him and she persuaded him to make his comeback as an artist.

Together they made an album described as a 'hymn of love.' They titled it 'Double Fantasy.' Their love became stronger than ever.

Seemingly isolated in New York, John found it increasingly difficult to return to England and reunite with Paul, George and Ringo.

Tensions grew between them and sadly John and Paul, whom I regarded as the greatest songwriters of the day, started slagging each other off in the weekly music magazines. It was the most bitter mud-slinging act two erstwhile friends could ever resort to. I remonstrated with them and told them to stop acting like a couple of squabbling schoolkids.

Paul said he would never write any more songs with John. John feeling stung, hit back telling me: "If that's what Paul wants, then so be it. Why would I want to get back to writing fairy tales? From now on I'll be writing music that reflects life as it is."

In my newspaper column I wrote: "It's time they both grew up. They should bury the hatchet and sink their differences with a pint in the nearest pub. If it's any help I'll buy them the first pint." Neither took up my offer and I didn't imagine they would.

Ringo faced the reality knowing that the split was impossible to repair and there was little chance of them getting back with one another.

"Besides, I couldn't go through the turmoil all over again," he told me. "We have had five years of Beatlemania and it is enough. No sleep. No proper meals, living out of a suitcase, being torn to bits mentally and physically... Oh, never again!"

George Harrison also gave me his views on the break-up and whether they could ever get back together again. "Everybody keeps asking the same question," George told me. "There are some people around who can't imagine the world without The Beatles. That's what it must be. But this had to happen. We had to find ourselves. It was the natural cause of events. The thing is that people think we know all the answers about the Beatles and we don't. Who are we? We can't give the answer, and I for one can't define that special something else that made us as we are. It wasn't just the records or our concerts. If you know then you tell me. But it's all unity through diversity, Don."

The Beatles' last single 'Let It Be' seemed to be an ironic pastiche of their split. George agreed. "You have to dig that title because it fits the picture of where we are now. Why try and fight the natural turn of events?"

Whatever I could write or say it was clear that the break-up could not be averted. All the signals were red. Most of the bitterness would heal in time but the Beatles, ignoring multi-million pound offers to reunite for just a single concert, were never tempted to perform together again.

I had to face the fact that this was the total eclipse of all the amazing and crazy times we had all experienced.

So many images flashed through my mind. Of the hilarity and dramas that broke out when the boys were filming 'A Hard Day's Night' and more so on their next movie 'Help!' from which two big hits were derived. Memories came flooding back too of the adventures on the Magical Mystery Tour, and of a fun day when I hitched a ride in John's psychedelically painted Rolls Royce which quite literally stopped traffic around town. And so many more happenings over the years. To quote Paul, it had indeed been a long and winding road.

Now, on that fateful evening in April 1970, I had to bring the curtain down on what had been an historical decade. It wasn't the story I wanted to write — the meltdown of the Beatles — but as a newspaperman this was a sensational exclusive that I could not hold back.

So the Mirror pitched the banner headline on Paul quitting. Many uptight journalist rivals poured cold water on my exclusive. One writer made lame excuses for missing what he described as being the scoop of a lifetime. He claimed he had already heard the news from John Lennon about the break-up but had failed to file the story. If so, his editor must have been livid.

So just why did the Beatles disband? There have been countless theories. Many blamed the arrival of Yoko Ono into their midst and her perceived meddling; then after the tragic death of Brian Epstein there was dissent among the group as to who should lead them. John wanted to appoint New York financial wheeler-dealer Allen Klein and Paul, then married to Linda, was suggesting his father-in-law attorney Lee Eastman. In the end, Klein took control but his tenure ended in court actions and acrimony. From that point on, The Beatles and their Apple empire disintegrated to a stage with John saying: "The way it's going on it will all go bust." John could only have been joking of course.

With record royalties worth millions of pounds pouring in almost daily from all around the world that fortunately could never become the case. Disagreements and feuds finally came to a halt. There were reconciliations. But whatever the troubles of the past the Beatles left the world with one precious and priceless legacy. Their inspirational music — a bequest for generations to come.

CHAPTER TWO

JOHN LENNON
AND HIS SEAFARING DAD

My role, as John Lennon blithely described it, was that of the 'peacemaker.' My ominous task was to heal a rift between him and his seafaring father Freddie Lennon, who he had not seen for seventeen years.

John, at the age of seven, and his mother Julia had been left in their Liverpool home by the errant Freddie who chose to go back to sea with the Merchant Navy. Nothing more was heard of him. Until, that is, in the early days of 1964 when I found Freddie. Or, more accurately, when Freddie found me.

I was at my desk in the News Room. I had been fielding the usual calls that morning, but this was one that made me sit bolt upright in my chair.

"I'm Freddie Lennon," the caller pronounced in a throaty voice. "I'm John Lennon's father. Can you help me contact him?"

Incredulous, I was momentarily lost for words. "John Lennon's father?" I stuttered in disbelief.

"Yes," he replied emphatically. "I know you must know my son well," he went on, "I keep reading your stories in the Daily Mirror about him and the Beatles. Is there any chance we can meet and I will give you proof of who I am?"

Two hours later I was sitting opposite him in a pub in Earl's Court. His thinning hair appeared uncombed, his jacket was well-worn and trousers were creased, but I could see a family resemblance to John: his straight nose, furrowed forehead and eyes were an instant giveaway. There was little need for him to produce the bundle of papers he thrust on the table to prove he was indeed John Lennon's dad. Over the odd sip of his beer, he began to relate his story, or as he put it, 'my side of the story.'

He told me of how he left home because Julia was pregnant with someone's else's baby. We talked for an hour or more before I motioned him to put a hold on his revelations as it would be necessary to get it all down on tape. He agreed and we arranged to meet later in the evening.

I returned to the office to get my tape recorder and — more pressingly — to put in a call to John Lennon to share the happy news of his lost father's sudden appearance. John did not see it the same way. He found it difficult to conceive that his father had chosen to come out of hiding after so many years.

"No I won't see him," John exploded angrily. "He walked out on us. He betrayed us. Why didn't he ever contact me all these years before? Now that he thinks I am famous..."

John, whose mother had died in a car accident, had been brought up by his mother's sister the fabled Aunt Mimi who had always detested Freddie and the way he had left his family.

I sympathised with John and his deep-rooted hurt. Somehow I had to calm his rage and talk him round into seeing his father. After all, for a reporter this was potentially a big front-page story, as good as it gets. I could not let it slip from my grasp. It wasn't easy but grudgingly John gave way.

"Alright," he said finally. "Bring him to the theatre tomorrow night but remember, I want no truck with him."

I escorted Freddie to the Scala Theatre in Soho the next evening. The Beatles were in the middle of filming scenes for their first movie 'A Hard Day's Night' and were going to perform a concert for the cameras.

Brian Epstein welcomed us at the stage door and led us through to the dressing room. Paul, George and Ringo greeted me and seemed fascinated as I introduced them to Freddie whose eyes were cast on the leering figure behind them.

"John!" cried Freddie in sheer excitement as he moved forward to hug his son. But John stepped back from reach and scowled at his father. "What do you want?" he snapped.

Freddie was taken aback by his son's cold demeanour. "I don't want anything John," he stammered.

"Then why are you here?" came the swift reply. "You've never bothered about me before."

"John, I am not here to jump on the bandwagon," said Freddie. "Isn't it enough that I'm your father? I know you think I deserted you as a child but I just want you to know it wasn't really like that... I'll tell you now..."

But that was as far as Freddie got. John was called to start filming and we had to leave the theatre. I gave Eppy a note with Freddie's workplace phone number should John have a change of heart and wish to see his father again.

Despite John's rebuttal, Freddie felt they had broken the ice, although I did not share his optimism. "Oh, he will come around alright," said Freddie, who was still in awe of his seeing his son after so many years' absence.

"I just could not believe it," Freddie added, "Do you know he looked so much like his mother? The eyes, the face — and that scowl of his. Julia could put on that kind of scowl sometimes."

I smiled. "Funny that. I thought he looked like you." Freddie beamed with pride.

My next move was to make contact with John to get his reactions. He was still feeling scornful about his father's motives. But I told him how Freddie had fallen on hard times and was working as a £10 a week kitchen porter at the Greyhound Hotel in Hampton Court. The Beatle's attitude began to soften. What's more, I related, his father was living in a shoddy boarding house room and only in the recent past had been forced to sleep rough on park benches.

"Okay," said John, "Let me think about it."

I offered to act as the go-between, and it was then that John dubbed me the peacemaker. I arranged to meet Freddie to transmit John's messages in a bar close to his workplace.

John occasionally sent him money and one letter containing £25 that he addressed to his father (whose Christian name was Alfred but known to his friends and old shipmates as Freddie) 'Dear Alf, Fred, Dad, Pater, Father, whatever...'

The Beatle's mood was one of sympathy when he next encountered Freddie and John invited him to stay with him and Cynthia in their St. George's Hill mansion.

"Meeting Cynthia for the first time and my grandson Julian was quite an ordeal," Freddie admitted. "Suddenly I had found my family."

Life was now to change for the down-and-out-Freddie. Cynthia gave him his own room in the luxury of the house and for once he was living and dining in style. But two months down the line Freddie began to feel like an isolated lodger.

"John was always away from home working on new records and giving concerts with the Beatles," said Freddie. "And Cynthia had her own social activities. It was Cynthia's mother who, on a visit to the house one day, suggested I should find my own bachelor apartment. John thought it was a good idea and he made me a weekly allowance of £10 to help me move into a large studio apartment in Kew. John told me: 'There's no need to work Dad. Just enjoy yourself.' One night John phoned me and told me to get ready as he was taking me to a fancy dress party at the Royal Garden Hotel in London. That put me in a bit of a quandary. I couldn't think of what to wear but for a laugh I finally decided to go dressed as a garbage collector. John roared with laughter when he saw me and we sang 'My Old Man's A Dustman' together in the back of the chauffeur-driven car."

Freddie, who had a good singing voice and could play the banjo, thought he might follow in his son's footsteps and make a record. "Music is in our genes," he said. A record producer took him on and Freddie recorded a song titled 'That's My Life.' He also cut three other tracks but none reached the charts. If Freddie thought he would have John's blessing then he had to think again.

John was outraged. "What in the hell do you think you are doing? You're just cashing in on my name because I am famous," he yelled at his father.

Freddie, reeling from John's wrath, decided not to pursue his career any further. Several observers suspected that John had deliberately blocked Freddie's new career but I could not find any evidence to suggest that was the case.

Trouble was ahead. I blindly suggested that Freddie, having sung a song about his life, should write his memoirs and I promised to help him.

John hit the roof when his father told him of the idea and I was glad I wasn't present to witness the scene as Freddie later described it. "John gave me the biggest verbal lashing of my life."

Once the dust had settled and the turmoil passed, the pair reconciled once more. John apologised and Freddie put the idea of a book out of his mind. When John next saw Freddie he was surprised by his father's news.

Freddie had fallen in love with an eighteen-year-old student at Exeter University named Pauline Jones. John was amused to learn that Freddie had met Pauline when she earned her summer pocket money by washing up glasses in the Toby Jug pub near Tolworth where Freddie had worked as a barman a year earlier.

Freddie said: "John congratulated me. He didn't think there was anything wrong with falling in love with a girl who was twenty-seven years younger than me. I thought he might have called me a silly old goat on top of everything else he had heard about me. But no — he was all for it."

When John got to know Pauline, he gave her a job as his secretary and putting her in charge of his fan mail. The whole family got closer.

Pauline and Freddie were guests at the Beatle's mansion home for Christmas. There was to be a big party and the rest of the Beatles and all their friends flocked in. It was going to be a night of fun and Freddie was not going to be left out of things.

Freddie recounted the whole of the night's escapades to me: "One of John's buddies produced a joint. He passed it to me and I could see by the glint in his eye that he was thinking he would get John's old man going." He continued: "I had once smoked hashish in the Mediterranean when I was in the Navy. I found it didn't do anything for me that a pint of beer couldn't do better. But to please them and to show I wasn't an old square I smoked one. Pauline declined. I didn't feel any effects from it. In the background they were playing The Beatles' latest records. I knew it was going to turn into quite a party and I thought I should make myself scarce and go to bed. Pauline had already gone upstairs to her room. So I asked John 'Where do I sleep son?' He replied: 'In your old room.' I shook my head. 'But Pauline is in there.' John shrugged and said, 'Well, you are going to marry her, aren't you? What are you worried about?' John didn't know it, but I had not slept with Pauline. So I had to knock nervously on her door and explained the position to her. She allowed me to sleep on the floor of the bedroom that night."

When the couple announced they were to marry, Pauline's parents fiercely objected and made her a ward of court. But three or four months later the couple defied the court order and eloped to Scotland with John's help. He engineered the elopement for them, booking them into a small hotel in the centre of Edinburgh under false names to ensure that Pauline's parents would not find them.

"As we went away together John told me 'You love the girl Dad, go and get it over and get it done with. Yes, marry her. To hell with what the court says.'"

The couple stayed for three weeks to qualify for residency in

Edinburgh and then they were married at a local registry office.

The Beatle sent a letter of congratulations to them and he picked up their hotel tab. What was more, he bought the couple a bright new house in Brighton to start their married life in.

I thought my job as peacemaker was done, as all seemed goodness and light. But as a reporter it was prudent to continue to be in touch with both John and his Dad.

Another situation had arisen that Freddie found difficult to understand. Was history repeating itself? As a seaman he had walked out on Julia and John as a boy leaving them to their own devices. Now he had just learned that John was walking out on Cynthia and their youngster Julian. He had fallen in love with Yoko Ono. But, as Freddie conceded when he talked over the situation with me, the circumstances were a little different. Cynthia and Julian would at least always be secure.

Nevertheless, Freddie was bewildered by the news. "John told me he was in love with Yoko and that he was leaving Cynthia. I could not believe it but I could not say anything. How could I pass judgement with my track record? Besides John is so independent and self-assured. I was deeply conscious of the heartache he must have been feeling in leaving Cynthia as he was set to do now."

Freddie's voice conveyed his emotion as he talked. "I had become so close to Cynthia. She is the loveliest daughter-in-law you could wish for. I knew she had practically grown up with John. They were so much in love and Cynthia is such a marvellous mother to Julian. But what could I say? I couldn't tell John he was doing wrong. I had to stay silent and take comfort from my own good fortune to have found happiness with Pauline."

One year later, John Lennon had a new infant half-brother when Pauline gave birth to a son that the couple named David Henry Lennon. John sent flowers and notes of congratulation.

But for the couple and their infant son, the next encounter with John was something much more bizarre than they could have anticipated. They were to be the guests at John's birthday party.

John and Yoko had moved into the magnificent Tittenhurst Park near Ascot surrounded by hundreds of acres of countryside.

When Freddie, Pauline and the baby arrived and took the long drive up to the house they were confronted by the wreckage of a car partly buried in concrete on the front lawn. They learned it was the car in which John and Yoko had been injured when driving in Scotland two months before.

John Lennon And His Seafaring Dad

More surprises were in store when they entered the house. Most of the furniture had been scythed in half and all of the walls were painted an icy white. They were greeted by a grey-faced servant. There was no sign of John or Yoko as they were shown in.

"The house was more like a museum or a mausoleum," Freddie recalled when he recounted the whole episode to me. "Pauline held David in her arms as we waited in the kitchen. It seemed like ages before John and Yoko came down the spiral staircase. They were both ashen faced. It was as though they were transcending from a cloud creating a strange inhospitable atmosphere. The whole room where we were standing went cold. John had grown a wispy beard. He looked as angry as thunder as he bore down on us. 'Why have you come here?' he shouted glaring directly at me. 'Get out. You're just a good for nothing drunk. Get back to the gutter where you belong!'"

Freddie reminded him that he had invited them only the day before and they had brought him his birthday gift: a leather-bound shaving kit. It made no impression. "John was just screaming at us. I recoiled in fear and horror. Pauline held David, in his boots and mittens, closer to her. I turned to Yoko — we were meeting her for the first time — hoping she would say something to relieve the atmosphere and tension. 'Was this the couple who were preaching love and peace throughout the world?' I thought. Where was the love and peace now? Yoko did not speak. She did nothing to help appease John and neither did she show us any welcome. John's rage went on unabated. He told us to get out of the house saying that I had left him to perish as a child. He became so violent I thought he was going to hit me. Then he threatened me with my life. 'I'll have you buried in a slab of concrete next to that car on the lawn' he shouted at me. I grabbed our youngster and took Pauline's arm and fled out of the house onto the forecourt. We still had John's birthday present with us. Pauline was in a dreadful state. She thought John meant his threat. So did I. I was so scared I immediately went to a solicitor and swore a statement of all that had happened at Tittenhurst Park that day."

More distress was to follow. Freddie and Pauline were to get a call from an Apple executive only two weeks later telling them they had to leave the house that John had bought for them in Brighton. John was evicting them.

Freddie cast his mind back to that moment. "We were allowed two weeks in which to get out. We were heartbroken. We had spent more than £500 of our own money on fittings and repairs in the house. I asked if we could be reimbursed when the house was sold. John must have got the message as he sent a cheque for £500 a couple of weeks later."

Freddie shrugged: "So he could not have been that down on us, could he?"

But the couple and their baby had to move out and they found a flat close by that they could afford to keep.

It was another year before the wounds healed and father and son were to get back on speaking terms.

Despite all that had happened between them, Freddie maintained that he was still proud of his superstar son and was able to obliterate all the friction that had existed between them.

"Every day of John's life is filled with some new ambition," mused Freddie "He can't rest like other ordinary human beings. Okay, he's impulsive but with that amount of energy inside him he's bound to be."

When I last saw Freddie, just before his tragic death from stomach cancer in 1976, he was still talking about John.

He was tearful as he told me of the old happy days when he would take John as a toddler out in his pram down Liverpool's Penny Lane. "Folks would look at us and say, 'He's a chip off the old block, all right, Freddie. How did you manage it?'"

CHAPTER THREE

VIVA
LA REVOLUTION

The revolution seemed unstoppable. The 'Swinging Sixties' took on the spectacle of a stampede. Music fuelled the nation while the latest fashion tumbled out of Carnaby Street. Discos and nightclubs mushroomed and the young were trying to break down the restraints of the past as they perceived them to be.

Cinema audiences dwindled to stagnating levels as millions of erstwhile film fans switched their affections from celluloid Hollywood stars to closer-to-touch music heroes. My brief was to crack the big stories of the day as the revolution swept through. I was flattered to read in the American magazine Newsweek that I was apparently considered a 'tenacious journalist'.[1] I was unaware of that title at the time, as my pressing need was to stay ahead of the pack.

Hardly a day passed without a star hitting the newsstands. Most were already on my radar. If I had secured the trust of The Beatles then it was necessary to gain that same trust with The Rolling Stones, as between the two of them, they had triggered the revolution.

The Stones and their manager Andrew Loog Oldham were suspicious of my motives because of my connections to the Beatles. My path was cleared by Les Perrin, the doyen of the day's publicists who acted for the group. His intervention broke the ice.

"Don Short is a newspaperman. He isn't taking sides. He's got one goal and that is to get a front-page splash for his newspaper. It could be you or anyone who makes the headlines," he told the group, clarifying my intentions.

Mick Jagger saw the logic. So too Brian Jones who had founded the group, and Keith Richards, Charlie Watts and Bill Wyman were in agreement. Having got that vital nod of approval, I was invited to join the Stones on many of their key concerts at home and abroad. Their legions of fans were as effusive as those who trailed the Beatles.

Backstage strategy dictated a very different image. The Beatles were clean-cut, wore smart clothes on stage, said the right things. In the words of Keith Richards, they could be labelled as "real gents" in theatrical circles.

So the Stones chose to cut a more rebellious form. While I was travelling across Europe with the group, I happened to ask Jagger once if he felt the Rolling Stones had any moral obligation to teenagers. Jagger was ready with his answer: "Everybody has their own moral code," he retorted. "I conduct myself as I think fit and what I do is my affair. In the same way I feel this should be the right of every teenager of today. Stars and celebrities should not try to set any level in morals. Who are we to say what is right and what is wrong? Let teenagers live as they please — they are nobody's fools."

Anti-establishment, anti-social with a seemingly truculent take-us-as-you-find-us persona. Torn jeans and sweatshirts became a trademark fashion.

It was this kind of casual garb that perhaps I should have adopted when travelling with the Stones after my experience in Warsaw where the group were to give their first ever concert. Going through Customs in the usual manner I was singled out and escorted to a back office for questioning. It was only a routine procedure, I was assured, as I was strip-searched. As I re-dressed the senior officer apologised as he verified my credentials. He told me that I had been identified as the most likely suspect in the party to be carrying drugs.

"Why so?" I inquired. The Customs man smiled: "You looked too smart in a suit against your pop group friends in torn shirts and jeans. Someone might have planted some drugs on you without your knowledge." Travelling with the Stones was clearly not without hazard.

Indicating his friendship Mick invited me to a Park Lane hotel reception where the Stones were going to be presented with a gold disc.

"Don't worry about a taxi. I'll pick you up," promised Mick.

True to his word, Jagger arrived at the Daily Mirror offices in

Holborn to collect me in his new red Ferrari. The front desk receptionist called me to tell me he was waiting. I took the lift down and Mick waved a welcome to me through the windscreen of the car.

I opened the car door and attempted to climb in. But the floor of the car was so low that as I slithered to get into the seat, I heard my trousers rip apart.

Mick laughed. "We've got to go. Otherwise we will be too late," he said.

We got to the hotel and the presentation suite was packed with record company people, celebrity guests and other members of the Press. I was only too well aware of the large tear in the seat of my trousers and the only way I could manage the situation was to cross the room walking crab-like from side to side. Mick was clearly tickled pink by my situation and I got amusing glances from the friends in whom he had confided my predicament.

Afterwards, I hurriedly took a cab to Oxford Street and went straight into the first men's clothing shop I could find. I bought a pair of new trousers and kept them on — the torn pair were deposited in the store's litter bin. I strode out into the sunshine brimming with relief and with fresh confidence to face the rest of the day's events in the newsroom. Things could only get better. Or so I thought.

I got a custard pie thrown at my face at the London launch of the Stones' new record album 'Beggars Banquet' in December 1968.

The Stones had organised a Tudor-style reception with costumed waiters and waitresses.

It started peacefully enough. Serving staff in the hotel brought a boar's head on a salver and dispensed mugs of mead to the guests. But really observant guests should have suspected something when Mick Jagger arrived with a plastic fork where his carnation should have been.

Lord Harlech beamed as Mr Jagger introduced him as "a groove, a lovely cat." His connection to the group was through his elder sister Jane who had once gone out with Mick.

Then Mick marched to the top table and, smiling, thanked everyone for coming. The reason for his gratitude became obvious when the waitresses brought on the pies oozing with a custardy-meringue mixture.

Lord Harlech quickly copped one. And the Decca executives. And the record columnists. And, finally, the Stones themselves.

Lord Harlech bravely called it "an absolutely topping party," as he swabbed down his jacket from a direct hit from one of the edible missiles.

Indeed, most people took it remarkably well. But they had to, really. After all that food, no one had the energy to duck.

Things were about to take a very tragic turn for the Stones. It was the night of 2nd July 1969 when, working late in the office, I received an anonymous call.

A gruff unidentifiable voice came on my line: "Brian Jones has been drowned. Get to Cotchford Farm." The caller rang off.

I put an instant call to Brian's home. But the line was dead. He had changed his number.

There was only one solution. I hastily left the Mirror office to take the road to East Grinstead and to Brian's home.

When I arrived at his home in Hartfield, I saw a lone policeman and Brian's distressed girlfriend, Swedish dancer Anna Wohlin and one of Brian's aides Frank Thorogood.

They had managed to drag Brian from his swimming pool and Anna had apparently kept saying he was still alive thinking she had felt a pulse. But ambulance medics shook their heads. Anna was told: "There is nothing we can do to save him. We are so sorry."

Once I had established the facts, I ran to a phone booth in the hotel opposite and dictated my copy in rushed takes. It was a world exclusive for the last editions, and once more we had managed to outstrip our rivals.

But at Cotchford Farm, there was an atmosphere of desperation and disbelief, and there was nothing I could do or say that would have helped the situation. I made my way back to Fleet Street as dawn was breaking.

The inquest produced a verdict of death by misadventure but it was not a verdict that was overall accepted. Anna, for one, believed that Frank Thorogood had murdered Brian after they had a terrible row of some kind. There were rumours that Thorogood, who had been hired by the Stones guitarist to do some building work, had kept his foot on Brian's head as he was about to climb out of the pool after an evening swim.

The mystery did not end there. Some time later I got another anonymous call. I could not recognise the voice as again it was too gruff in tone and could have been made by speaking through a handkerchief. Whoever it was, the message startled me. "If you want to know who murdered Brian Jones. Go to Mick and Keith. They organised it." The call cut off.

I did not heed the words from the phone call. It was widely known that Mick and Keith were at odds with Brian Jones, having sacked him from the group some weeks earlier. They had viewed his attitude within the group as being destructive, largely due to what they believed to be his extreme drug addiction. Mick later confessed to the Rolling Stone magazine that he didn't feel any guilt about Brian's death. "He was very, very jealous, very difficult, very manipulative."[2] But there was not a shred of evidence that either Mick or Keith were involved in Brian's death. They had already dismissed him from the group, and he was out of their lives as far as they were concerned.

I had interviewed Brian Jones only a few weeks after his expulsion from the band. He told me, "The Stones' music is not to my taste anymore. I want to play my own kind of music. We had a friendly meeting and agreed that an amicable termination was the only answer."

Brian's gaunt, chiselled face and green-blue staring eyes had glowered disdainfully as he talked. He explained that he was often sore that practically all of the group's records were composed by Mick Jagger and Keith Richards and his compositions were ignored. "It's not that I dislike their music. It's great," he confided. "But there must be a fair crack of the whip. As a group we've got to consider all channels of music, mine included."

I then recalled how Brian had once told me that when the Rolling Stones' days were over, he would find what he really wanted to do. He wanted to develop his own rhythm and blues style of music — the rhythm 'n' blues that he loved so well.

It was with this pursuit in mind that he bought and settled into the fifteenth Century Sussex farmhouse where A.A. Milne wrote his immortal 'Winnie the Pooh' stories. At the time Brian called his friends and announced: "I'm the new Pooh of Pooh corner."

Brian was an intense introvert — far removed from the rebel we knew. He wasn't proud of his drugs trials he had faced and come through. He did not glorify in the hysteria and uninhibited life of a Rolling Stone. At a Court of Appeal hearing, at which Jones's nine-month gaol sentence for drugs offences were quashed in December 1967, Jones was said to be an intelligent and extremely sensitive young man who had been catapulted to fame. One psychiatrist described him as "an extremely frightened young man," while another told the judge about four interviews he'd had with Jones. He said: "He came in most extraordinary clothes which one could only describe as flamboyant. I think he had gold trousers and something which looked like a fur rug." Surprisingly, he added, he found the man inside the clothes quiet, thoughtful and courteous.

When Brian died, I thought back to what he had told me earlier: "No one would choose to live the kind of life I lead. Do you really think I enjoy it? But I mustn't complain or be bitter about it. It's brought the bread and the opportunity."

Brian's tragic death became a shroud that haunted the group for many, many months. The group's chauffeur and minder Tom Keylock went on Crimewatch in 1994 and told how he had visited a sick Frank Thorogood in hospital, who in his last hours confessed to murdering the Rolling Stone. Keylock claimed that Thorogood told him: "It was me that done Brian."[3] He died before he was able to reveal a motive.

Only days after his death, the Stones paid tribute to Brian Jones with a free concert in London's Hyde Park and hundreds of white butterflies were released in his memory.

Now, they had to move on and rise above the tragedy. Success and glory were still on the horizon. Another tour, another gold album were crucial stepping stones and once more I packed my bag and portable typewriter to continue trailing the band.

Many more intriguing stories were to unfold but in reality, the spotlight for Fleet Street was always focused on Mick and his love life.

It was a colourful subject. Monitoring his friendships became interesting. His relationships with aspiring actress Chrissie Shrimpton and singer-actress Marianne Faithfull provided me with many headline grabbing stories. Scandals and drug busts regularly exploded into the open. Marianne, once confessing to heroin addiction, figured in many such episodes. There were break-ups and stormy scenes. Nevertheless, it seemed odds on that they would eventually marry.

But it was not to be. It seemed that Mick transferred his affections to a married American singer Marsha Hunt who had his child — a girl named Karis.

The News Desk might have been forgiven if they concluded that this was the end of the story. But Mick's adventures were far from over.

Out of the blue, Mick announced he was going to marry Nicaraguan diplomat's daughter, Bianca Perez Moreno de Macias, whom he had met in Paris in the Spring of 1971. Another front-page story in the making.

But then came a surprise twist and one that I had not anticipated. It came as a request from Les Perrin. Would I agree to be the bridal couple's bodyguard throughout the nuptials in St. Tropez?

"Bodyguard?" I gasped in astonishment.

"Yes," confirmed Les. "Well?"

I did not have to think twice, although I could not promise any degree of fitness for such an onerous task.

Fear of the expected furore the wedding would cause clearly meant we needed a second bodyguard and my trusty colleague Patrick Doncaster agreed to play the role with me.

Our prize in return for our 'services' was to be granted the first and exclusive interview with the couple after the nuptials.

We flew to the South of France and twenty-four hours before the wedding in St. Tropez, we met Mick, Les Perrin and the local police chief to put the plan in place. It felt as though we were being briefed and sworn-in on some secret SAS mission. Mick told me: "I dig marriage, yeah." He grinned, "Living in sin has become too conventional."

I was excited to report on another possible union that day. The Beatles had also been invited to the Jagger wedding. We knew that if all four made it then it would have been their first get-together for eighteen months. Mick had chartered a private jet plane to bring more than thirty celebrity guests to St Tropez. John Lennon said in London the day before: "It will be good to see Paul. There will be no ill feeling between us. I'm wondering whether we should take our guitars in case we have to do a number at the reception." In the end, only Ringo appeared.

The big day arrived. Apprehensively, we made our appearance the next morning. Just one glance at the baying fans and invading paparazzi already gathered outside the St Tropez town hall where the ceremony was to be conducted made us realise that Perrin had not underestimated the commotion that he and the French police had predicted would evolve.

There seemed to be thousands blocking the precincts to the Town Hall which the town's mayor had failed to seal off. The Mayor threatened to call the whole ceremony off, such was the tumult. Mick, in his best suit, and Bianca, in an Yves St. Laurent white jacket and a long skirt, left it to Les Perrin to talk the Mayor round into allowing the ceremony to go ahead.

So, risking all and sundry against the huge tide of fans and cameramen, we managed to guide Mick and Bianca through to the hall.

Trouble and tempers again escalated when the couple emerged as man and wife. The crowd went ballistic. We placed ourselves either side of the hemmed-in couple now marauded by the flash-popping paparazzi, rival journalists and hysterical fans. Punches were exchanged between the frantic crowd.

Patrick Doncaster was elbowed and almost bowled over. My own battered frame was savaged relentlessly, but inch by inch, we achieved our aim to get the couple into the waiting limousine to make their escape.

Our next stop was the region's Catholic church for the couples' blessing and, again, the heated scenes were overwhelming. We battled on through the day and once back in the safety of the Byblos Hotel, we recovered and took stock of the situation.

Some hours later, we were able to talk in more peaceful surroundings to Mick and Bianca in their private hotel suite. We had got our scoop and to our delight the story was spread across the front page of the Mirror the next morning. One published photo of our struggle on the Town Hall steps became iconic — a picture in which we figured in the full thralls of our bodyguard duties.

Coincidently, in 2014, my daughter Amanda was redecorating her home. At a West End store, she stumbled on the same picture, clearly having survived the years. Only now it was being reproduced as an entire wallpaper mural. "Dad, you've become a wallpaper," my daughter teased. Some might have considered that it was a snip at £163. I do not know how many customers might have invested in such a mural but my daughter commendably resisted the temptation!

Not long after his marriage, Mick, then twenty-nine, was assuring me that he was going to quit the scene when he reached thirty-three. "After that I will find something else to do. I couldn't bear to end up as Elvis Presley and sing in Las Vegas with all those housewives and old ladies coming in with their handbags. It's really sick. Elvis probably digs it. That's his good fortune if that's the way he wants it. Not me." He must have had a change of heart.

A week after the wedding, I met with Keith Richards and his girlfriend Anita Pallenberg, who had once partnered Brian Jones. I was to dine with them at their villa near the coast at Villefranche. It proved to be a long night filled with lots of vintage wine and indiscreet chatter about many of the stars of the day and their misdoings and foibles.

Said Keith: "Who was surprised Mick got married? Not me. I guessed he would. That's his scene. Me and Anita don't have to do that. We don't want to be fed into a computer and come out on a ticket."

Keith had come to the South of France to escape English taxation. "England is too expensive to live in, man," he told me. "Everything about England is prohibitive." I knew this was a common concern amongst the pop fraternity as Paul McCartney had once told me that they lost nineteen shillings and sixpence in every pound they earned.

What about music and recording sessions? I asked.

"We've taken over a closed-down cinema along the street which we're using to rehearse in. Just now we're scoring the next album and we're half-way through. No, Mick and I don't sit down and write it just like that together. We're not your Rodgers and Hammerstein."

Time wore on and Keith realised that it was far too late for me to travel back to Cannes where I was staying.

"Why don't you pitch down here for the night and journey back in the morning?" said Keith. It was a nice gesture and I was more than happy to accept.

Anita, who had kindly prepared dinner for us, was now showing me into one of their spare bedrooms. The room was empty, other than a chest of drawers and a large bed sprawled out on the bare floorboards.

"It's not five star," joked Keith, "But you'll find the bed comfortable. Good night," he sniggered as he closed the door.

When I climbed into bed, I found the reason for his humour. Pitching down was an apt description. It was a waterbed and I was swaying around on its mattress like a child playing on a bouncy castle. My worry was that the mattress might have burst if I didn't remain still and it was on that daunting notion that I finally fell to sleep. When I departed the next morning I wondered how many other house guests had coped with the waterbed, but friends back in London told me that waterbeds were all the rage. We live and learn.

In the sixties, he and the Stones and the Beatles were routinely occupying the front pages. But they were not alone, as many other groups came to the fore determined to grab the attention of the rapturous, indoctrinated fans and claim their space in the day's newspaper columns. Bands like The Who, Status Quo, The Byrds, The Monkees and The Beach Boys to name just a few were making their mark and could not be ignored. Nor so a galaxy of solo artists in the mould of Roy Orbison, Bob Dylan, David Bowie, Elton John, Tom Jones, Engelbert Humperdinck, Dusty Springfield, Cilla Black, Lulu and Jimi Hendrix.

But the revolution had its casualties. It was hard to believe that the biggest victim of all was Elvis Presley, the King of Rock 'n' Roll and without doubt the music industry's most worshipped star.

Elvis had vanished from the public eye, seemingly in retreat from the international blitz of the Beatles and the Stones. The revolution had apparently forgotten him. No one had seen him for nine months. Neither were there any new records from him. His fans had become puzzled and disconsolate by his mysterious absence. Just what had happened to him?

My telephone line was abuzz with rumours. One of my contacts was led to believe that Elvis had been imprisoned in an ivory tower and given little communication to the outside world. Could that be why his name had been virtually expunged? It was an engrossing theory.

There was only one way to get the answers. I took the night plane to Los Angeles in 1965.

It was an on-spec assignment and I realised that getting to Elvis would not be easy. And once out there, would he see me? He was always surrounded by a posse of aides and cronies known as the 'Memphis Mafia.' Breaking through the barrier they imposed was not an easy task.

Installed in my room at the Chateau Marmont on Sunset Boulevard, I knew I had to rely on my network of contacts. Calling in old favours, I eventually managed to get through to the right source. I got my break — Elvis had agreed to see me. So just where was this ivory tower? The outcome was a little different from the one I imagined.

Elvis's ivory tower transcended to the shape of a luxury caravan on a Hollywood film studio floor, where he was working on a new movie: "Paradise, Hawaiian Style."

Like all Hollywood stars, Elvis had been assigned his own private caravan which doubled as his dressing room and homestead for the duration of the shoot. I knocked on his door and Elvis, in a beige shirt and trousers, answered. He looked tanned, fit and well — a replica of his star image.

"Come on in, sir," he said. "Make yourself at home," motioning me to sit on a narrow couch beneath a small window. I had been called a lot of names in the past (many of them derogatory) but I couldn't recall being addressed in such stately tones as 'sir.'

"It's Don," I persuaded Elvis. He smiled.

His manner was courteous and sincere and there was no flicker of emotion as we talked about the rumours flooding Europe. I could not help but admire his self-discipline, an asset he may have gained from his days as a U.S. Army conscript. He kept calm and patient. No sign of any tantrums or temper.

Was he a prisoner caught up in an ivory tower? I pointedly suggested to him. Elvis shrugged. "Look around you. Is this the ivory tower you are talking about?"

I peered through the caravan window. The Paramount studio floor was crawling with film props, crews, extras and technicians. I couldn't argue the point — not in the midst of this setting. But I persisted. So just where had he been and, more importantly, why had he never performed a single concert in Britain where millions of fans were exasperated by his absence? Was it any wonder they were switching allegiance?

"Oh, I like The Beatles and I've got all their records. Your British groups have really been something. I mean it. I'd say that — even if they put me out of business," Elvis joked with another smile.

I knew that two years earlier Elvis had been invited to London to appear on the Royal Variety Show being attended by the Queen. But Elvis had turned the invitation down. To avoid giving offence by his rebuttal and to ensure there would be no further approaches he sent a cheque for £1000 for the show's charities.

Didn't he want to meet the Queen? I asked him. Elvis sighed: "It would be a great honour, sir."

So why had he not come? Had he been prevented from coming? Elvis was about to answer but at that precise moment we were joined by the singer's mercurial manager Colonel Tom Parker, the man I was told kept Elvis under virtual wraps and kept him guarded by the Colonel's own squad of cronies.

The Colonel cast a hard stare at me. "Does Elvis wish to see your Queen?" he roared rhetorically, as if I had said something incendiary. "That's not the question. Let's find out whether the Queen wants to meet Elvis. If she doesn't — then we've got no place to go."

I realised at that point I had no place to go either and I moved the conversation on to his helicopter pilot role in the film he was making, and what he thought of his vivacious leading lady, the twenty-one-year-old actress Suzanna Leigh from London. Elvis was effusive. "She is causing quite a stir here. She is bubbling with personality and I couldn't wish for a better co-star."

We parted on friendly terms and the Colonel assigned a photographer to take a picture of Elvis shaking hands with me as I stepped down out of the caravan.

The Colonel[4] — not a military colonel but a title he had adopted from the days he spent in Kentucky where he was a circus showman — was a Dutch immigrant to the States and he did not hold a passport.

It was said that he would not have allowed Elvis to go on any concert tour abroad without him as he feared losing control of his star. His influence on Elvis was that of a Svengali. He didn't welcome journalists or anyone else probing Elvis's finances, or like them questioning the fifty per cent cut he deducted from the star's earnings. The Colonel was a high stakes casino gambler and he needed all the funds he could get to ensure his seat at the gaming tables. But I could not help being taken in by the old rogue.

Over lunch in his studio suite, the Colonel was all smiles as he defended his strategy in looking after Elvis's career.

"Elvis always tells me that I have made him the star he is, so he relies on all the decisions I make for him..." the Colonel explained. "We're making movies now and that's what Elvis wants to do. He's happy doing it. Listen, if Elvis wants to do something — then he'll do it. I wouldn't stand in his way but I will always give him the advice he needs..."

I wasn't entirely convinced by the Colonel's assertions, and the picture of Elvis being trapped in an ivory tower had not gone from my mind.

We lunched on the Colonel's huge mahogany desk which had been cleared of all his trays, files and papers and a white tablecloth spread out over the surface. Two flunkeys appeared with dishes of salmon, prawns and salads and another waiter appeared with bottles of white Californian wine. The Colonel lit a cigar and leaned back in his leather chair. He knew how to win people over.

Suddenly he started looking round his office. There were gold discs hanging on the wall and, on an upper ledge, lots of Elvis pennant flags and paraphernalia. I could see that the Colonel was searching for something.

"Don, are you married?" he asked. "And you've got kids?"

I nodded. "Married and two children," I replied. The Colonel glanced to the far corner where a very large toy dog — the unmistakable replica of the one that appears on the face of the old HMV records and affectionately known as 'Nipper' — was poised sitting. Colonel Parker got up and lifted the enormous creature and thrust it into my arms almost bowling me over in the process.

"Here Don. Elvis would want you to have this for your two little kiddies."

I had to peer over the dog's head to thank him. I didn't want to appear ungrateful, but I was travelling to five other US cities with a typewriter and lots of baggage. Carrying the huge toy dog around was going to create some problem for me. But as I walked out of the studio to get into a stretch limousine that had been laid on for me, I reasoned that I could give the toy dog to the first deserving children I spotted in the lobby of the hotel where I was staying.

The Colonel must have read my thoughts. "Don!" he shouted to me as I was climbing into the car. "Can you do the Colonel a favour? When you get back to London, can you take a picture of your two kiddies with Elvis's dog?"

I heaved a sigh but I could not help admiring the Colonel's brilliant piece of thinking. Maybe he did have telepathic powers. He had truly outflanked me.

So Nipper and I travelled the States as companions together. When I returned to London, I took a picture of my two children hugging the dog and sent it to the Colonel as he had requested.

A year went past and, finding myself back in California once more, I paid the Colonel a surprise visit at his studio office. When I walked in the first thing I saw was the picture of my daughter and my son with the HMV dog now framed and hanging on the wall behind him.

"There you are!" greeted the Colonel, pointing to the picture. "I'm glad your children like Elvis's doggie."

How did the Colonel know I was coming? I thought that he may have been alerted by security guards at the studio gate. It was unworthy of me perhaps to suspect that the Colonel kept similar pictures of guests who visited him and rotated them on his wall to meet the occasion. But as a PR ploy, I realised it could work wonders.

Elvis was to make his comeback to the live stage at the end of July 1969. It was not an occasion to miss and the greeting from 2,000 fans packed into the auditorium of the International Hotel in Las Vegas for the opening night was as manic as I had seen for the Beatles or Stones.

It was a bewildering and incredible moment. A moment many of his loyal fans across the world didn't believe they would see again. But the gamble he took was whether he could still cling to the legend he had created, now that he was married and a father, or be cast out as an unwanted relic of the rock 'n' roll age.

There was no doubt. Elvis (or 'Elvis the Pelvis') pranced the boards like a panther in his bell bottom trousers and black tunic. Out poured the hits 'All Shook Up,' 'Jailhouse Rock,' and his newly cut song 'Suspicious Minds' which would go to No.1 in the charts within weeks. Fans besieged the stage and one girl threw her knickers close to his feet. Elvis picked up them up, mopped his sweaty brow and threw them back to her. It was a performance of raw emotion as the King flipped and cartwheeled across the stage. At the outset he had told the fans: "Before the evening is out I'm sure I will have made a complete and utter fool of myself — but I hope you get a kick out of watching." He need not have feared. These devoted fans were all won over before he sang the first note.

On the following day I joined three other English journalists to talk to Elvis in one of the hotel private lounges.

Wearing a dark jumpsuit, he looked as fit and well as I had seen him those years earlier. He was sat on a settee with a bunch of his cronies sprawled around him and looming in the background was the keen-eyed figure of the Colonel standing like Elvis's custodian to ensure his star didn't say the wrong thing.

Elvis explained he had been in a rut and that was why was he had not made any public appearances for so long. He had also been working on a string of film musicals that the critics had unanimously panned.

Surprisingly Elvis was not going to defend himself. "I can't hide my feelings," Elvis began. "I am ashamed of some of the movies I've made and some of the songs I've had to sing in them," he told us. "I'd like to say they were good but I can't. I've been extremely unhappy with that side of my career for some time. But how can you find twelve good songs for every film when you're making three movies a year? I knew a lot of them were bad songs and they used to bother the heck out of me. But I had to do them."

Elvis went on to say he had wanted to perform on stage again for the past nine years. "It's been building up inside me until the strain became intolerable. I've got all het up about it and I don't think I could have left it much longer. It was something I missed a lot. I always wanted to get back into live concerts but I've been too busy filming."

American audiences were ecstatic to see Elvis's return to the stage and he performed many sell-out concerts in the country in just one year. The King was back and he was happy to reignite his glittering career.

****

There was one musician who steadfastly believed that the revolution was actually triggered in the Fifties. Jerry Lee Lewis, a wild living veteran of that era, and known to his fans as 'The Killer' had certainly been influential in pop history. Stars like Elvis and the Beatles had been influenced by him.

And, in the spring of 1972, the American pianist-singer, then at thirty-seven years of age, was in London on a comeback concert tour.

His fresh series of gigs were to attract the retired Teddy Boys and loyal fans of the past as if he were a multi-ribboned war chief recalling his reservists. They were in thrall to his full-frontal attacks on the piano keyboard. He literally lit up the venues with his blazing hit 'Great Balls of Fire.'

For Jerry Lee, it was a tour that helped to wipe out the memory of his debacle in 1958 when he arrived in Britain with his bride, his 13-year-old cousin Myra — his third wife. So much hostility erupted that Jerry Lee and Myra had to flee back to America and his £40,000 nationwide tour of the UK was cancelled after only three concerts. Jerry Lee was branded as a 'child snatcher' and when he got back to the States he was blacklisted and his career almost stuttered to a halt.

No one believed the marriage would last but Jerry Lee claimed he proved his critics wrong when the marriage survived thirteen years before they were to divorce. Jerry Lee said he was sad when the marriage broke up: "But when Myra went to a private eye to check me out and he came on me with a scroll of names of a flock of women I'd been to bed with — that was it. Myra asked me if I could remember any of them — I couldn't. But I couldn't say I didn't enjoy 'em. She couldn't forgive and forget and I can't blame her. What do you think Myra did? She landed up marrying the private dick who had assembled the evidence against me!"

The American singer was ready to admit his weaknesses. "Booze and women," he confessed. "And I've gotta have them both when

I need them."

We talked in his hotel suite in London and Jerry Lee, wearing a red tunic sweater and jeans and a pair of plimsolls without socks, lit a cigar.

He went on: "I've never asked a woman to marry me. All the women I've married asked me to marry them and damn it, I've let myself get talked into it."

Jerry Lee got talked into it seven times over, as I was to note through the years.

[1] NEWSWEEK 'Baby You're a Rich Man, Too' by John McMillian https://www.newsweek.com/2013/12/20/baby-youre-rich-man-too-244952.html Date: 19/12/13

[2] Rolling Stone Magazine 'Mick Jagger Remembers' by Jann S.Wenner. 14th December 1995

[3] Independent Newspaper 'Tom Keylock: Rolling Stones Fixer from the 1960s' Wednesday 9 September 2009

[4] Born Andreas Cornelis van Kuijk in Breda, Netherlands, 26th June 1909. Died 21st January 1997

CHAPTER FOUR

THE REVOLUTION
RAGES ON

I was making almost routine visits to Las Vegas, the showbusiness capital of the States, a city of clubs and neon lights and of casinos without clocks. I had become such a familiar face on TWA and Pan Am flights that the air crews welcomed me as one of their regulars.

My assignment in May 1970 was to see Diana Ross make her solo debut after breaking away from The Supremes.

The blue upholstered theatre of the Frontier Hotel was half empty and the audience seemed stricken with suspicion — as though they were putting Diana on test on her opening night.

"It's like starting all over again," Diana told me. "But I am determined to go through with it. I don't mind. That's the way show-business is. Ten years with The Supremes and now I have got to introduce Diana Ross as though no-one knows me."

She was conscious of the fact that most people blamed her for the break-up. "I know that is true and to a degree it was my fault. But Mary and Cindy had come to the same decision. We had all grown up and we had all acquired different ideas and opinions, and there was no longer any communication between us. But there wasn't any bitterness over the parting. I have no regrets. The only time I miss them is after a show when there's no-one around to argue with."

The Supremes had continued without Diana. They were also going their own route and I learned they were in San Francisco with newcomer Jean Terrell joining Mary Wilson and Cindy Birdsong.

The Beatles and Beyond

In her dressing room, Diana reflected on a performance in London two years earlier when the image of The Supremes was tarnished on the night of the Royal Variety Show. I remembered the night well. Diana slotted a freedom message into one of the songs. The Supremes had obviously planned it as a moment of high drama, but its impact was lost by the cool reaction of the audience.

The message came in the middle of Leonard Bernstein's hit 'Somewhere.' Diana cut into the ballad's lyrics to plead for freedom for blacks and whites and said, "Let our efforts be as determined as those of Dr. Martin Luther King who had a dream that all God's children, black men, white men, Jews, Gentiles, Protestants, Catholics could all join hands and sing that spiritual of old, 'Free at last, thank God Almighty.'"

There was a little uneasiness in the theatre, although the Queen Mother and the Royal Family applauded. Some critics were shocked but Diana, as she thought back on that eventful night, explained to me: "It was not meant to be offensive, it was a message of peace."

There was certainly an aura of peace now for the singer. The audience welcomed her as she treated them to her new chart buster: 'Reach Out And Touch.'

Diana told me: "It's too late to go back. If I've made a mistake in pursuing a solo career then I can only blame myself. But I am not a loser. I might lose the odd point sometimes like everyone must. In the end, yes, in the end, I am a winner." So it proved.

Diana's wishes for equality and peace were shared by Nina Simone, who I interviewed at the May Fair hotel in London in the spring of 1969. She told me her thoughts on being regarded as the 'High Priestess of Soul,' and we talked about gospel music and black power.

She was frank. "The message is more important than the music to me, although the two cannot be separated. It is said that I inspire Black Power and I like to think I do. Because through this movement comes new hope and strength for coloured people who have suffered for centuries."

She added, "My real message is for love and care. People don't care enough about one another in this world."

She was thirty-four and had just returned for a European concert tour during which her audiences rampaged her stage nightly.

"It was a thrilling experience," she said. The tour showed the immense strides Nina had made in the previous six months as a result of two successive hit parade smashes. She had earned a silver disc for 'I Ain't Got No, I Got Life' while sales were almost as big for 'To Love Somebody,' penned by the Bee Gees which she cut two years before.

Her husband and manager Andrew Stroud, once a New York detective, and their six-year-old daughter Lisa travelled with her on the European tour and shared her new fame.

But in London, she arrived to a slight setback: her latest record 'Revolution' had fizzled into apathy. She couldn't hide her disappointment. "Of course I am sensitive about my records. It means money to the record company and," with a flash of a smile, "and to my husband."

She told me how she came to write her new song.

"It was inspired by the Beatles' 'Revolution' but I didn't understand what their lyrics meant. So I wrote my own 'Revolution.' It's about revolt all over the world. Not only the racial one, but the young versus the old, the rich against the poor and the new breed against the Establishment."

Her final words in our interview showed her spirit: "I am carving my own little niche in this world by my own music in its own style. I live for my music and when I die I want to leave some kind of mark that is all my own."

Just over a year later, I met Aretha Franklin in Britain, who had similar concerns to Nina Simone about the reaction in Britain to her music.

She had given a concert in London, but audiences were disappointed in her performance, saying that it was devoid of the magical aura she normally created. Days before she left to return to America, I interviewed her in her Savoy Hotel suite.

I wondered how many of the audience knew that for Aretha Franklin it was only her first month in her comeback to the concert stage after a year of total nervous exhaustion?

The twenty-seven-year-old talked to me about the lost year in her career. "I'd given as much as I could to show business. Concerts night after night, hotels and travelling. It all caught up with me. I just couldn't go on any longer."

Aretha added, "I had to go into hospital and then I was really foolish, believing that I was well enough to keep one of my engagements in Las Vegas where I had been booked for a season. I got out of my hospital bed in New York, and, against my doctor's advice, I went there. But it was too much for me. I did the first night, but the next day I collapsed and I was back in hospital."

There had been a grapevine of whispers that Aretha had been under the influence of drink, and maybe even drugs. No show had ever opened and closed so fast in the show capital before.

"That's how people talk," said Aretha, as she clasped her hands together. "And you can't stop them thinking what they will. But none of it was true. I was a physical wreck and I stayed in hospital until I recovered enough to go home."

The previous month, the queen of soul picked up her career and she did precisely what any other star would do. She went back to Las Vegas to live down the nightmare of the year before. She got a royal greeting and was a huge success, and from there she flew on to Europe and England.

But, as Aretha was to find out, a comeback bid is never without stress and strain.

Aretha was booked for the Royal Albert Hall but had to cancel for what she told me were personal reasons. She then decided to substitute it with a Hammersmith concert to appease her fans.

In the Savoy, she was trying to be as happy and as relaxed as she could be, sprinkling her conversations with a funny dig at English accents and making humorous remarks like, "Splendid, old chap."

Aretha and her husband Ted White had parted and with her four young boys, moved from their home in Detroit to an apartment in New York. "I'll find something more permanent when I get back," she told me. "But please don't ask me about marriage. It's something I don't want to talk about."

I respected her wishes and admired her grit and perseverance. She had thirteen gold discs to her credit with 'Respect' and 'Say a Little Prayer' among them. It was clear that she would battle on and the queen of soul was not going to abdicate without a fight.

"My career and my music, apart from my children, are the most important things to me," she told me, with the determination of a star who planned to reign again.

The Byrds had had a similar resolve when I met them in 1968.

The American group had got a cool reception from British fans on their first visit in 1965 but they planned a second tour three years later. They were determined to put things right.

I flew to Rome to intercept the group just four days before they were due in London. They were making the final preparations for their visit and it was virtually a new line-up in the ranks but Roger McGuinn (one of only two original members of the band) was ready to admit the mistakes that were made on their ill-fated first tour.

"Everything went wrong for us on that trip. We left England nursing strong feelings," he told me, lager in hand. "The English Press claimed we were poaching on Beatles-Rolling Stones territory. And the fans just didn't take to us after that. It was all so wrong. We even had our only Gold Disc stolen in Britain."

He went on: "We were ready to blame the British then. But now we realise the fault was at our door. We just weren't ready for the tour and your fans saw through us."

The Byrds, he conceded, had presented their image badly. He explained honestly: "We blew up because we didn't have the experience behind us."

McGuinn was also to confess that he was the only member of the Byrds who actually played an instrument on their smash hit of the Bob Dylan composition 'Mr. Tambourine Man.'

"They were our voices okay but the rest of musicians were session men," he revealed.

After that unsuccessful tour, internal troubles broke out. There was a management dispute and later three of the Byrd idols left. New recruits were taken on and it was clear to me in Rome that The Byrds were ready to project a different image and were setting out to veer towards a more Country and Western sentiment in their music.

They had just recorded a new single, another Bob Dylan song. McGuinn looked at me apprehensively as he unveiled the title 'You Ain't Going Nowhere' and dissuaded me from suggesting it was a bad omen.

McGuinn caught my thought. "Don't worry. We know where we are going. And that's a promise," he said.

Another star who had been fretful about a cool response in Britain was Barbra Streisand. It was the first night of 'Funny Girl' at the 1100 seater Prince of Wales Theatre in April 1966.

The show was a sensation. But Streisand bit her lip tearfully as the curtain came down. She said: "I don't think it was electric out there. They were so quiet, I only felt the things that were going wrong. I wish they didn't have opening nights."

Barbra had taken six curtain calls, and I felt she could have taken more. Showman Bernard Delfont, who presented the musical with Arthur Lewis, told Barbra: "It was a much better reception than Broadway."

Then he added: "This is natural. Most young artists react like this on an opening night. It was a tremendous ordeal for her. But really this is the most fantastic West End premiere we've had for years."

Barbra stayed only a few minutes at the champagne party on stage for the cast, but she was smiling as she arrived at a second party in Leicester Square. It had been a brilliant night and I thought the only problem facing the management was: Who could possibly replace Barbra when her fourteen-week contract ran out?

****

Personal secrets often have a strange way of emerging. The cool look of American folk singer Julie Felix never once betrayed her secret that she was married.

She gave the impression of being single and was once heard to remark: "If I don't marry soon, I am going to be an old maid."

She almost gasped, she said, when she heard herself saying such a thing but it was all part of the camouflage protecting her secret.

"Then I told myself: 'Why should the public know about my personal life anyway? Can't I just keep something to myself?'"

From that point on, Julie vowed never to talk about her marital status and whenever she was asked about romance and marriage, out came her elusive touch: "A marriage maybe one day... only when it means security."

My column produced a copy of Julie's wedding certificate, revealing she had married advertising manager David Evans in 1966 when she was aged twenty-seven and he was twenty-three.

The American star, her long black hair tumbling over her shoulders, sighed as she said: "I am glad it has at last come out."

She was surprised that no one had found out before — "I've always worn a wedding ring — even on television." No one seemed to have spotted it.

Julie could have gone on living with her secret. She could have also gone on with the disguise, had it not been for a bunch of fans of an American pop group who were refused a renewal of their work permit by the Ministry of Labour.

"How is it Julie Felix manages to stay here and work all the time? She's American too," one of the angry fans demanded when confronting a Ministry official.

It was then the truth emerged. Simply, the authorities had no reason to interrogate Julie. She had married a Briton and she was entitled to stay and work in Britain.

Julie reflected: "The world really does go round and round with a lesson each day. And we learn with each revolution."

She added: "Perhaps I should thank those kids. Now there will be no need for pretence." The folk singer was clearly relieved.

****

The Bee Gees could thank one man for their stardom. That man was their Australian manager Robert Stigwood.

His was a rags to riches story. He had once worked in a hostel down under looking after the elderly, those in need, and the homeless. But a chance meeting with a theatrical friend set him out on the path to the entertainment industry. He hitchhiked to London with only thirty shillings in his pocket when the sixties started. His rise to the top was phenomenal.

When I met with him in 1969, he was the head of a £5,000,000 showbusiness empire with the Bee Gees as its showcase stars.

But Stigwood implored me not to relate his story as one of rags to riches. It was a scenario difficult to ignore. For the Aussie, from his poverty-stricken past, was now living in one of the country's finest sixteenth-century mansions where we had lunch in the heavily beamed dining room.

It wasn't all plain sailing for Stigwood at the outset. London's Tin Pan Alley wasn't the place for the meek and mild, and Stiggy got caught in many affrays but his bruises only served to motivate him further. Attempting to poach an act from a rival agent (which I shall relate in a chapter ahead) may have been a fatal mistake. But somehow Stiggy survived.

When he started in the fickle pop scene, the signs looked promising. But Stigwood's first-registered company went into liquidation with £40,000 worth of debts.

One might have thought that this was the end of the trail. But Stiggy's energy and ideas fascinated a fresh circle of financial angels who were willing to back him in new enterprises. Stiggy then made his master stroke. He signed the British-born, Australian-raised brothers Barry, Robin and Maurice Gibb — the Bee Gees. New horizons opened up.

I had listened to the Bee Gees' acetate of 'New York Mining

Disaster 1941' and knew it was going to be a success. It was to pave the way for a whole string of chart busters like 'To Love Somebody' and 'Massachusetts' and many others. As Stiggy's career flourished, so did that of the Bee Gees who expanded the band for a time with two co-opted members Colin Peterson and Vince Melouney.

Stigwood moved into television, theatre and films, bringing into London's West End theatres the controversial shows 'Hair,' and 'Oh Calcutta!' before staging the epic Tim Rice musical 'Evita.' Hollywood became in awe of this new entrepreneur intruding on their sacred ground when he produced 'Saturday Night Fever' and 'Grease', two movie blockbusters with the talented Bee Gees contributing to the music.

It was inevitable there would be setbacks in the film business and Stiggy experienced one or two failures, but when he suffered them his resilience to disaster was astounding. Simply, he took another step forward, conducting his affairs through his multi-offices in Hollywood, London, Paris, Berlin and Sydney.

So how could I dismiss the compelling rags to riches story? I reasoned that it was something to be proud of, his journey could inspire so many. Stiggy smiled. "I can see that's a dilemma for you," and reminded me of our conversations in earlier days when he and Brian Epstein were exploring the idea of an alliance.

It didn't pan out but when Epstein died the door was open for Stiggy to sign the Beatles.

"I was offered a sizeable stake of their company Apple but it didn't give me overall control. So the deal broke down. I must have control of everything I get into."

I didn't want to hurt Stiggy's feelings, but I knew that the Beatles were not great admirers of the Australian interloper. In fact, it was they who had blocked the deal.

But then there were no regrets from Stiggy. He was the one impresario who could have afforded to say: "Who needs the Beatles?"

****

Scott Walker described himself as an American delinquent because he refused to go home and become a soldier. So he chose to remain in Britain and found himself in another struggle he detested — the battle for stardom.

"I loathe the showbusiness ladder and the way it operates and

I loathe more the people hustling behind it. I don't want to be a pawn in it."

That was why, Scott confessed, he was sceptical about popularity polls and one in 1969 which placed him as Britain's top singer. Scott believed that was a spot occupied by Tom Jones.

"I'm not in any showbusiness bag. I don't sing to please the public as much as I sing for myself, and I only do it for the bread," he told me candidly. "I hate being identified with the pop scene. I'm not a pop singer and I don't swim with the scene. I'm not trying to be snobbish about it, but I'm trying to go my own way... I don't want to be pigeonholed. I don't write my music to be commercial and I don't sing for the hit parade."

Maybe he didn't sing for the hit parade, but his records had an uncanny way of appearing there.

Two years had elapsed since Scott split from The Walker Brothers, but no one doubted that it was Scott who would find instant stardom when he chose to go solo. His immense baritone voice typified on 'The Sun Ain't Gonna Shine Anymore' was the forerunner of many great hits. Scott, who was applying for British citizenship, told me: "I can't go back to America. It could mean going to gaol for three years and I don't feel I would dig life in gaol very much."

Scott's family home was in Ohio and he was the son of a wealthy geologist. He was quite frank about his homeland. "It's a cruel scene there, man. I'm thinking of the race riots, Vietnam and the rest."

Many might have cast him as a draft dodger but there were so many other stars who were pacifists like the singer and vehemently protested at America's involvement in the Vietnam War. Scott Walker's fans weren't ever going to see him that way. To the contrary they hailed him as a hero. He was going to win the chart-conquering war.

****

Elton John had first appeared in my column in the early days of 1970. He was making a huge impact with early hits such as 'Goodbye Yellow Brick Road' and 'Candle in the Wind.'

There was something about Elton's fashion choices too that reminded me of David Bowie's love of stage outfits. Elton also created his stage identity in sparkly, sequined clothing, statement glasses, and an added extra — a pair of torturous platform boots. I don't know how he managed to walk in them.

In the sixties and early seventies, it was not acceptable to come out as being homosexual. Elton struggled to disguise the truth.

There was gossip spilled on the grapevine of rival girlfriends vying for his arm, and hints of potential marriages, all conjured up by his management team to ensure the feverish girl fans were not alienated. I formed the impression that Elton, at that period, was not sure of his sexuality himself.

He told me how he had the chance of marrying a millionaire in 1969 but chose his music instead.

"We arranged the wedding but three weeks before the ceremony I called it off. She wasn't very happy but in the end she realised music was the only thing I was in love with."

Elton did go on to marry a German recording engineer Renate Blauel in 1984, but there was speculation that it was a cover for his homosexuality. The marriage was dissolved four years later.

****

Perhaps the most famous for his sartorial choices was Liberace. He seldom went anywhere without his 'Momma', his brother George and his gold candelabra. But he flew to Britain in 1968, his first visit in eight years, without 'Momma' or George, but with a fantastic wardrobe, including a light-up suit.

"Momma is 75 now," Liberace explained. "She is at home with the great grandchildren she has been blessed with." He added: "None of them have anything to do with me..."

He was forty-eight years old, immaculately dressed, and was eager to talk non-stop about his favourite subject: Liberace.

He kept his press conference waiting for an hour in London. But it was not because he was lost for words. "I lost my wardrobe at the airport," he explained. "And you know what that means to me."

He breezed into Heathrow in a white tunic-style suit, a peace medallion and a candelabra-style ring.

He later talked of his work as a pianist-extraordinaire and quipped: "I like today's music — once you take the noise away."

A journalist reminded him of the time he told a critic: "Okay, so I cry all the way to the bank." He smiled at the memory and said: "Now I've bought the bank..."

****

The Revolution Rages On

The Sixties revolution had left one man broke. Andrew Oldham, an expelled public schoolboy, tea-maker to fashionista Mary Quant, club doorman, discoverer of the Rolling Stones, founder of a record company empire and one-time millionaire, was on skid row.

He had only two assets left at the vulnerable age of twenty-six as he told me when I went to meet him at his home in Richmond in Surrey.

"This house I stand in — and my head. That's it, man. That's all that's left," he said coolly, as though he had conditioned himself to a situation so close to the nitty-gritty.

Outside on the forecourt of his beautiful historic mansion stood a Rolls Royce, a Lotus, an Aston Martin, a beach buggy and a couple of other jalopies.

Without so much as a sigh, he glanced through the lattice windows and said: "They've all got to go."

He was even able to force a smile.

"Why, man, I've even been on the Tube lately. I might have to get used to it."

His record company — Immediate Records — had crashed just a month earlier in April 1970 with debts of £300,000. Since then the red-haired, bearded man of pop had become a recluse in his own home. His palatial offices in London's Oxford Street had been closed, so too his branch office in New York.

One of the marker points in the rise and fall of Andrew Loog Oldham came two and a half years earlier when he and the Rolling Stones severed links.

"We split because we all got to the stage of mutual boredom," explained Oldham. "We had made so much bread and I for one didn't want to know anything anymore."

I had heard things a little differently. Oldham had made the mistake of hiring Allen Klein, the American producer to be the Stones business manager. As a result, Oldham's own relationship with the Stones became strained because of his cocaine habit and his long periods of absence. Klein saw his chance and took control, leaving the Stones no option but to fire Oldham.

Oldham did not stay out in the cold for too long. It was then he formed Immediate Records and a roster of artists were signed to the label including the Small Faces, Rod Stewart, Eric Clapton and others. It had all looked so promising, but finances were stretched and when the company went into liquidation, the artists signed to the label had to find fresh mentors. Oldham did not show a flicker of distress or any emotion. He shook his head.

"I couldn't find any new group to match the Stones," he told me. "Whatever else is said about them they were as close to professionalism as any five artists can get."

As I left Oldham, I saw a thin tight smile appear on his lips, like the smile of a gambler who made one feel his game wasn't lost. He was clearly contemplating the next throw of the dice. We had not heard the last of Andrew Loog Oldham.

****

Fashion model Twiggy, very much part of the Swinging Sixties revolution, was talked into making a record by one of London's major record companies. But when I came to review the record 'Beautiful Dreams' it was hard to believe she had been persuaded to cut such a drum beaten platter. I feared it was going to flop and tarnish Twiggy's flourishing career.

No one could dispute Twiggy was the ultimate face of fashion with her striking androgynous looks. But when it came to singing, she sounded like a shy schoolgirl at morning assembly who is hoping that no one will notice her. Her voice was timid and strained.

Her manager at the time, Justin de Villeneuve, was harbouring regrets. "If this doesn't win out then I doubt if Twiggy will sing again. She hates her own voice and we hadn't thought about this until Ember Records approached us. We then thought it might be a good idea as the fashion and pop worlds are so closely linked. But now we will have to see what happens."

I did not blame Twiggy as much as the record company chiefs. They liked to sign celebrities like Twiggy to sell their records on big name values.

Also stepping into this contentious arena was Barbara Windsor, best-known then as a star of the 'Carry On' films. She cut a novelty record titled 'Don't Dig Twiggy' — a record she claimed she made just for a joke. It was composed by socialite writer Robin Douglas-Home. There were no holds barred on the lyrics.

"I just hope Twiggy won't think I'm insulting her. She's a tremendous kid and she has a lot to offer. My disc can't do Twiggy any harm. Or upset her. Besides, the fact I have made a disc about her must be complimentary to her. Don't you think?"

Complimentary? Barbara was ready to elucidate.

"Well, when you start singing about other people they must be well known. Isn't that true?"

Twiggy took it all lightly, but how wrong had I been in dismissing her vocal powers so quickly in the first place? Twiggy, with real determination, entered the pop affray on a more cultivated canvas recording numerous singles and albums and many of them breaking into the charts worldwide. She went on to sing in concerts at the Royal Albert Hall and broke into movies. She even won two Golden Globe awards as 'best actress in a film musical' for her role in The Boy Friend.

Some of the older generation saw the Sixties as an age of promiscuity and decadence. They chose to stay with the evergreen troupers like Sinatra, Andy Williams, Tony Bennett, Matt Munro, Perry Como and their contemporaries. These stars had withstood the battle against the young and raucous — against the revolution itself. And their records were still in demand. Tony Bennett put a seal on it. "We are the survivors," he told me, not without a sense of relief.

CHAPTER FIVE

EARLY DAYS

Whenever I drive past Croydon's Aerodrome Hotel facing the Purley Way, memories flood back at the sight of the de Havilland: a four-engine Heron aircraft planted like a sculpture on its imposing forecourt. It has been given a nice new coat of white paint over the name of its airline, but it is unmistakably the same plane in which I often travelled in my early days as a news reporter with the Daily Mirror.

If there was a ship floundering at sea, an urgent mountainside rescue, or a similar drama occurring beyond normal reach, then the Heron was at the Daily Mirror's instant call. It was on standby at Gatwick Airport to transport the Mirror's reporters and photographers to the scene or to an aerial observation point.

The Daily Mirror retained the Heron and two of its sister aircrafts (a twin-engine Dove and a Dragon Rapide) on a long standing contract for such emergencies with their operators Morton Air Services. Their fleet was also based at Gatwick Airport, where it relocated when Croydon Airport became defunct in 1959.

I lived closer to Gatwick than most of my colleagues on the editorial staff, so I found myself in the firing line of duty in or out of my regular shift patterns whenever it was necessary to take to the air.

It was the Heron that I boarded with a photographer to fly to the Alpine ski resort of Innsbruck in March 1964, to report on a tragic disaster when a Britannia passenger airliner with eighty-three Britons aboard crashed into the snow-covered-fog shrouded peak of the 8500ft high Mount Glungezer.

The Austrian city of Innsbruck, with the towering Alps flanking the approach to the main runway, is still regarded as having one of the most dangerous airports in the world for pilots to navigate and land at safely.

We flew over the crash scene the next morning when the fog had cleared. It looked as though the Britannia had hit the peak, snapped in half and toppled into a deep ravine. The tail section of the plane stood out starkly against the snow. Peering out of our plane flying overhead, we could see rescue workers dotted on the mountain.

I had to cling on to the waist of our zealous photographer while he leaned out of a partially open door of the Heron's fuselage in a bid to capture the horrific scene beneath us.

Sadly, there were no survivors from the crash, and it emerged that most of the victims were British families happily bound for a winter sports holiday. It was a tragedy that occupied our front pages for several days.

Covering a jewel raid in Jersey brought the Rapide into action and I flew out alone with the plane's pilot and navigator. Twenty-four hours later, my story was wrapped up and filed to London. We were homeward bound, but I sat in the cockpit next to the pilot as his navigator had been taken ill overnight and was being attended in St. Helier by a doctor.

En route we ran into thick fog, which developed into a real peasouper as we neared Gatwick. Suddenly the intercom radio crackled into life.

"You cannot land here at Gatwick," a stern voice from the airport control tower commanded. "We've got a blanket of fog over the runway. You must divert elsewhere."

My pilot, an ex RAF squadron leader with a swashbuckling nature who had averted many aerial dramas in the past, retorted: "Can't be done. We haven't got enough fuel. We're coming in."

There was no answer. I could only imagine he switched off the intercom to ensure there would be no further discussion on the subject.

Through the thick fog we made our approach and I doubt if we could have seen more than thirty yards ahead of us. Then, as I strained to peer through the cabin windscreen, I finally caught sight of the lit runway at the last minute, only well starboard to the direction we were heading. We were landing on a grass strip parallel to it, some twenty yards adrift, but my Squadron Leader was unperturbed and put the plane gently down on the green turf with only the slightest of bumps.

I was not privy to what the Control Tower operatives might have said to him later. I could only guess. But this was when Gatwick was not as congested with the heavy volume of air traffic it handles today. Otherwise we would have been in real trouble and my pilot's actions would not have been countenanced!

Working at the Daily Mirror was like living a new adventure every day. Court cases at the Old Bailey, militant union activities in the docklands, political chicanery, gangster feuds, eloping couples, art robberies — all the sequences of human life were about us. This was the daily diet for the news reporters on the floor. The breaking stories were individually assigned to us by the News Desk team headed by Ken Hord, a disciplined, bespectacled headmaster-like news editor who did not fit the image of the widely imagined stereo-typed newspaperman. But he was scrupulously fair to his staff and was widely respected in Fleet Street.

I was a keen tennis player and I managed to persuade Ken that it might be worth sending a news reporter to cover the Wimbledon tennis fortnight. It struck me that there were many newsworthy events during the fortnight that could make good copy which went unnoticed by our sports writers who were totally glued to the play and result of the matches.

Ken stroked his chin thoughtfully. "Alright Don. Let's go," he said.

I had effectively created a new role in Fleet Street which other newspapers were quick to follow as an abundance of stories materialised.

Many stories from Wimbledon made the front page: there were tempers and tantrums erupting on court, romances between players, athletes who fell injured, exciting line-call incidents, weather interruptions and so many unexpected happenings.

The All-England Club decided to reinforce their strict all-white dress code for the players after top Brazilian star Maria Bueno wore shocking pink underwear on court in the 1962 event. Other players like the American Gussie Moran had flouted the rules in earlier years with colourful underwear beneath her shortened skirts. Wimbledon frowned on such conduct saying that Gussie (or "Gorgeous Gussie" as she was then known) had brought vulgarity and sin into the game.

Maria Bueno did not believe she had broken any rules and an Italian player, Lea Pericoli, complained of Wimbledon's dictate: "It's so, so sad. How can a lady dress without just a little colour somewhere?", while tennis player Pat Stewart disagreed and said,

"Tennis, white and tradition go together."

My features department asked me to contribute a piece on the coloured clothing controversy. When the article appeared, I received letters from one or two irate readers accusing me of being a voyeur, and another reader branded me a pervert.

Fortunately, the majority of the post I received was in full favour of players being allowed to make up their own minds on what to wear on court. Tennis fashion designer Teddy Tinling thought Wimbledon's crusty, twelve-strong all male committee had made the wrong decision to re- impose the dress code so strictly.

"Outdated thinking," he told me. "I have designed everything with white and that's as far as I can go with it."

Today, Wimbledon maintains the all-white code but uses discretion if players prefer just a hint of colour in their court attire.

My role as a news reporter at Wimbledon lasted for eight successive years and was extended with the same aims to cover Henley Regatta and then Cowes. Little came out of Henley (other than champagne corks popping and picnic parties) but Cowes produced a stream of headlines.

In the summer of 1962, Prince Philip was taking part in the yachting festival as a competitor with his friend and famed boat builder Uffa Fox, and I was sent to report on their presence and activities.

The Duke of Edinburgh had narrowly missed a terrible accident. He was standing under the thirty-foot arm of a crane as his yacht — the 'Coweslip' — was being winched on to a jetty at Cowes. Suddenly there was a crack. The crane snapped at its base. Instinctively, the Duke glanced up and leapt aside.

The split-second leap saved him. The massive crane arm crashed on to the spot where he had been standing. The Duke was cool and turned to Uffa Fox and said: "That was a close shave, Uffa."

It was the second drama of the day for the forty-one-year-old Duke and sixty-four-year-old Uffa. Earlier, they both took a ducking when Coweslip capsized during a Cowes race.

From the Mirror office in London came immediate instructions.

"You must find a way to get to Prince Philip!" Ken Hord rattled out. "No? Okay, then see if you can get hold of Uffa Fox..."

A score or more of my journalist rivals must have received identical instructions from their news rooms as there was a gathering of reporters outside Uffa Fox's harbour boathouse. Despite constant knocks on the door and notes pushed through the letterbox — no reply came.

Some thirty minutes later, during which time the Prince and Uffa had showered, an aide came to the door and said: "There are so many of you here. But the Prince has agreed to see one reporter on behalf of you all."

We all went into a huddle and I was nominated as the pack's sole representative.

I pressed the bell resolutely once more. The aide opened the door to welcome me in. I followed him up a small staircase and into a front room where Prince Philip and Uffa were languishing on a couple of armchairs facing one another. They were drinking whisky and a bottle of a fine Scottish malt was in my eyeline on a small glass-topped coffee table.

Uffa ushered me into a chair and said, "Would you like a whisky young man?"

Prince Philip, with a mischievous glint in his eye, said: "I'm sure he would Uffa. They are a hard-drinking bunch in Fleet Street."

The atmosphere was convivial and Uffa, stripped to the waist, told me what had happened when the boat capsized. They were jockeying for position half a mile out when a rival cut across their path. The Duke turned the tiller about — and just missed a collision with another yacht, Blue Heaven. Then Coweslip capsized. The Duke and Uffa were flung into the sea in their oilskins. Coweslip, with the Duke and Uffa clinging to the waterlogged hull, had to be towed back to Uffa's jetty at Cowes. It was there that the crane arm crashed. Fittings at the base of the two-hundred-year-old crane were torn apart by the weight of Coweslip. The yacht was taken to another jetty a hundred yards away. The Duke and Uffa, still in their soaked sailing clothes, baled out Coweslip with buckets before she could be hauled on to the quay. Uffa added, "It's the first time in the fifteen years we've been racing together that we've ever fouled another boat — or ever been in the drink."

Prince Philip nodded confirming Uffa's description. By then, two more large glasses of whisky had been poured for me by the obliging Uffa. And when he poured a fourth, I attempted to desist but Prince Philip intervened.

"I thought you chaps were hard drinkers," he said. "You can't let the side down." I drank it swiftly and explained that my colleagues outside would be waiting for me. The Prince and Uffa both laughed. They had staged an ambush for their own merriment.

Uffa said: "There you go then."

I crawled out of the armchair and staggered down the staircase.

In the fresh air outside, I realised I was finding it difficult to walk evenly. My colleagues surrounded me with notebooks poised for me to read back my shorthand notes. I looked despairingly at my scribbled notes trying to decipher the squiggles but I could not make head or tail of them, no matter how close I pulled my notebook to my squinting eyes. I was getting more and more flustered.

Someone at the back cried out: "He's pissed!"

With that, Guy Race from the Daily Telegraph grabbed my notebook and, with amazing skill, was able to read my shorthand as though he had written himself.

Drunk? Maybe. But at least my shorthand was impeccable. The pack was delighted and the Express man patted me on the back.

"Well done Don!" he said. "There's a drink waiting for you in the pub across the road."

It was a reward, for good reason, that I had to decline. Nevertheless, it was mission accomplished: we all made the front page with our stories the next morning.

My previous encounter with Prince Philip had brought out similarly mischievous behaviour. He was at the Chelsea Flower Show in 1959 and was being shown round an exhibit called the 'Garden of the Future.' By chance, I was only a few yards behind him when he noticed a control panel for the garden's watering system. I heard him ask one of the guides: "What does that button do?" He was told: "It waters that area of the garden, sir." "Oh," said Prince Philip, glancing at a pack of photographers who were encircling him on the lawn.

Suddenly, a jet of water hit the air and spiralled over a bunch of cameramen. I could not help but see a wry smile cross the Prince's lips, but in gentlemanly fashion, he went over to two of the drenched photographers to sympathise with them.

True to form, and later in the day, a Buckingham Palace spokesman denied that it had been Prince Philip who had actually pushed the button. Time for me to go Specsavers.

Another event bestowed on me for coverage was the yearly Miss World contest. It was one assignment envied by some of my chums in the office tied to more mundane duties. For me and photographer Kent Gavin, it became a regular seasonal stint. Betting shops generally relied on our preview of the contestants at rehearsals in readiness for the big night. Our coverage gave the bookies enough information to set odds on the contestants.

I later wrote a book about Miss World and all its winners over the years. Unfortunately, the publishers blighted the book's purpose as a true record of the event by using a picture of a girl's naked derriere on the cover. It had no bearing on the content of the book. It was clearly a commercial stunt and when I saw the printed book in the shops, I felt wretched and apologetic to those who had given their time to relate their personal stories to me. Through the years, the pageant itself ran into lots of controversy, but one story, which I shall recall in a later chapter, involved Tom Jones and it really scorched the headlines.

****

I had always dreamed of being a newspaper reporter. At my secondary modern school, we were asked to fill in a form citing three possible occupations we would most like to get into.

My first entry was that of a reporter, my next a BBC radio sports commentator and finally — for reasons I cannot recall — an estate agent.

I won a scholarship to Chiswick Polytechnic where my studies were centred on shorthand, typewriting and English. All necessary ingredients to fulfil my journalistic ambitions.

My family were working class and we lived in a rented terraced house in Staines, then a part of Middlesex but now repositioned in Surrey. My father Herbert, a cabinet maker by trade, ran a second-hand furnishing store after the war, and my mother, Lilian, remained at home to look after me and my four younger siblings. We had been lucky to survive the war. Two or three bombs, a doodle bug and a V2 rocket hit houses only a few hundred yards from us. Our ceilings and windows crashed around us in one raid, but none of us was hurt.

One of my earliest memories was the day war had broken out and my mother, who could not help but panic when faced with such dire moments, hugged me in tears and said: "Daddy will have to go to war. We will not see him again."

I imagine many wives and mothers would have had the same uneasy feeling.

In fact, my father didn't go to war but, owing to his carpentry skills, was dispatched to the foliage-hidden hangers at Windsor Great Park to help build Wellington and Lancaster bombers for the RAF.

I was born in the Great Northern Hospital in Gray's Inn Road.

We moved to London to a basement flat in nearby Kings Cross, before moving to Staines not long after the outbreak of the war to be close to my father's parents. They had moved there from Wantage, where my mother's own family lived. When the tensions of war grew, and the 1940 Blitz came, we went to stay for the year as a family with my widowed grandmother in her tiny terraced house where she had brought up ten children of her own. Most but one had left home and some had been called up for active duty.

My father remained at home in Staines, looking after our house, and cycled to Windsor Great Park and back every day throughout the war. At night, he was on duty with the ARP. It was not an easy life for him.

Our close-knit community, like thousands of others across the country, threw a wonderful celebration street party with a huge tent decorated with bunting and flags when Winston Churchill declared the war was over. It was a joyous year, although rationing was still in place and would remain so for many more years.

My father opened his furniture store with a friend, and one day brought home several cases of second-hand books he had gathered in a house clearance. I had the idea of forming a library with them and logged each one before announcing my little enterprise to the neighbours in the road. I would charge them one penny per book per week to take out. But, of course, many of the books were never returned and not too many pennies exchanged hands.

By running the little library, I had perhaps unconsciously instilled the future pattern of my career. A career which began at the age of 15 when I left Chiswick Polytechnic to go to work to help the family income. Through shop gossip on the High Street, my father had learned that the Staines and Egham News were looking for a boy as a trainee in the local newspaper office.

I applied and got the job for the princely sum of fifteen shillings a week, giving seven shillings and sixpence to my mother for my keep.

It was a meagre wage compared to the salaries that some of my fellow students were earning but I had taken my first step into a newspaper office. I shall always remember my first day. I wore my one and only best suit only to be given a massive pile of dusty old newspapers falling from a cupboard to sort out and restack in date order. But the local editor, a ruddy-faced Bill Norsworthy, was soon to take me under his wing and accompanied me to local council meetings and to the Press benches in Feltham's magistrates court. Within a year, I was seen as sufficiently competent to take on such tasks on my own and I was made a member of the National Union of Journalists. I was now able to show my Press card with pride at any function I was assigned to. In my free time at weekends, I liked to cover local football matches and I would produce reports for the next issue of the paper. I also took up tennis. I had been with the paper for three years when, at the age of eighteen, I was called up for the obligatory National Service.

I served with the RAF and occupied the lowly rank of a LAC — Leading Aircraftsman — and remained so throughout the whole term of two years. This might be explained by a photograph I still have of me from my RAF days in a training march. I am easily identified in the picture, as mine is the only foot out of step.

I had turned down the opportunity of a commission, because it meant enlisting for a minimum of three years which I was not prepared to do, as my only interest was resuming my career in newspapers. Once in uniform, we were asked if we would rather occupy a clerical position at home or have a role overseas. I opted for the job at home, given my experience in office work gained at the newspaper, and I applied for a possible post in the RAF's Press Office. But the service ignored my credentials as I had shown them to be and plonked me on the troop carrier the Empire Ken for East Africa, making long stops in Egypt and Aden. It was my first trip abroad.

I reached Nairobi and the RAF's Eastleigh base where I was given the unlikely job of running the camp's clothing store. It proved fortuitous. It afforded me lots of spare time and within weeks, I was moonlighting as a reporter having made contact with the East Africa's daily newspaper the 'East African Standard.' The Standard's sports editor Steve Mitchell hired me on a freelance contract and I began covering tennis tournaments, boxing, football and hockey matches. I was paid one penny per line of print face and I received a regular monthly cheque.

Inside the base, I launched a station magazine I named 'Focus' featuring all the news of the airmen's activities to include soccer, safari jaunts into the bush, mountain climbs to Mount Kenya and Kilimanjaro and a whole range of other interests and hobbies. I charged sixpence per copy, and along with the revenue gleaned from local advertisers, was able to meet the costs of the printing bill.

It would have been difficult to survive on RAF pay as it was just a few shillings a week. But with the additional income I was making from the Standard, I was able to pay other airmen to undertake my guard duties whenever they came around. An act which did not please a particularly muscular Geordie who felt I was skiving out of things and chose to vent his feelings by throwing a punch or two at me in one of the hangers that served as a storeroom. I was left black and blue but the Geordie came out a little worse. He had hit me so hard he broke his arm in the process and the arm was still in a plaster cast when I next confronted him, taunting him for an immediate re-match. We both laughed and became good friends.

Perhaps the most memorable moment, and one of historical significance during my stay in Nairobi, was the arrival on 1st February 1952 of Princess Elizabeth and the Duke of Edinburgh. They were visiting for a holiday break in the hope of seeing some of Kenya's teeming wildlife and were to reside at the famous Treetops hotel.

I got a camera to photograph them as they stepped out of their BOAC airliner after it landed on the Eastleigh runway. I intended to use the pictures for my 'Focus' magazine, but the pictures were not published, overtaken by a tragic event which was to occur just five days later when news came through of King George VI's death in London. The sensitive but stoic Princess was declared Queen and she and the Duke hastily returned to England.

Nearing time on my RAF days, I was invited to stay on in Nairobi by the East African Standard, but realised I might have been instantly enlisted by the military to fight the dreaded Mau Mau terrorists. What I really wanted to do was to return to my family at home in England and get back to my job with the Staines and Egham News. Once home and demobbed, I was welcomed back by family and by the weekly newspaper which had kept my job open for me.

Romantic pursuits were on the horizon. Very soon I was to meet Wendy Foster, a very attractive and witty optician's assistant, who worked opposite my office. We got married and I left the Staines and Egham News for a new post at the Richmond and Twickenham Times. But I had to break with protocol and, on my first day, I handed the editor who greeted me a letter giving him my one month's notice to quit. He was bewildered having not experienced such a bizarre welcome before. I explained to him that I had accepted another post that offered not only better prospects, but also a semi-detached house for us to live in, which would become our very first home. Jobs at local papers sometimes came with accommodation (and occasionally a car) as part of the deal. The editor graciously accepted my situation and allowed me to work for the paper for the month before releasing me from his employment.

So my beautiful bride and I moved to the Cotswolds where I was to become a district reporter in charge of the Cirencester branch of the regional evening newspaper, the Gloucestershire Echo. We were very happy there and we were blessed with the arrival of our daughter Amanda. In later years, we had our son Ashley, and second daughter Louise, to complete our family.

My wife had no wish to leave Cirencester. I was earning good money and we were paying a peppercorn rent for our house. We had also made many good friends there.

But after two and a half years, I could no longer resist the call of Fleet Street — every reporter's dream. I joined the Daily Sketch at their invitation. We moved to Surrey, leaving the beloved Cotswolds behind and a region where, coincidentally, my father and his twin brother were born and had spent their childhood.

I stayed with the Sketch for eighteen months. It was a chaotic office with the news editor Bert Pack under constant pressure from the executives mulling over him like hornets.

When the first editions of our rival nationals dropped nightly on the news desk, it was catch-up time on stories we had missed out on. On-duty reporters had to crib those stories from the pages of our rival papers to reproduce them for our own late editions. I took home a classic edition one morning when I found I had four different stories and by-lines: 'from Don Short in Paris', 'from Don Short in Rome', 'from Don Short in Madrid,' and best of all 'from Don Short in New York.' Some journey! I wondered how many readers would have noticed. That was the Sketch. Always in a frenetic, urgent mode. Corners, like our expenses, always had to be cut.

In 1959, I joined the ranks of the Daily Mirror and, having survived the general news voyage, I was appointed the paper's showbusiness reporter the morning after I had managed to get a world scoop on Elizabeth Taylor and Eddie Fisher.

My life was to change tack from that moment on. When I departed from the Mirror, I formed a new company I named Solo, whose journalistic and publishing activities will thread through these memoirs.

CHAPTER SIX

STAR TRACK

Elizabeth Taylor flew into London in 1960 to take the title role in the epic movie 'Cleopatra.' That, in itself, was marked as a major event that I was assigned to cover. But an unscripted drama was to unfold, like a bolt of lightning from an unexpected thunderstorm.

The actress was struck down by a mysterious virus that initially confounded Lord Evans, the Queen's physician, and several other doctors. Her life was seen to be in great danger as she was moved from her luxurious suite at the Dorchester Hotel to a private wing of the London Clinic hospital. She was diagnosed with 'meningism' — an inflammation of the membranes of the brain or spinal cord — which had the symptoms of meningitis but without its often fatal effects.

Her husband Eddie Fisher visited his stricken wife daily and he came to regard me as a friend when I helped him to evade the paparazzi. Such was his gratitude for my support that when his wife was allowed to recuperate back in the comfort of her own hotel suite, he invited me to visit her. It was a breakthrough on the story that I could not have dared to hope for.

Before taking the lift up to their Dorchester suite, Eddie warned me that Elizabeth was still weak, and one other thing: "She doesn't like newspapermen, but I have told her that we can trust you and she is willing to see you." Eddie also gave me an added briefing: "Please don't call her Liz. She only likes to be called Elizabeth."

I had a bouquet of flowers in hand, but I soon realised they were a little superfluous. It was like entering London's finest florist. Glorious flowers tumbled from every corner, having been sent by a multitude of well-wishers. The whole suite was bathed in a beautiful fragrance.

Eddie showed me into the star's darkened bedroom, lit only by a bedside light. Elizabeth was sat up in bed wearing a yellow nightdress. She looked pale and nervous, but in a whispered voice she said, "Eddie tells me that you have been helping us. That's very kind. I'm sorry I have not always had a good experience with reporters in the past."

She smiled. "Now, I've never felt so happy in my life. I've never been so glad to be alive. There were moments in the last seven weeks when I thought I would never see another day. But just now the world seems a wonderful place to live in."

She added: "I don't know how or when I picked up this virus or when I went into hospital. I just don't remember. All I know is that it's wonderful to be back with Eddie and my children. Now I am longing to start the film. It means more to me than any other I have made. To those who put their faith in me I would like to say, 'Thank you.'"

Her illness had caused unwelcome delays on the filming schedule of Cleopatra at Pinewood studios and was said to have cost Twentieth Century Fox £1,250,000.

There was profound relief when Elizabeth appeared on set and the cameras were rolling. But not for long.

Just as the clapper boards struck back in rotation, Elizabeth Taylor fell ill again. Only this time, she had gone down with pneumonia and she was rushed back to the London Clinic where she was given a tracheotomy to save her life. The physicians had nothing but admiration for the twenty-nine-year-old's fighting spirit. One doctor told me: "At least on four occasions during her illness she was as near to death as she could be."

Eddie Fisher turned to me again for support as a friend. With Elizabeth on the mend, he invited me back to the Dorchester to see the family.

A relaxed, casually dressed Eddie was surrounded by Elizabeth's three children from her earlier marriages. I had equipped myself with boxes of chocolate for the youngsters who were happy to see their mother safely home, although eight-year-old Michael and six-year-old Christopher from her marriage to actor Michael Wilding and five-year-old Liza from the star's marriage to producer Mike Todd, could not have known how close to death their mother had been.

"We always travel with the children. They are never left behind," confided Eddie, diverting the conversation away from any possible mention of his wife's illness which might have disturbed the children.

Elizabeth appeared dramatically from one of the bedrooms. She made her entrance as though she had just stepped out of a movie screen, a moment perhaps from 'Cat On A Hot Tin Roof.'

She was dressed in a shimmering blue night gown. Her famed violet eyes fixed directly on me. I noticed the scar from her tracheotomy on her neck. She must have caught my passing gaze.

"I am lucky to be alive," she said quietly out of the children's earshot as they played. "The surgeons saved my life. They told me that at one point I had stopped breathing. They thought I was going to die. Thank God they did not give up on me."

I was now the invited guest and we had a pleasant evening with platters of Mediterranean dishes passed around the table which the children clearly enjoyed. Our chatter across the table was no more than small talk. The children's plans for the next day, what they wanted to see in town and inevitably the British weather! Between them they visibly lifted their doting mother's spirits.

As her health improved, her filming schedule was back on track, and it was not long before Elizabeth was again in front of the cameras.

Only a few months before, an astonishing offer came from Hollywood producer Walter Wanger when he asked Elizabeth Taylor to play the eponymous 'Cleopatra.' Wanger told her to name her own figure. Elizabeth, not to miss an opportunity, obliged. "One million dollars and ten per cent of the box office takings," she suggested tentatively, not believing she would be taken seriously. To her surprise Wanger did not blink. "Fine," he agreed. "Let's do that."

Overnight, Elizabeth Taylor became Hollywood's highest paid actress of the era. Filming began at Pinewood Studios but quickly moved to Rome. Suddenly into the mix, came the Shakespearean actor Richard Burton who was to replace Stephen Boyd in the role of Mark Anthony.

I was pleased for Burton. I knew him well and had spent many convivial evenings in his company. He possessed a unique presence in the theatre and on the screen. Several of my peers regarded his acting talents to be parallel with those of the formidable Laurence Olivier.

Billboards for 'Cleopatra' could not have carried two more glamorous names: Elizabeth Taylor and Richard Burton. It was a magnetic fusion of casting. And so it proved. 'Cleopatra' was a conduit for searing, torrid love scenes and almost inevitably, it was a match to spiral off-camera into real life. Astoundingly, under the very watchful eyes of Eddie Fisher.

The singer had been married to Elizabeth for less than three years. Now the marriage was crashing about them like rocks falling from a cliff edge. Eddie, so confident just a few months earlier, did not know which way to turn.

There was anger in his voice when I caught up with him in Rome. He shook his head in disbelief of the evolving situation. Woefully, he told me, "I don't know what is going on. What can I do?"

There was no objective advice I could give him. Commiserating with him would have been insincere. My gut feeling was that Eddie should have known and seen the dangers. There were so many warning signs and gossip among the film crew.

Meanwhile, all sorts of problems were hitting the running of 'Cleopatra' and budgets were soaring, threatening Twentieth Century Fox with bankruptcy.

But for Eddie that wasn't an issue. He was more anxious about things closer to the heart and his relationship being beyond repair.

At the end of a day's filming, Burton's obsession with Elizabeth saw him regularly make himself a guest at the couple's rented villa on the Via Appia.

Burton's high-spirited ribald stories of the past visibly entertained Elizabeth at dinner and Eddie shrunk tamely into the background. One night he wanted to make his presence felt. He started to play the piano and sing, only to be told by his wife to shut up and not to interrupt the conversation she was having with Burton.

Eddie admitted to me later: "That was the final straw."

Divorce loomed and lawyers were consulted. Things weren't going to be easy and frustrations boiled over.

In Rome, Elizabeth and Burton grew close: days at the seaside thirty miles away; champagne parties at Burton's villa. It was not realised at the time, but Burton also faced marital strife. His wife Sybil sued for divorce.

With 'Cleopatra' premiered and widely panned by the critics, and yet another movie completed, Burton moved on to film in Mexico and the woman he dared to call Liz joined him there. They took a cottage in the fishing village of Puerto Vallarta. For weeks they waited for Liz's assumed quickie divorce to go through. The actress had even chosen her wedding dress that had been expertly stitched to the last seam in readiness for the big day. But the nuptials had to be put on hold.

Bitter, angry words were being exchanged. The happy couple claimed that Eddie was demanding one million dollars in cash for granting the divorce. The cuckolded Eddie, appearing in a stage show in Las Vegas, denied he was demanding a cent.

Richard Burton was in dispute. He blazed back: "We are told privately by our lawyers that Mr. Fisher's demands are in the realm of the fantastic and quite intolerable."

Liz was seemingly more sympathetic but not without a touch of cynicism. "Eddie is right in a way. He hasn't asked for a cent of my property — just a million dollars in cash."

The story was now making headlines all around the world. I felt it was time to catch up with Eddie in Las Vegas. I found him just as he was in the process of packing his bags to fly out to New York. He claimed he had come to terms with the situation but wished to put things into perspective.

"I am not seeking vengeance. I have no reason to. But everyone seems to have a short memory, especially those involved," he told me. "They want to forget the past too easily. Remember, this was the girl I loved. This was my wife and this was my family. But I have learned a lot from the moments of hurt. I am not bitter about it now."

Why, then, I asked, the delay over the divorce? "It's not a squabble over money," said Eddie. "And I am not demanding a million dollars. The issues involved are human problems — the kind of problems that any couple have to sort out when their marriage breaks up."

Eddie harked back to the previous year when Burton and Liz were in London filming 'The V.I.P.s' together. "I went to stay for three months in the State of Nevada, and on three occasions I tried to contact Elizabeth about our divorce," he confided. "But I got no answer. Now, when it suits them, they plant themselves in Mexico and say what they want — and demand it now. Like children asking for a lollipop. I am not going to be part of a slanging match. I'll leave that to Burton — he is famous for making statements."

Eddie paused when I suggested that he was holding them to ransom.

"No. I haven't got them on a string," he countered, with a shade of sarcasm. "I'd rather have a yo-yo on the end of a string now I

come to think about it." He went on: "Everything is being manu-
factured. The fantastic demands I'm supposed to have made don't
exist. Just let me out of this snake pit — that's all I plead. And if
we all stop talking and show a little sense we can get the divorce
through. That's essential for the sake of the children. Then perhaps
we should all sit back and count our blessings."

Another six months passed before the divorce went through. Just
eleven days later in March 1964 Burton and Liz were married in
Montreal.

It was a bitter, emotional moment for Eddie but then there was
not much public sympathy for him in losing Liz in the way he did.
Some felt he had got his just deserts as he had divorced his devoted
wife actress Debbie Reynolds (with whom he had had two children, the
late Carrie Fisher and her brother, Todd Fisher) in order to comfort
and marry Elizabeth. At the time, Elizabeth had been grieving over
the tragic loss of her third husband, Mike Todd, who had been killed
in a plane crash. Eddie had been best man at their wedding and was
reliably on hand to support her through the ordeal. Their affection
for one another through this period led to their marriage.

After their divorce, it was some years before I saw Eddie again.
Unfortunately our friendship was to sour somewhat when we did
meet, which I shall relate later.

My focus now was to move more closely to the travails of Liz
and Burton who were rarely absent from the front pages.

I flew to Budapest at the end of February in 1972, where the
actor had organised a glitzy star-studded party to celebrate Liz's
fortieth birthday. It was the party of the year with David Niven,
Michael Caine and Ringo Starr among the high-flying guests.
Parisian designers had given new décor to a hotel suite ahead of the
arrival of Princess Grace of Monaco.

Photographers and journalists from all over the world laid siege
to the Hotel Continental where the lavish party was being staged.
Despite my advantage of knowing the couple, I thought that there
wouldn't be a chance in a million of cornering Elizabeth and
Richard on their own, so I had no alternative but to join the melee.
I was lucky to get a few words from the joyful couple as they posed
for the barrage of cameras hemming them in.

Burton presented his wife with the famous Taj Mahal diamond, a
heart shaped gem with origins in the seventeenth century. Liz was
ecstatic. From all accounts, it had cost a cool £380,000 at the time.
Mr Burton kindly draped the pendant round his forehead — Cleopatra

style — for the assembled photographers. Managing a brief aside, I wished the couple well and thought that would be it.

Fortunately, on the Sunday morning, I was able to meet with him while Liz was dressing in their tenth-floor suite at the International Hotel in time for the next event in the weekend festivities — brunch.

"I tried to buy the Taj Mahal, but I couldn't transport it," Burton told me, jokingly. "But I managed to find this diamond. I suppose it has enough carats to make it the size of a turnip. It was designed by the prince who commissioned the Taj Mahal."

I heard afterwards that the birthday gift was purportedly first presented to Mumtaz Mahal by her adoring husband Shah Jahan who also built the Taj Mahal for her some time before her death in 1631.

The lemon-tinted diamond was beautiful, surrounded by rubies and other gems.

"I don't know what they all are," Richard went on. "I don't know much about stones — I only pay for them."

Liz had enjoyed the party tremendously — in spite of an unfortunate incident.

Welsh writer Alan Williams, the son of Emlyn Williams, happened to tell Elizabeth Taylor that he thought the money spent on the party would have been better spent on the refugees in the Hungarian revolution. A four-letter word was heard.

Miss Taylor dissolved into tears, and the offending guest was politely asked to leave, an instruction he duly followed.

Burton was remarkably composed about the party when he talked to me. "Undoubtedly this is an extravagant one," he said. The final bill, he added, could be between £25,000 and £30,000. "Whatever the figure, we'll be donating the same amount to UNICEF," he said. He added that he would also give the equivalent of the price of that pendant to a British charity.

Together, Taylor and Burton were a box office bonanza. They appeared side by side in eleven films. Liz won an Oscar for playing a high-class hooker in 'Butterfield 8' and claimed her second Oscar for her role in 'Who's Afraid of Virginia Woolf?' Many critics also applauded her performance in 'The Taming of the Shrew' again with Burton playing opposite her.

It seemed the world was at their feet. Richard bestowed more diamonds on the appreciative Liz and they adopted a little girl named Maria from a Munich orphanage. But such emotional and kind measures were not enough to seal over the ever-increasing turbulent rows that were to break out between them.

Both possessed explosive temperaments. Both loved to drink into their cups. Disharmony would follow disharmony with every miniscule issue of the day causing controversy between them. Neither cared who was listening. They became known as the Battling Burtons.

It was inevitable they would split and Liz Taylor cut a lone figure when she appeared at the gala opening of the San Sebastian film festival in the late summer of 1973. She was greeted with tumultuous rapture by 5,000 spectators. They lined the garland-festooned pavements to catch a glimpse of her and she waved cordially back to them from her chauffeur driven limousine. But just a few hours later Liz was in for a shock.

As the star entered the auditorium for the premiere of her new film 'Night Watch', she was met with a barrage of boos and jeers by 1,100 members of the Spanish aristocracy who formed the select audience. She had never been booed before in her life and it was a shattering experience that she would never forget.

They were furious at being kept waiting eighty minutes for her arrival in the near-suffocating heat of the old opera house where the film was being screened. The bow-tied and bejewelled audience hissed and cried "Fuera, fuera" ("Go, go.")

When the film began, there was a period of silence. But not for long. One of the film's scenes featured Liz insisting that a maid should serve dinner on time. Ironic jeers boomed around the theatre.

When, finally, the curtain came down, there was a modicum of polite applause. Baffled by all that had happened to her, Liz regained her composure and bravely smiled to attend the reception being staged in her honour in the ballroom of the elegant Government House.

There she relaxed with a champagne cocktail and explained to me why she was late.

"It was exasperating — but there was nothing I could do about it," she said. "The customs delayed my baggage and so I could not get to the clothes that I wanted to wear." Her face flushed a little as she added. "To think I busted my ass to get here — and walked into this."

Waiters wheeled in trolleys of lobster and crab before her. But her appetite was not apparent. She was clearly upset by what had happened.

"At least those people in the street — the real people — were wonderful to me. They were touching my hands, trying to hold me. They were the ones who really mattered."

The party was lavish and long. The champagne did not stop flowing. The actress tried to relax. She looked every inch the movie star in a green sari-style evening gown. She wore long pearl earrings, but none of the famous diamonds that her estranged husband Richard Burton had given her.

Burton was far away in America and Liz seemed happy about it. She told me: "This is how my future is going to be from now on. I'm going to work and work and work. I can't lose everything. Life has to go on." Those words, so deliberate and final, meant that there was to be no reconciliation between the squabbling and distant couple.

Once more the lawyers were readily on hand. Divorce came swiftly in June 1974.

It was not the end of the story and I was not alone in missing the sequel just one year later. Browsing in the newsroom one morning my attention was drawn to a cable message carrying a report from Africa that Liz and Burton had remarried. Unbelievable!

Phone lines were jammed as global newspapers tried to confirm the report. Apparently, Liz had become ill once more and Burton was immediately on the scene to care for her. As he nursed her back to good health, he tentatively suggested they remarry. Liz accepted his proposal once more and the wedding was quietly arranged. Few attended the very simple ceremony conducted on the banks of a Botswana river.

When the couple returned to London, I was able to offer my congratulations. With a twinkle in his eye Burton told me: "The truth is we cannot live without each other."

Liz just smiled. "We were meant for each other. We were just a little rash last time round."

Those words still rung in my ears when just a few months later the couple gave up the ghost and decided to divorce for a second time. I was flabbergasted.

I was not to see Liz again. She went on to wed an American politician. When I ran into Burton, he was perplexed as to why Liz had chosen to be a politician's wife.

"I can't imagine Liz in that role," he told me when we met for a drink.

Diversifying, there was news he wanted to convey and he could not contain his excitement. He had fallen in love with Suzy Miller, the twenty-seven-year-old fashion model, who had stormed out of her marriage to the glamour boy hero of the racing track James Hunt. It was all hush-hush for that moment. But soon Richard opted to walk out in public with Suzy. They flew to New York which afforded the paparazzi a field day.

The Formula One racing and showbusiness fraternity combined were asking why Suzy should ever wish to leave the racetrack superstar that was James Hunt for the less handsome, less athletic, paunchier and much older Richard Burton. There was a twenty-four-year age gap between them. Burton's answer was simple. "Because we love one another."

Remarkably James Hunt didn't seem to care a jot. To him there was no great trauma.

He took the whole episode casually, almost amiably, when I went to see him race at Long Beach in California. He told me: "I just want Suzy to be happy."

Past girlfriends were left in no doubt that Hunt's only love in his life was his car. One friend summed it up: "The reality was that Suzy was left alone too much. While James was out on the track she just didn't know what to do with herself. Even at home James only talked about his car."

Richard Burton and Suzy married in 1976 but their happiness together was short lived. Richard was collecting another lawyer's bill in 1982 when he and Suzy agreed a divorce was the only solution.

I asked myself what more could happen in Burton's dramatic life. I could not have provided an answer. Nor could I have guessed what was to transpire. It was to some the impossible dream.

Richard, I learned with some credulity, was back with Liz. On stage at least.

They were starring on Broadway playing opposite each other in a production of Noël Coward's play 'Private Lives.' They ruled out marriage this time round but it was obvious they could not deny their enduring love for one another. Both, however, went on to marry new partners. Even though Liz was married eight times to seven different men, the film industry's verdict is that her greatest love in life was always Richard Burton.

CHAPTER SEVEN

HOLLYWOOD ENCOUNTERS

There was another legendary Hollywood star who overtook Liz in the marital stakes. The gregarious Hungarian born actress Zsa Zsa Gabor. She could count nine husbands on her fingertips, including hotel magnate Conrad Hilton whose playboy son Nicky Hilton was by remarkable coincidence Liz Taylor's first husband. Another of her husbands in the Hollywood mould had been the actor George Sanders.

Zsa Zsa also installed herself at the Dorchester Hotel. She was enjoying an illustrious career and to encapsulate her colourful life in a biopic magazine series was a tantalising prospect. It was a shot in the dark but I felt I could not miss such an opportunity, having learned she was here on my doorstep in London. So I posted a note to Zsa Zsa by way of introduction and suggested that her career would make a great cover story. To my pleasant surprise she returned my missive the next day.

"Of course dahling," she said in her melodic Hungarian accent. "That sounds like a wonderful idea. Why not? Can you be here tomorrow afternoon?"

I cleared my diary and I went out to buy a new tape recorder. It was a rather complex and bulky device but I took it along with me to Zsa Zsa's suite on time.

She was in an effervescent mood and ready to start recording once we had finished the Dorchester's traditional afternoon tea. Zsa Zsa, wearing a floral summer dress, relaxed on one of the settees as I inserted the tape and pressed the recorder's start button.

I was quickly impressed by the actress's ability to recall, without a moment's hesitation, almost every twist and turn in her life. Her films, her marriages. There was hardly a pause in Zsa Zsa's narration of her highs and lows. She was creating brilliant copy. I had no need to prompt her on any detail.

Time wore on. I changed over the tapes giving us a brief interlude, but Zsa Zsa was in full exuberant cry and insisted we carried on.

Three hours had elapsed before Zsa Zsa finally looked at me to call a halt and said: "There dahling. Have you got enough?"

I assured her that indeed I had. I could not have been more grateful. She had been a newspaperman's dream.

Thanking her profusely, I promised I would send her a copy of my article when it appeared. I made my way back to my office and placed the recorder on my desk ready to play back the next morning.

I was in for a nullifying shock. When I switched on the recorder, the two tapes were blank. Disaster on a Richter scale of ten. Not a single word had been recorded. The wretched machine had malfunctioned. Panic descended like a lead weight upon me. What could I do? I opened my notebook and found a few scant words in a mix of shorthand and brief longhand notes. How could I tell Zsa Zsa what had happened? I went through a dozen or more excuses that she might accept. But I just had to admit the truth. It was the only option I had. I rang the hotel and they put me through to Zsa Zsa. I could not remember another occasion when I felt so nervous.

"What is it dahling?" said Zsa Zsa when I stumbled over my words.

"I'm so sorry," I managed to utter, "But I am afraid the tape recorder was not working. The tapes are blank. I can't apologise enough…" I shuddered as I anticipated Zsa Zsa's response. Three hours of wasted time. How could I expect her to react? Any other star would have exploded in anger.

I could hardly believe what was to come. Zsa Zsa, with a calm voice devoid of any irritation or anger, purred: "Don't worry darling. We will do it all again. Are you free tomorrow morning? We can do it then."

And she did. Only this time I took a tried and tested recording machine and Zsa Zsa insisted on hearing some of the playback before I departed. I could not blame her. A bouquet to her suite was the small token of a gesture I could only make in return for all her patience and understanding of my predicament. She was so considerate. No wonder she had been so well-liked by so many people.

There are some stars who are a little more reticent to talk. One of the industry's film publicists rang me one morning to see whether I would like an exclusive interview with one of Hollywood's leading heartthrob hunks, Robert Mitchum.

"He very rarely gives interviews," explained the publicist Theo Cowan. "But I told him about your column and that it will be great publicity for his new film."

Needless to say, Mitchum took some persuasion but to Theo's delight he agreed to see me.

I was to meet him in the foyer of the Westbury Hotel the following morning and Theo was on hand to make the introductions, dissuading me from using my tape recorder which was apparently an anathema to the great man in his hate of interviews. I nodded my head. In any event, I always carried a pen and notepad.

"That's fine," I assured Theo as we waited for the star to come down from his room. We didn't have to wait too long.

Mitchum, in a grey suit and open neck shirt, strode almost business like from the lift.

"Okay," he declared as a way of greeting and dispensing with the need of a customary handshake, or even affording a quick glance at my presence. "I am taking my morning walk round the block," he said with the kind of drawl I could recognise from his film roles. "Tag along with me and we can chat as we walk."

An unusual invitation and hardly an ideal setting for a serious one-on-one interview. For his part Theo imagined we would have staged the interview in a quiet corner of the hotel's lounge. He shrugged and rolled his eyes conveying to me it was not as he intended it to be — but what could he do?

So I tagged along as Mitchum suggested. It was a very cloudy day as we stepped out of the hotel and Mitchum, clearly in a keep-fit mode, zipped away at a fast pace. I struggled to keep up with him.

I thought carefully about the situation and Mitchum's brusque attitude. I decided to open things softly. That would be the easiest solution and there is nothing like the unpredictable British weather to discuss as an opening gambit.

"It's not looking too good this morning. We might have rain pretty soon," I said, looking to the sky.

"Yep," Mitchum nodded, skipping lightly over a pavement edge.

"Is this your first visit to London?" I asked to get the conversation moving.

"Nope," came the short, curt answer.

"Do you like London?"

"Yep."

"Tell me about your new film — 'Anzio' isn't it?"

"Nope."

"Oh, so you've got another film to make first?"

"Yep"

"Is it another war film?" I asked thinking back on two earlier pictures 'The Enemy Below' and 'The Longest Day.'

"Nope."

"Can you tell me what this new film is about?"

"Nope."

"Oh, so you don't know the role you are going to play?"

"Nope."

"Have you got a favourite leading actor or actress you like working with?"

"Nope."

"Do you have a say on your co-star?"

"Yep."

I posed another half a dozen questions trying to get him to talk, but they only brought the same "Yep" or "Nope" response. He was acting like a cricketer blocking the ball with his bat at every delivery bowled at him.

We had been walking for almost half an hour and we were heading round the block for a second time when it started to rain hard.

Mitchum turned up the collar of his jacket and accelerated his stride. There was no point in asking him another question. It had become a futile exercise.

I was relieved when I saw the hotel just ahead of us. Getting into the hotel foyer, Mitchum swept past Theo who had been waiting for us, and disappeared into the lift, presumably to change into some dry clothes.

"How did it go?" inquired Theo, looking at me as I stood pretty drenched before him.

I found it difficult to conceal my frustration. I could not help but tell him all about my morning with the monosyllabic Mitchum. As he had set the whole operation up, Theo was apologetic for the star's behaviour. But he could not resist putting a humorous spin on the situation.

"At least the exercise will have done you good!" he quipped as a parting shot.

Driving back to the office, I reflected on the whole episode and imagined a cod headline for my next column: 'Robert Mitchum —

Nope' — but who would have understood it?

No hard feelings would linger. Robert Mitchum: a movie great? I guess there was only one answer: "Yep!"

Thankfully, there were to be no more interviews of that kind.

****

Cary Grant, the debonair romantic Hollywood star was in London after spending a few days exploring his family roots in Bristol.

Cary invited me for some drinks at the London Hilton and we met in the Polynesian bar below the stairs of the main vestibule in 1972. It was a quiet night but the glamourous staff were in no doubt about the identity of the actor and smiled effusively when they served us with an array of colourful drinks. It was a long night and Cary talked about his early upbringing and his school day memories in Bristol where he had visited his ninety-four-year-old mother. "She's still in wonderful health. I hope I live to be that age. No, I mean 194."

Cary's childhood memories poured back into his mind. "You can never deny or forget your family roots." Cary was proud of his English heritage and it was only his pursuit of his acting career that took him to Hollywood and to become an American citizen in 1943. He had no regrets in having taken that decision, but he was never going to wipe out the past.

"Don't we all ask ourselves 'where did I come from?' Can you ever break ties?" he reflected.

In his early career, Cary had starred in a string of Alfred Hitchcock thrillers but then moved on to occupy a more romantic persona as in his portrayal in the award winning 'Charade' with Audrey Hepburn.

It was no coincidence that the actor's romantic screen image was one that he appeared to duplicate in real life. He smiled a little ruefully when I mentioned it was on record that he had eloped with several actresses and had been married five times.

"We're not going to get into that, are we?" Cary laughed and then with a more sober thought, "I just hope I have not hurt anyone on the way."

So was it just good looks and acting talent? "I guess some of us got a little luckier than others," he smiled back.

Cary Grant had taken his leave and his footprints out of the Hollywood cement seven years previously and refused to return.

"Why should I go back when it took me so many damn hard years to talk my way out?" he asked.

At the time, he was the director of an American development company who had plans of opening a new development in Ireland. He was also the director of America's Western Airlines and an executive of Fabergé, the giant perfumery outfit. Together with Roger Moore he had made a new "with it" perfume the year before.

He said he was not going to be lured back in front of the cameras himself. "I'm sticking to my role of consultant. Advising them of the pitfalls of the movie industry. Besides, I'm an old crock now. The fans might not accept me back."

He talked about his family and his six-year-old daughter Jennifer. "You know one of my old movies came up on television not so long ago and Jennifer spotted her Daddy being kissed by Deborah Kerr. She went over to the set and scolded the lady: 'You just leave my Daddy alone.'"

His reminiscences were providing me with excellent copy but neither of us were prepared for the brazen interception that happened at the end of the night.

It came as we were about to leave the hotel. We both headed for the men's cloakrooms and, as I was joking about our extravagant cocktails being dispensed into the urinals, a young man who had followed us through the foyer clutching a restaurant menu in his hand, cried out to the star: "Hey Cary Grant! Can I have your autograph? Here sign on the back of this menu."

Cary who was in the course of zipping his flies turned angrily and retorted: "What do you want me to do? Sign with my dick?"

The young man seeing Cary's anger beat a hasty retreat. As we departed and climbed into a cab Cary said: "You get used to autograph hunters and normally I am happy to go along with them. But not when you are having a pee. That's the first time I have been marauded in a bathroom. Why couldn't he have waited in the foyer and perhaps then I might have signed it for him?"

Could I relate the incident to those reading my column the next morning? Tempting as it was, I feared not. Not the most appetizing story to consume over bacon and eggs at breakfast time.

Cary's close friend, the definitive English gentleman of the screen David Niven shared much of his contemporary's concerns about the shady under seam of the Hollywood system. Casting couch scandals are nothing new. They were as rampant in the past as they remain today.

David Niven had good reason to be wary of the practice not long after he married the Swedish fashion model Hjordis Genberg in 1948.

The memory of the unfolding events was still vivid in his mind. He told me how he watched from the sidelines as Hollywood attempted to lure Hjordis into the net. Her picture appeared on the front cover of Life magazine and triggered an avalanche of offers.

"Everyone wanted to sign her," Niven recounted over drinks at Pinewood film studios. "They all thought she was the greatest thing to hit Hollywood for years. Even David Selznick was among them. The blandishments were electric and they really turned it on for her."

Niven felt relieved when his wife rejected all of the offers that were presented to her. He smiled: "Hjordis amazed them all by saying no."

The actor expressed concern about the film industry's diversion into sordid low budget porn movies. "They are a stain on the industry," ruled Niven. "Skin flicks are so awful. One should pity the girls who appear in them and the things they are expected to do."

Niven praised the girls who set their hearts on becoming bonafide actresses and who refused to be lured into the film business when they learned of the sordid blandishments. It became customary for some to take jobs in fashion, airlines, retail or offices until they made it. "I don't blame them a bit. I applaud their good sense," Niven said.

The actor was at Pinewood filming a Disney comedy-drama 'Candleshoe' with the fourteen-year-old Hollywood actress Jodie Foster who was determined to succeed and ready to brush away any obstacles in her path. Niven admired her grit and courage.

He smiled: "The thing I liked about her most was her comment that she prefers working with adults — as long as they remember their lines!" Niven took the hint. "Since then I have tried to be word perfect!" he laughed.

David Niven, always the most charming star on the circuit, was the supreme raconteur whose hilarious anecdotes reaped from Hollywood's golden years regaled countless house parties. Many of the stories he resurrected from his two bestselling books of memoirs: 'The Moon's A Balloon' and 'Bring On The Empty Horses.' Guests never complained that they had heard some of the tales on earlier occasions because Niven could re-tell a story with renewed freshness. He recounted magical and mirthful days spent with the likes of Errol Flynn, Humphrey Bogart, Marlene Dietrich and many others. There was never a dull moment when Niven was around.

One summer Niven invited me for lunch at his home in the South of France and again I was to enjoy some of the classic and riotous tales from Hollywood. Pouring a glass of wine, the actor noticed I had gained weight from when he had last seen me.

"You should try the white wine diet," he joked. It was a beautiful sunny day and we strolled out into the immaculately manicured garden. David pointed to a lattice window chalet at the end of the garden where he liked to write his books in complete silence and solitude. "How can you write otherwise?" he said, "And of course you need time. Time is a precious commodity."

I could not imagine how the actor found the time to write his books. Few stars could be as busy as Niven. His catalogue of films was mind-boggling and included 'Separate Tables' for which he got an Oscar playing opposite Deborah Kerr. He had appeared as the aristocratic jewel thief Sir Charles Lytton in two of the Pink Panther films with Peter Sellers.

"They were great fun to make," said Niven who admired the ingenuity of Sellers who played Clouseau as much off-screen as on. "Peter just lives the role in every film he makes," said Niven, who like other thespians saw Sellers as a brilliant but complex man who struggled with uncertainty and depression.

Coincidence is never far away. Peter Sellers was to become the focus of my work for a long period. In 1980 I was engaged to write Peter Sellers's life story through the eyes of his three children and two of his four wives.

World movie audiences loved Sellers, especially in his Clouseau role which also brought wide acclaim from the critics. But for his family, the star was a very different man — more akin to a Jekyll and Hyde — whose persona could swing alarmingly from one extreme to the other. There was rarely room for laughter. Melancholy, depression and spates of uncontrollable temper were regularly witnessed by the family. In fits of utter pique, he would often disown his children Michael and Sarah from his first marriage to Australian-born actress Anne Howe, and his daughter Victoria from his marriage to the Swedish actress Britt Ekland. They would only have to say one word out of place to displease him.

If pricked with conscience, Sellers would write them conciliatory letters signed with the appendage 'P.S. I Love You', which was to become the title of their book.

Anne was to relate some of the most bewildering stories during their traumatic marriage. When Sellers was filming the romantic comedy 'The Millionairess' playing the role of an Indian doctor, he fell madly in love with his co-star, the Italian beauty Sophia Loren. Anne was to bear the consequences of his unquenching passion for the actress.

Anne told me how her husband woke her in bed one night as though an apparition had appeared in the room with them. "Shush, don't say anything," Peter whispered to her. "I can feel her presence coming into the room. Yes, she is here with us."

"Who is?"

"It's Sophia... Sophia." Peter uttered.

Anne felt she had heard enough. She moved into a guest room. "I left those two together," she told me.

Sellers' pursuit of Sophia was relentless. On-set, off-set he was at her side. When he could not see her, he bombarded her with calls. The Beatles producer George Martin saw a sequel to the film in which Sellers and Sophia would cut a novelty record 'Goodness Gracious Me' followed by 'Bangers and Mash' and an album titled 'Peter and Sophia.'

All three made the charts and heightened Sellers' manic desires to marry Sophia. He was sure he could convince her to leave her husband producer Carlo Ponti but Sophia had no intention of doing so. She returned to Italy at the end of filming and she cut Sellers out of her life.

Sellers was left sobbing and morose and took weeks to recover from the rejection. But then, in his tangled mind, he construed there was another actress he had fallen in love with. It was Nanette Newman, the lovely actress who had played his girlfriend in an earlier movie titled 'The Wrong Arm of the Law.'

At the height of another confrontation with his family, Sellers inexplicably announced that he was going to marry Nanette. It was all the more shocking as she and her husband actor-producer Bryan Forbes were close family friends.

Anne shook her head as she recounted the shocking moment. She asked Peter: "Whatever are you thinking about? Just what has got into your head? They are our friends. They are happily married."

Sellers ignored her and retaliated by picking up the phone and put a call through to Bryan Forbes. Without even bothering to pass the time of day he told his friend: "I want to marry Nanette. Is that all right by you?"

Clearly Bryan Forbes was accustomed to his friend's wild fantasies and irrational behaviour. He responded with commendable patience: "Of course I understand. I'll talk to Nanette about it and call you back."

The call was never made.

These were episodes, I imagined, that could have found their way into any of the scripts of The Goon Show, one of the nation's favourite radio programmes that starred Peter Sellers, in which he played many different characters along with his fellow artists Harry Secombe, Michael Bentine and Spike Milligan.

Spike, like Peter Sellers, also suffered from periods of severe depression which would emerge when the cameras and microphones were switched off.

Spike often locked himself away for days on end and refused to answer the front door or take any telephone calls. When normality resumed, Spike would reappear in the public eye once more to be hailed as a genius for his ad lib creations.

Such versatility was illustrated by his star role in the stage play 'Son of Oblomov' based on a nineteenth century Russian novel.

I was there on the night in 1966 when he made the shock announcement that he was going to quit the show after eighteen months in the role.

When the curtain went up, Spike told the seven-hundred-strong audience that they might like to eavesdrop on a Press conference before the play would proceed.

One of the production assistants led the contingent of journalists on to the stage where Spike, still dressed in his Victorian nightclothes costume, was sitting up on a four-poster bed ready to elaborate.

Several chairs were placed by the side of the bed for us to sit on. Yells of delight came up from the audience. They could see us visibly wriggle with embarrassment. More discomfort followed.

He told the audience: "You must be puzzled as to what's going on. It was raining outside and I couldn't talk to these gentlemen there, so I invited them in. You see, I'm having to leave the show."

The forty-seven-year-old actor added: "I've had enough. At weekends the kids were asking: 'Who's that funny man who's come home?'" He said that he would leave the show at the end of the month.

His announcement came five days after he had stormed from the stage because of ill-mannered hecklers in the audience, and he had the curtain brought down thirty minutes early. He apologised to the people who had made advanced bookings for the show.

Suddenly to our astonishment, he turned to us on the stage: "Now, Gentlemen of the Press, what do you want to know?"

We exchanged uneasy glances before one of us asked meekly: "Are you going to miss playing this role?" Spike repeated the question loud and clear to the audience intending to show just how pedantic our questions were going to be.

They laughed at the next question. "Was this role inspired by the Goons?" Again, Spike relayed the question to the audience. At this juncture, we were overtaken by stage fright and scuttled out of our seats to make our exit amid cheers from the auditorium.

The irreverent, irritable Spike who once got away with calling his Royal friend Prince Charles "a grovelling little bastard" at the British Comedy Awards ceremony, had transformed a serious stage play into a mirth-splitting farce. The nightly audiences were invited to cheer and boo with the cast being given the freedom to respond while Spike remained in his four-poster bed to command the whole direction of the play. Every performance brought a different script. It had been a very successful show. The Queen made it her birthday celebration outing the previous year, and Princess Margaret saw it four times.

Spike was known for his irate behaviour. He set out on one occasion to kill Peter Sellers after the pair had a row. He was armed only with a potato peeler and on reaching Sellers's home ran into a plate glass door and became hospitalised as a result. It had no effect on their friendship.

Some years later, I was in the throes of doing an interview with Spike in his hotel room prior to filming in Madrid. We were in the middle of our interview and I had my tape recorder running when Spike said he heard a noise from the outside corridor and went out to investigate.

I sat patiently waiting for him to return but there was no sign of him. Time wore on. When I peered down the corridor it was quiet and empty. Confusion set in. Where had he gone? I looked at my watch. Forty minutes had gone by. I knew I could not depart and leave the room unlocked. Just as I was giving up hope, Spike suddenly reappeared but gave no explanation for his absence. You would assume that most interviewees to restart the interview would have asked something along the lines of: 'Now where were we?' Not Spike. He picked up his previous unfinished sentence exactly from where he had left off, as though it had been mere seconds since he had last spoken, and not nearly an hour. I was staggered. Equally so by the unsolved mystery of his disappearance.

Spike had another friend who suffered from depression. Tony Hancock was one of the nation's most loved comics. His show Hancock's Half Hour was listened to by millions and the television sequel with iconic episodes 'The Blood Donor' and 'The Radio Ham' gave the BBC top audience ratings.

But Hancock suffered greatly from inner battles. He was constantly critical of his own work and would often blame others when he became uncomfortable with a script or felt a fellow actor impeded his own performance. Hancock worked alongside Sid James for many years but then broke away from him because he feared they were going to be seen as 'a double act.' He also broke away from his loyal agent Beryl Vertue and sacked his scriptwriters who had been largely responsible for his fame. From thereon he was on a downward spiral.

Hancock, seeing no future, needed a shoulder to cry on. When his showbusiness friends lost their patience with him, he would often call on me to unburden his woes. I would meet him in the relaxing basement bar of the Ritz Hotel.

"I come here because it is so quiet," Hancock explained. "If I go anywhere else the customers always look at me and harass me to tell them a joke."

I nodded, agreeing with him that must be one of the afflictions of being a comedian. Most comedians suffered the same intrusion.

There was one particular night in 1965 when Hancock had convinced himself that his career was truly over. He had not worked for several months and his phone had fallen silent. When I joined him in the Ritz, the barman gave me an anxious look when Hancock ordered another vodka. I could not guess how many he had drunk before. It seemed he was determined to drown his sorrows. Hancock, unhappy to be out of the public eye for so long, was truly in the doldrums.

"Everything is going wrong," he lamented. "No one liked the film and they said my last television series was a flop. Where do I go from here?"

It was almost impossible to lift his spirits by telling him his film 'The Punch And Judy Man' in which he played a struggling seaside entertainer wasn't the flop he believed and that millions of fans were on his side.

"Yes. Yes," said Hancock. "But what now?"

It was a long night and when one or two more customers arrived in the bar, I felt it wise to get Hancock home. I walked him to my car parked close by and we drove to his Surrey house just a few miles from my own.

His wife Freddie Ross was there to greet us. She was well accustomed to her husband's bouts of melancholy and his desire to drink problems into oblivion. She threw her caring arms round him, saying she would get him something to eat but as I was leaving, I heard her tell him "Tony, please don't do this again."

But Hancock relied too heavily on alcohol to listen and in June 1968, as their divorce was going through, the comedian committed suicide. He was in Australia where he had been contracted to make a new television series. An empty bottle of vodka was found at his bedside in his Sydney digs and it was clear he had taken an overdose of barbiturates. There was also a suicide note. Hancock wrote: "Things just seemed to go wrong too many times."

Commenting on Hancock's tragic death at the age of forty-four, Spike Milligan was quoted as saying: "You felt sorry for him. He ended up on his own. I thought, 'he's got rid of everybody else, now he's going to get rid of himself' and he did."

It was a hard but truthful epitaph. The world had lost a comedy genius.

I was reminded of this sentiment when I dined with the legendary Charlie Chaplin when he was eighty-two years old. He said, simply: "There's no laughter anymore. That's the truth."

CHAPTER EIGHT

MUHAMMAD ALI AND OTHER HOLLYWOOD HEAVYWEIGHTS

Hollywood's film studios are as alive with action as the films they produce. Stars and directors who have been unceremoniously sacked, prima donnas whose demands have put movie budgets into jeopardy, and stories of rows, tears and tantrums, surround film sets.

But the man who gave Hollywood one of its biggest frights was none other than the world's most famous boxing champion, Muhammad Ali.

Ali was playing himself in the planned movie of his life 'The Greatest' in early spring 1977.

It was the first day of filming on the Columbia Films set in Miami and it was an occasion not to be missed. I was given exclusive accreditation to be there, and it was certainly a day that remains long in my memory.

True to character, Ali seemed to be his animated self as he arrived on the set looking relaxed, in his half sleeve shirt and beige trousers and chatting and joking with the film crew and cameramen. Everything was in place. Everything was ready to go.

Suddenly, the cheery atmosphere was abruptly shattered by the film's British producer John Marshall who had got tired of all the frivolity and the champ's bantering. Marshall shouted across the set harsh words towards Ali: "You'd better stop clowning around now and get on with your work!"

Silence descended as heavily as an iron curtain on the visibly shocked film crew. Every face turned to witness Ali's reaction. The boxer's dark eyes flashed like laser beams.

"No white man is gonna boss me about! I am the heavyweight champion of the world! Who do you think you are?" he exploded.

Marshall, with a reputation of being a tough egg, stood his ground. Nervous Columbia executives groaned when they heard Marshall's response.

"I don't care a damn who you are, 'black man.' Get on with your work — or go!"

The two men stood eyeball to eyeball screaming at one another as if they were about to get into the ring.

"Any more trouble," Marshall yelled, "And I'll kick you off."

Then, to the horror of the cast and film crew glued to the unseemly scene, Marshall slapped Ali's face.

Ali's bodyguards moved in and Columbia's own security hirelings grappled to part the two men. For one horrendous moment, it looked as though the £4,000,000 film of Ali's life would never be made.

Ali's face was contorted with rage as he was led away to his dressing room, and Marshall instructed the production office to cool down.

But a few minutes later, when I dared to risk opening the champ's dressing room door, I discovered Ali and Marshall slapping each other on the back and rolling with laughter.

Their "big row" had been secretly staged as Ali thought it might help ease the tensions that usually exist on the first day of filming.

Needless to say, Columbia's film chiefs did not share the same view. They were not amused. Too much was at stake. "It was heart attack time," one executive muttered. "Why didn't they confide in us?" he added, shaking his head.

Ali and Marshall were unrepentant in their charade. The two men were in fact remarkably close friends. Ali told me: "He is like my brother. I would never had made this film with anyone else."

Marshall, at the age of forty-three, was known in the industry as something of a maverick, an opportunist with a flair for enterprise. Ex-frogman, ex-lumberjack, he was the son of an English banker. Earlier in his career he had produced two television documentaries on tennis stars Stan Smith and Arthur Ashe. But his biggest break by far was signing a contract with Muhammad Ali in what he predicted would be the most successful movie blockbuster of the day. At least it appeared to be his biggest break.

Marshall was nonplussed when he failed to find any investors to back his film. A contract with the legendary Muhammad Ali? Wasn't that enough? It was like holding a poisoned chalice.

Amazingly, no one wanted to back a film about the boxing champion. Marshall clung on to the contract for three desperate years travelling the world to find backers to make the movie. He gambled £100,000 of his own money and finally he managed to get some backers — and Columbia Films — on board.

An exhausted Marshall sat down with me one evening to explain the troubles he had come through.

"Initially the major studios would be wildly excited but when they sat down with their advisers they got cold feet. No one in Hollywood knew Ali personally. Nor did they know anybody who worked with him. They wanted to know things like: How is he to get along with? Is he punctual and reliable? Are you sure he won't get bored and drift away? They also felt that Ali was very much his own master and not used to taking orders. But the real anxiety was whether they could really put up £4,000,000 for a man to play in his own life story without any acting experience."

One of the Columbia hierarchy phoned directly to Muhammad Ali to inquire about his rapport with Marshall.

Ali's reply was incisive. "I won't be making a movie without Marshall," he declared.

There was no doubt that Marshall's success in signing the boxing champion was the cause of jealousy: an Englishman with no Hollywood experience, and from other quarters — a white man producing Ali's film?

"There was enormous resentment at one stage," Marshall confided. "Especially among Ali's hanger-ons and entourage. They regarded Ali as their property and how was it an outsider had acquired the rights?"

The two men first met in Las Vegas after the champion had fought and defeated the English contender Joe Bugner. Soon Ali and Marshall became great friends.

Now Ali, keeping his bond with Marshall, was in Miami facing the film cameras for the first time and he proved to be a true professional.

"Man, no one is gonna have to prompt me," said Ali as they rehearsed lines.

After filming Ali confessed: "Sometimes I amended lines that I wouldn't normally say, but I don't think I slipped up otherwise."

Indeed, the film crew applauded Ali after his first challenging one-to-one scene with Oscar winning star Ernest Borgnine who played the part of his trainer Angelo Dundee. There was also praise for actress Annazette Chase portraying Ali's second wife the famous Belinda Boyd.

Even the champ was startled and often halted filming to tell Annazette incredulously: "You are so like her — it's uncanny."

Annazette got the role after producer Marshall had auditioned nearly one hundred actors.

"Naturally Ali wanted to have some say on who was going to play his screen wife as well as other relatives portrayed in the movie," said Marshall. "When he met Annazette he thought she was perfect."

Annazette discovered another side to Ali that his fans never saw. She told me: "The one thing that amazed me about Ali was how different he is in private. To the outside world he is clowning and boastful — but in reality he is gentle, gracious, sensitive and childlike."

Ali's confidence was clear and he was so positive about the film: "Is there any other film worthy of my talents?" he asked. "No screen script can compare with all I've been through in real life."

He added: "I'm blessed to be so popular in real life that I challenge every movie star in Hollywood to take me on. I challenge your John Waynes and Clint Eastwoods and Richard Burtons — you name them all — to take a walk with me around the world and let's see who's the most popular."

Another actress on the set, Mira Waters who played one of Ali's old flames, admired Ali's sensitivity in his approach to the movie. They exchanged only two mild kisses in the film.

Ali insisted that there would be no sex, no nudity or profanity in his movie. "No sir. Not for me," he told me. He chattered on, harshly condemning his old boxing rival Ken Norton who had turned actor two years earlier.

"I ain't gonna do what Ken Norton is doin'," he snorted. "He makes X-rated movies and what's he doin' playing a black man who rapes a white girl? I ain't gonna do anything like that."

Cast as Ali's younger self was a nineteen-year-old supermarket packer named 'Chip' McAllister who got the part when he sent in a picture of himself with the cryptic footnote: "I'm pretty, ain't I?" His sheer impudence won him the part.

It amused Ali whenever he crossed the teenager on the film set with an audible passing mutter: "There ain't no one prettier than me," to the smiles of the surrounding crew.

Normally, it would take a pack of high-powered publicity teams to help a new recruit. Muhammad Ali didn't need any advice. "I ain't kissing no behinds and I ain't doing no Uncle Tomming," he warned.

When I left Miami, I was convinced that Ali was a natural. When the movie was premiered, most critics praised Ali for his performance. One observer wrote that: "Ali brought the film an authority and a presence that left John Marshall's production above some of the limitations inherent in any film bio."[1]

On my return to America a few weeks later, Ali invited me and my close friend and photographer Terry Fincher to dinner at his snow-covered Chicago home. Terry and I undertook many joint word-and-picture operations together over the years, and the features we produced were successfully syndicated to newspapers and magazines across the globe.

Ali shared the elegant mansion with his future wife Veronica Porsche and baby daughter Hana. He was proud of his home and took us on a tour of the house numerating £300,000 worth of furnishings he had bought on his boxing travels from all around the world.

Beautiful crystal chandeliers hung from the ceilings, lavish chairs and settees were installed from France and Italy and a 12-place dining table dominated the entertainment room that Ali had shipped in from the Lebanon. Though furnished in the last word of luxury, the house was accessible and not cut off on a private estate. It was positioned close to a mosque and nestled among the shops and tenement blocks of the Muslim community.

Ali had committed his life to Islam and the Muslim faith. He had poured untold millions of dollars into the religion. Ali made no secret of his will to preach his faith: "People listen to people who have got money, they'll listen to movie stars and I reckon they will listen to me because God didn't give me the most recognised face on earth for nothin'."

Over a chicken roast dinner, kindly prepared by Veronica, and served unpretentiously on plastic plates — a facet which amused my companion Terry as we sat amid so much luxury — the boxing champ looked relaxed and was in a playful mood, setting free from their cages a parrot and cockatoo he kept as favourite pets in the household. It was an image of Ali that we felt privileged to witness.

Sometime later, Ali came to England and stayed with Marshall and his wife Liz at their country home near Basingstoke. I joined them at several luncheon parties and, arriving early one afternoon, we took Ali for a photo shoot to the village pub. The landlord invited Ali behind the bar to pull a pint of beer for one of the awe-struck villagers but Ali declined to the disappointment of the photographer. "No, I can't do that," Ali explained. "It's against my faith."

When Ali was embattled with Parkinson's disease and died in 2016, I could not help but recall his conversations with me on his profound feelings about life and death.

"There is a heaven and there is a hell," he told me. "And one day I'm gonna die. But I don't want any confusion about where I'm goin'."

Through his life Ali had helped so many who had faced poverty and deprivation. But he rarely talked about such deeds. He told me: "Doin' service to others is the rent we pay for our room in Heaven. What's a man's wealth? His wealth is his knowledge. If he's got money in the bank and no knowledge then he's not wealthy. Look at Howard Hughes. He was the poorest man who lived. Two billion dollars in the bank and only sixteen people at his funeral and just a single teardrop. That's not how I wanna be remembered."

Muhammad Ali's perspective of life and death rang true. Tens of thousands were to come forward to show their respect to The Greatest when he died. Millions more across the world mourned his loss on social media. Just as Ali might have wished.

****

I knew John Marshall from 1972, before Miami, when Mario Puzo made me an offer I could not refuse. "Come over and have a drink," he called. "I've got a deal for you."

Who could turn down a request like that from the man who wrote 'The Godfather'? So, brimming with intrigue, I drove to John Marshall's Hampshire countryside home where Mr Puzo was staying as a house guest.

Only to find that Mario had run out of opponents — at table tennis!

There were a dozen or more guests and they were all limp bodies, devastated by the flaying bat of the granite-sized Puzo who had won the weekend's table tennis championship.

The amiable Mr Puzo looked at me through his specs and said: "I'll give you a ten point start."

Then, without removing his twelve inch cigar from his lips, he swept me off the board — in two straight sets.

He had just finished writing the screenplay of 'Godfather II' and his book giving the lowdown on his success, 'The Godfather Papers,' had just been published. He told me; "Some people thought that when 'The Godfather' was being made, the Mafia would murder me. Now it's such a huge success, they're saying the Mafia paid me a million dollars to write it. But I don't know one member of the Mafia."

Mario, son of a Sicilian railway worker, had become a millionaire because of his phenomenal book.

"I love making money," he told me. "Who wouldn't — having been without it for so long?"

Outside of writing, his first love was — ping pong and tennis. He also loved gambling, but he recounted how a Puerto Rican casino had refused to let him enter as he was wearing shoes but not socks.

Said Mario, barefoot in his leather sole shoes: "Why don't I wear socks? It's too much trouble taking them on and off."

****

There were many other heavyweight champions who crossed my travels. Not least among them the Irish star widely regarded as the ultimate hellraiser. Richard Harris, perhaps best-known today as the actor who played Dumbledore in 'Harry Potter and the Philosopher's Stone' and 'Harry Potter and the Chamber of Secrets', thrived on such a reputation.

I met up with him in the American bar of the Savoy Hotel one evening as he was planning a world concert tour. He invited me along for the ride. He told me that he had appointed a new manager John Marshall and he was surprised to learn that we were good friends from the past. "Well John will be joining us right through the tour," said Harris.

I was a little wary of the scenario. I wondered whether I could live with Harris's hellraising exploits in which booze, brawls and women seemed to figure in his daily lifestyle. But on the plus side Harris had everything going for him. His screen track record had made him one of Hollywood's greatest stars. He had earned buckets of plaudits for his appearances in 'The Sporting Life', 'Cromwell' and 'Camelot' and now he was hitting the concert trail as a singer. I decided to take up Harris's invitation just part of the way covering the States and Europe.

So in the summer of 1972 I packed my bags and followed Harris into New Orleans where he was booked as the star of the nightly cabaret at the aptly named Blue Room of the luxury Fairmont Roosevelt Hotel. He was being meticulously shadowed by Marshall (a teetotaller, a requisite asset to possess while living in the midst of Harris's erratic slipstream). There were frequent mornings of rehearsal in readiness for his cabaret act — a mixture of songs, poetry and theatrical anecdotes. This gave us many free hours to explore the famous neon lit French Quarter, home to a labyrinth of blues and jazz clubs with veteran old timers taking to the stage with their saxes and trumpets and never-run-dry drinks. Harris soaked up the booze like a sponge in a bathtub. One night as many of the clubs were closing their shutters, Harris was holding court on the last solitary table as the patient and perspiring jazzmen on stage played on. Many of the hostesses were in his thrall.

"I resent sleep," Harris explained to his bevy of glamorous listeners. "It steals my precious time. I'm a nomadic person. I love the night and all of its intrigue." He laughed: "I'm always out to break more records by pushing my mind, body and spirit beyond the boundaries of normal human endurance."

It wasn't a hangover that disrupted his good mood the next morning but an urgent call from London telling him that his nine-year-old son Jamie — the youngest of his three "wonderful rascals" — had been taken to hospital with appendicitis and suspected peritonitis.

"That's it," cried Harris. "I've got to be there with him!"

Distress flushed across John Marshall's disbelieving face. "But Richard — it's opening night tomorrow. I realise the concern but Elizabeth is with him..."

Elizabeth — Harris's ex-wife and socialite then married to actor Rex Harrison — had taken their son into hospital for an emergency operation.

"No," said Harris with visible tears flooding his eyes, "I've got to go to him. John cancel everything. Put back the opening night. I don't care what anyone thinks. There's nothing in this world more important to me than any of my boys."

John Marshall was told by management that Harris would forfeit £3,000 for cancelling his opening concert but the star remained adamant. "Even if it cost me £3 million I wouldn't care!" blasted Harris. "My career doesn't matter a damn."

Harris made another phone call to the London Clinic and found that Jamie had pulled through his operation and was able to talk to him. Said Richard: "This is Daddy. How do you feel Jamie? I'll be with you tomorrow..."

Harris, relieved, said: "He's on the mend thank God. But I am still going. I promised him I would. His mother is with him and as always she's been marvellous. If she hadn't got him to the hospital in time... oh God I can't bear to think about it."

John Marshall stared forlornly at the star. "But..."

"I am sorry John. Just delay the opening night by twenty-four hours and I will be back. I won't let anyone down. I just need to hug my son for ten minutes..."

At that precise moment I must have stepped into his eye-line. "Don. Will you do me a favour and come with me back to London? I need the company," he beseeched me.

It was a staggering thought: there and back in little more than thirty-six hours and spanning thousands of miles — all for a ten-minute hug with Jamie? Of course the stress of this journey would be tempered slightly by the first class seats that John booked for us. But then who was considering the cost of the return plane tickets? Not to mention the waiting limousine at Heathrow to take us to the London Clinic and at our call just thirty minutes later.

But now in New Orleans all was set. "Don this means a great deal to me," said Harris, patting me on the shoulder. Three hours later we were in the air.

"I just couldn't go on stage and face an audience as I feel now," Harris confided. "But once I've seen Jamie I know I will be all right."

Throughout our journey he kept repeating: "I know I've done the right thing. Wouldn't any father do the same?"

Before we boarded the plane, Harris had bought some toys for Jamie in the shopping arcade after we had passed through customs, but promptly left them behind in the transit lounge of Miami where we had to change planes.

During the flight Harris reminisced on his own childhood. "I know what it means to be in hospital. When I was eighteen I got tuberculosis and I was confined in a hospital bed for a very long time. I used to have lots of friends — or so I thought. But few of them made the effort to come and see me." Harris looked back on his childhood with mixed feelings. He was one of eight children born in Limerick, the son of a man who ran a flourmill that was taken over by a conglomerate, which he bought back for his father when he became a wealthy star.

For much of the tedious journey Harris slept clutching in the palm of his hand a rosary given to him by an Australian psychotherapist named Sue Petersen with whom he had had a three-day fling on earlier travels. "You know," he whispered to me when he woke "Maybe I will marry again. You should meet Sue. She is beautiful." He gazed down at the rosary and said: "I will give it to Jamie for good luck."

Finally we landed at Heathrow and the actor instantly headed for the terminal shops and replaced the bundle of toys, games and puzzles he had left in Miami. Our limousine was waiting for us as we emerged from the terminal and less than an hour later Harris was at his son's bedside.

I took coffee in the waiting room keeping a constant check on the time as I was only too well aware that our turnaround flight was booked in the early afternoon, and we could not afford to miss the flight to get back in time for the star's opening night, which the Blue Room had managed to postpone for twenty-four hours. When after only thirty minutes Harris reappeared from his son's room he was like a man who had just had a huge weight removed from his shoulders. "He's fine!" exclaimed Harris joyfully. "He really is fine. He'll be out of hospital in a day or two. I've given him the rosary and the toys. He loves them." Then he slapped me on the back again and said, "Let's go. We've got a concert to do!"

Of course, our return trip to New Orleans was not without incident when the air crew mockingly suggested having a whip-round for Harris when he mislaid a two-hundred dollar travellers' cheque buried somewhere in his hand luggage. The irony of it all was not lost on Harris. "I've just signed a three million dollar contract and here I am broke," he chortled to the amusement of the cabin crew.

We made it to the hotel with only a few hours to spare and much to the relief of John Marshall who had patiently waited for our return. But Harris rose to the occasion. His opening night was a great success, although newspaper critics gave him mixed reviews; one wrote that Harris couldn't sing for the life of him, another described him as the greatest entertainer that New Orleans had seen in the last decade. Either way, the star didn't seem to mind.

"I have my good nights and my bad nights," he reflected. "It doesn't worry me because I know it doesn't worry my kind of audiences. I tell them a story, recite one of my poems and give them a song or two. Sometimes I might miss my cue and get four bars behind the orchestra or four bars ahead of it!"

Few other entertainers could be as candid about their failings, I felt. It was some admission.

Mid-week came and just as the audiences were packing in for his show John Marshall called me up to his suite to tell me that he had to go to New York for a business meeting. "Don, would you take over as Richard's manager for a few days? Everything is in place and there shouldn't be any problems. But any snags then just call me in New York." Chronicling Harris's adventures was one thing but acting as his twenty-four-hour carer? "It will be a doddle," responded John reassuringly.

I should have known. Trouble was afoot on my second night in charge. All was set for the nightly concert with the audience packed in and the thirty-piece orchestra striking the opening bars of Jimmy Webb's epic composition 'MacArthur Park' as the curtain went up. I stood in the wings anticipating that Harris would appear at any moment in the opposite wing but there was no sign of him. The strains of 'MacArthur Park' were now rapidly reaching their climax and the grim faced, baton-waving conductor Walter Levinsky stared desperately at me with exasperation clearly on his face, which asked: Where the hell is he? Seeing the dilemma afoot, I turned and ran to the elevator and pressed the button for the sixteenth floor where our rooms were located. I had the duplicate keys to Harris's suite further along the corridor and as I opened the door I shouted: "Richard where are you? Everyone is waiting and going mad!" No sound came.

I made my way into the bedroom where Harris was making love to a young lady of the night. I grabbed Harris around his neck and hauled him out of bed and threw him his denim trousers and green jumper. "Sorry, but he's got to go. He's got another engagement," I explained to the bewildered girl, who pulled the sheets around her. I ran with Harris along the corridor and into the lift.

"What's going on?" said Harris angrily while finding his crumpled hat lodged in the sleeve of his sweater.

I glared at him. "It's your show. You are on stage now." When we finally got to the wings of the stage and Walter having persuaded the orchestra to repeat 'MacArthur Park' for a third time, Harris — a picture of innocence — walked onto the stage. I thought he would be booed back off but to my amazement he got a standing, tumultuous ovation from the 1,000-strong audience. Without a moment of hesitation, Harris broke into the fourth rendition of the song as though nothing had gone wrong.

After the concert I thought Harris would like a celebratory drink.

"Sorry Don" said Harris, "I've got another appointment. I have got some unfinished business to attend to." He winked and he was gone.

The next morning, however, I was obliged to conduct an inquiry at the behest of Walter the conductor who said: "Don those theatre goers paid fifty bucks a seat tonight. Okay they got their money's worth at the end of things. But what will happen tomorrow night? You must get Harris to the stage on time!" I made it a priority in my new role as the acting manager. I was greatly relieved when John returned to take over the helm once more.

Our travels took us on to Rome where Harris, a devout Catholic, hoped to visit the Vatican and present to the Pope a copy of his newly recorded poem: 'There Are Too Many Saviours on My Cross', the royalties of which he was dedicating to the victims of the Northern Ireland troubles. When he read the poem during an appearance on American television some 30,000 viewers went out to buy a copy, so strong and significant was his influence. Harris hoped that millions more across the globe would similarly go out and buy the record and the funds would go to the families of all victims on either side of the conflict.

"I am not taking sides," said Harris appalled by all the scenes he witnessed on television, careful not to mention the IRA or the Protestant splinter groups at loggerheads with one another. He shook his head. "The world needs peace... Not only Northern Ireland, but the Israeli-Palestinian conflict too and all the other trouble spots around the world."

Before we had left for Italy, the actor had already posted personal letters to many of the world's leaders urging action to be taken to curb the international crises. He was serious now, showing a rarely seen side of his public persona. Adventurer and hellraiser maybe, but I realised in that moment that if you chipped away at the nugget you could see a man of real depth.

We set out for the Vatican and by sheer coincidence we bumped into the vivacious actress Diana Dors on holiday in Rome with her husband. Spirited conversation exchanged between them and Harris could not resist playing a charade with Diana by stepping into the confessional booths for the benefit of the camera hugging paparazzi who were pursuing our every move.

"We are old friends," Harris told me "Diana is great fun. Pity her husband is with her!"

"That's enough frivolity," I remonstrated with Harris, reminding him that he had got his record to deliver. We marched on leaving Diana and husband to enjoy the rest of their holiday. At the ornate doors of the Vatican we were met by a priest apologising for the Pope's absence but accepting the disc with gratitude and grace. As we walked away, Harris was convinced the Pope would play it.

Harris was in a relaxed mood during our days in Rome. Over dinner one night, he told me about the film he made five years earlier in the Eternal City when he was cast as the screen lover of Princess Soraya the ex-Queen of Persia.

"She was a highly intelligent, gracious and a very, very beautiful woman but I think that in allowing herself to be pushed so young and so early in her acting ambitions into a movie she was utterly ill-advised," Harris reminisced.

Harris agreed with the critics of the day that the Princess had been exploited. "The thing of course was that Soraya didn't have the necessary temperament for an actress because having been brought up in that royal circle one is taught and conditioned to be extremely reserved, and cautious, and not to give anything away in an emotional sense," he opined.

As it transpired the film was a disaster and the candid Harris didn't try to make out that it was anything else. It was only screened in one or two countries before it was shelved into the archives.

I was back in London for some months and often spoke with Richard as he marched on abroad, playing in more theatres and considering a mountain of film scripts. He had signed to play the lead in 'Juggernaut', a suspense film about the hijacking of an ocean liner and he was enthusiastic about the script. But another episode was to occur that he was even more excited about.

Out of the blue, and very late one night, Harris called me at home. "Come on over! We're having one hell of a honeymoon!" roared the very familiar throaty voice. Harris was calling me from his newly acquired home on the sea-lapped peninsular of Paradise Isle in the Bahamas.

"Honeymoon?" I asked. "Have I got this wrong? You told me the wedding wasn't until the Spring?"

Was the world to understand he was already married to actress Ann Turkel, who had recently been voted America's most beautiful cover girl?

"No. No," retorted Harris, indignant at the suggestion that he was so impetuous that he couldn't wait until the nominated day. "We're having the honeymoon first," asserted Harris, "because there'll not be time for such luxuries after the wedding. We're both committed to work in the same week."

It shouldn't have surprised me: it sounded very unconventional — Richard Harris all over. What man would ask a friend and newspaper journalist to come and intrude on a honeymoon? I asked myself.

"Are you sure I won't get in the way?" I asked coyly.

"Not at all" he retorted. "As long as your foot doesn't tread the bedroom stairs!"

So in the echo of his laughter I began packing my bags and took the morning plane out to the Bahamas.

Harris, in a red and black rugby shirt and blue denims, greeted me at the door. His usual weather-beaten face had a fresh and youthful look. Bride-to-be Ann Turkel stood just behind Harris and said: "Welcome. Richard has told me a lot about you."

There was a bottle of champagne on the table and a tempting bowl of fruit and the couple took delight in showing me all over the house which Harris had bought for £200,000 from the American tycoon Huntingdon Hartford. The Colonial style homestead was surrounded by a rich growth of cypress and palm trees, and the shoreline lapped by the sea on all sides. I learned that Paradise Isle was once the haunt of pirates and smugglers and Harris laughed: "And now it has got me! Don't you think I will fit in well?" Ann laughed at his jokes.

She truly was as beautiful as her cover girl magazine shots and appeared regularly in Vogue and Harpers. It was not too difficult to see why Harris fell in love with her. I likened her stunning looks to Lauren Bacall, although Ann was a little taller. "Isn't she just perfect?" Harris asked me as if he needed reassurance from an outside witness.

Harris affectionately called her "Turkey" but more often a simple endearing 'Annie' and at that moment she was cooking a delicious chicken hot pot dinner for us. Ann, who had broken off a three-year relationship with David Niven Jnr., told me how much she loved the Irish hellraiser. "Hellraiser? Richard is more of a lamb than a lion. He's kind and gentle and I haven't seen him once lose control."

So she was already taming him? "There's no need. Oh I have heard all about his one-night stands, his boozing and the brawls but I can tell you he hardly drinks more than my folk who live in New York. It's not the past but the future we should think about."

Muhammed Ali and other Hollywood Heavyweights

The actress played with her engagement ring, a chain of four daisies set in yellow and white diamonds which she and Richard designed for Tiffany's to make in New York. Ann told me they had first met four months earlier on a film set in Hollywood but prior to the shoot Richard had objected to her casting because he believed she was an unknown talent. Harris explained: "All that changed when I clapped eyes on her and realised too how talented she was. She is going to be a sensational star and maybe one day she will keep me in the style of life I am accustomed." Ann thought the actor was alluding to their sixteen-year age gap. She was twenty-six at the time and Harris forty-two. "That's not going to make a scrap of difference," said Ann.

I invited one of the UK's leading photographers David Steen to fly over and picture the couple in situ in the Bahamas at play. Two days later they were posing for him and his portfolio was reproduced in the world's top magazines and newspapers.

We left the honeymooners happily romping on the beach and returned to London. A couple of weeks later I was pleased to hear that Richard and Ann had officially tied the knot and I sent them a congratulatory telegram. Together they pursued their plans for films and records in which they could jointly participate and they starred together with Sophia Loren in 'Cassandra Crossing.' At that point the world seemed on their side.

But Hollywood, a cauldron of hot gossip, was speculating on rifts in the marriage only two years later. 'It's all over' screamed the gossip column grapevine with the kind of delirious satisfaction that America's film capital derives from matrimonial breakdowns. At first glance it seemed that way: home-alone Ann out on the town in Hollywood letting her hair down while Richard was in Malta working on another film production titled 'Orca' about a fisherman's feud with a killer whale. Could all the break-up rumours be true? I flew out to Los Angeles to catch up with Ann as she greeted Harris back at the airport with a passionate embrace telling him how much she had missed him. Back in their Beverly Hills home, just one of many homes they kept across the world, Harris laughed off all the gossip.

"It was all my doing," claimed Harris. "Annie was with me in Malta for most of the time but eventually I packed her off home as life became so tedious for her. She also had her own work to think about, not only in films but as a singer too, now that she has her own record company. 'Go home' I told her and do your own thing.

Don't miss out on any of the Hollywood parties and dinners. Go out and flirt. Have a good time. I meant it. Because like me she is an excitement freak."

It was hard to make sense of Harris's protestations. But there was more.

"My philosophy is this: I have never believed in vaginal fidelity. I have always said it is not where the body lies but where the heart rests. The only moment that I would regard Annie as being unfaithful to me would be if ever her heart went to someone else."

Ann looked at me and smiled. "No man on earth could interest me as much as Richard. He will never have cause to worry."

The atmosphere appeared to be governed by bliss, and I returned to London in the knowledge that their marriage seemed secure, if Harris's interpretations were, typically, rather unconventional.

In the early autumn Richard Harris flew into London and checked into a suite at the Savoy Hotel. I joined him for breakfast one morning and by coincidence his bedside phone rang. I was soon to learn it was his ex-wife Elizabeth on the line. "Woman!" roared Harris down the telephone. "You have made me out to be a bloody one-dimensional bore. I am many things but never that. It's unforgiveable!"

He dropped the receiver forcefully. "That was Elizabeth," he said, in case I hadn't guessed. "She wanted my verdict on her book."

Elizabeth had quietly slipped into the hotel the previous evening and given a copy of her memoirs 'Love, Honour and Dismay' to a hall porter to deliver to her ex-husband. And he had read it overnight. As a waiter wheeled in the breakfast trolley laden with croissants, marmalade and coffee Harris tossed me the copy of Elizabeth's book.

"Oh, this is a signed copy," smiled Harris. "Just look at the dedication."

I turned the first page and saw Elizabeth had penned: 'To Richard — with fond memories and thoughts for the children that we were.'

"That's quite touching," I remarked.

Harris flustered. "Are you joking? Wait until you read the rest. She's made me out to be the wildest living monster on earth — a man of booze, birds, brawls and bloody battles."

But wasn't there an essence of truth in all of that? Harris crumpled in laughter, the roar vibrating the sugar bowl and silver cutlery.

"Of course I was hell to live with. Everyone knows about my

character. I've gone around the world on a bottle, not a broomstick. With my zip down and waving my fist in the face of controversy."

Harris's twelve-year marriage to Elizabeth, daughter of Liberal peer Lord Ogmore, ended in 1969 when she divorced him for adultery.

"Elizabeth wrote this book because she is a woman scorned. She can't bear the fact that I've found happiness with Annie. My marriage to Elizabeth was a sham. She was hooked on high society and I didn't fit in. Remember she was once a deb. So she lived like one. All she cared about was keeping up appearances in the social circle. I just couldn't live life like that. It had to end."

The furore, I gathered, went on for the rest of the week. Annie arrived in town and she delved curiously into the book. Her verdict didn't surprise me.

"Elizabeth has obviously written about a total stranger, because I don't know this man she describes," she said, softly kissing her husband on the cheek.

[1.] Arthur D. Murphy 'Film Reviews: The Greatest' Variety Magazine May 25 1977

CHAPTER NINE

A NIGHTMARE IN THE BUSH

L ike two travelling circuses, Richard Harris and I crossed paths once more in South Africa in 1977. Annie accompanied Harris on the journey.

Harris had landed a starring role in Euan Lloyd's movie 'The Wild Geese' alongside Richard Burton and Roger Moore. All three were cast as leaders of a group of mercenaries attempting to rescue an African leader from gaol.

The production company had rented the site of a college campus. Cast and crew were all accommodated in various log cabins and bungalows within the grounds which were heavily fenced in and protected from the wild bush flanking its perimeters. Euan had set aside a large bungalow for myself and compatriot Terry Fincher, my friend and talented photographer, in which to organise our week's work.

The three stars were ready to help us with obliging pictures and interviews and we worked well with them on set. With only another couple of days left of our week-long stay, we thought it was high time for a celebratory drink with our material safely intact.

We joined Richard Harris and Roger Moore in the bar of the campus restaurant and the South African choice wines went down exceedingly well. Richard and Roger left the bar saying that they were on call at dawn the following morning and Terry Fincher decided to return to the bungalow to pack his photographic equipment, leaving me to talk to two white bull-necked Afrikan security guards.

The conversation, fuelled by the fast flow of excess wine, turned into a heated discussion about current affairs and politics in South Africa with the two men.

In my cups, I criticised the South Africans' apartheid system under which Donald Woods, the anti-apartheid activist and editor of the Daily Dispatch, had been arrested by the authorities and had a five-year ban placed on him.

"That can't be right. What is your Government thinking?" I argued with the two men both dressed uniformly in white shirts and shorts.

It became clear that they had formed the impression that my role as a reporter was merely a disguise for being an undercover agent of some kind. Or, that if I was a journalist, I was there to conduct a probe into the gaoling of anti-apartheid protestors.

I left the bar and set out on the unlit dusty track just before midnight to return to my bungalow which was four or five hundred yards away.

Suddenly, the headlights of a car flashed up behind me and, as I heard its engine grow closer, I stepped aside on to the verge to allow it through. But the car (an open-top wagon) screeched to a halt. I was immediately aware of a large, burly figure hurling himself at me and knocking me unconscious from what could only be described as a karate chop to the back of my neck.

I knew no more until dawn the following morning. I woke up supine, concussed and dazed looking up into a clear blue sky. I was slumped on the ground. I could only hear birds screeching in the distance.

I found myself inchoately thinking: 'What has happened? Where am I?'

My thoughts were reeling. Only then did it hit me. I knew I must be in the wilds of the bush. An instant memory of the night before came flooding back. The wagon... the men in white suits... From that point on, the predicament I was in became only too clear. After I had collapsed unconscious, my assailants must have thrown me into the back of the wagon, driven miles away and dumped me in the wilderness in the belief that in the night I would be taken by lion or leopard or find death by a snake or scorpion.

I managed to rouse to my feet and I could see nowhere but the wilderness itself. I started to run in sheer fright. I tore on and on through the undergrowth, pounding the ground beneath me, not knowing which direction to take. The fear and horror of my desperate situation caused me to lose bladder control as I ran. I was at a point of exhaustion when suddenly I spotted a wind chute maybe a mile away at the end of the tiny airstrip where our little

A Nightmare in the Bush

plane had landed earlier that week. I decided that I had to get there in the belief that later that day an incoming plane might come into land and find me.

As I got closer, I saw some outbuildings to my left and I set course for them. It was a farm and leaning on the fencing were three or four African tribesmen. As they saw me running towards them from the bush, their eyes widened in fright and disbelief. One of them spoke a little English and I tried to explain my ordeal. He told me that the farm was run by a white man and he was due to be with them very soon. One of the tribesmen got me some water and I sat on a bench trying to recover and make some sense of it all. Within the hour the farmer arrived and he was astounded to see me and the state I was in. My safari suit was blackened, creased and torn.

"What has happened?" he asked with an incredulous voice. He shook his head and fixed his eyes on me. "You are lucky to be alive. I don't know how you survived out there," he said, looking out into the bush as I recounted my story.

"I can't believe it," he kept saying. Fortunately, he knew the location of the film set on the college campus. "I had better get you back there," he said.

I thanked him and he drove me back to the college grounds. By now, Terry had alerted the production assistants to my disappearance. He was aghast when I turned up on the doorstep. "What on earth..." began Terry, but I stalled him.

"I will tell you everything. But let me get into the shower first." Euan Lloyd the producer came to see me after I had dressed into a welcome change of clothes. Once more I related the whole incident. Again, the story was met with disbelief. Euan brought along one of his aides and they asked me if I could identify the two men.

"Were they the two men you were drinking with in the bar?" they said as they questioned me.

"It was too dark. I cannot be certain who they were, but I can only assume they were the same men..."

Euan took counsel with the local police but unless I could make a positive identification then I could not make any unfounded allegations against the two Afrikaners.

"But for the rest of your stay I am going to make sure that you have your own personal bodyguard," said Euan. The following night I dined quietly with Terry in the restaurant. I saw the two

Afrikaners that I suspected of having attacked me. More so when they stared at me with guilty disbelief written in their eyes.

"They thought I'd be dead," I murmured to Terry. We returned home. Two weeks later, the London editor of the Afrikan newspaper 'Rapport' carried a front-page scoop on the incident. Woefully I had become the story rather than the assignment I had set out to cover.

Later I learned that Euan Lloyd had taken out extra insurance to cover any misbehaviour or hellraising antics of Richard Harris. "From what I hear I should have extended that cover to Don Short," he told an aide.

For weeks and months after I suffered nightmares about the incident, reliving the horrors I had experienced. It is only now, so many years later that I have been able to write about it.

Safely entrenched back in London, I was persuaded to spend more time in developing my freelance work. In the process I sadly lost contact with Harris and all his exploits. I was more saddened to learn that he and Annie were to divorce after only six years of marriage. I reasoned that in the film world, where egos rule, love lives are never less than volatile. I thought about sending Richard and Annie a note but in the end felt there would be no purpose.

Happily Hollywood recognised that Harris was still a big box office actor. There was a run of massive budget films before he accepted the role of Albus Dumbledore. Initially he was apparently reluctant to take the role because he felt that it would diminish all his earlier classic works. But he had been persuaded to take the part thanks to the pleadings of one of his infant granddaughters who threatened not to talk to him anymore if he didn't appear with her hero Harry Potter!

I was stunned to hear that Richard's health was beginning to suffer and in 2002 he was diagnosed with Hodgkin's disease. He was taken into hospital from the Savoy Hotel where he had resided for several months. It was said that as he was being carried out of the hotel on a stretcher into the waiting ambulance he leaned up and joked with incoming guests "Don't have the fish," as though that was the cause of his ailment. In hospital Richard fell into a coma and died peacefully on 25th October. He was seventy-two.

He was cremated and his ashes scattered on Paradise Isle in the Bahamas. He was now rested in a beautiful place bathed in sunshine — a place, a paradise — he loved. Peace had at last descended on his turbulent life. There was only one thing I would have liked to

A Nightmare in the Bush

have said... Goodbye, my friend. Thanks for everything.

****

Finding myself in California once more, I was to become involved in an intriguing episode in the life of another of Hollywood's combatants — the actor Lee Marvin.

It was the extraordinary case of three 'Marvins'. Marvin, the star of 'Cat Ballou' and 'The Dirty Dozen', his live-in partner of six years Michelle Triola Marvin, and the famed celebrity attorney Marvin Mitchelson.

When the actor walked out on Michelle and left her empty handed, Mitchelson advised her to sue him in what was to become the first palimony case to be tested in the courts in any part of the world.

Mitchelson asked me to talk with Michelle and hear her side of the story. It was one of heartbreak for her.

Michelle, a jazz and blues singer, had met Lee Marvin when they worked together on the film 'Ship of Fools'. He was one of the stars and she had a small part. Both were in the throes of divorce and they quickly took comfort in one another. They fell in love and set up home together.

"We were like a pair of puppy dogs together," she recalled when I dined with her in Los Angeles. "Having fun, laughing at one another. We were friends and lovers. He was my husband and I was his wife. The fact that we weren't married made it terribly exciting."

Michelle unofficially adopted Marvin's name — but ran into an embarrassing moment when she accompanied Lee on a visit to London.

"Whenever we travelled together like that I went as Mrs. Marvin but at Heathrow that day the immigration official after inspecting my passport asked: "How long will you be staying Miss Triola?" Others behind me in the line gazed apprehensively. I found the incident embarrassing."

So, returning home, she changed her name by deed poll to Marvin.

"Lee convinced me early in our relationship that the only reason women push for marriage is because they regard it as an insurance policy. He used to tell me, Michelle, you don't need one."

Michelle paused as she reflected on that moment. "Huh, the way things worked out, obviously I did!" she countered.

A telephone call from Las Vegas one night in 1970 shattered her illusion of a happy-ever-after future.

It was Marvin calling to tell her he would no longer be seeing her. More to the point, he confessed, he had married Pam Feeley, the girl he had known in high school and who had four children by an earlier marriage.

"It was a bolt from the blue," said Michelle. "After all that Lee had said about marriage... and then to go out and do just that, like he had changed all the rules overnight. It left me totally confused."

Michelle had to move out of their Malibu beach home and take a small apartment offered to her by a friend. "It was a crisis," Michelle went on. "The man I had relied on for so many years was no longer there. Lee promised to send me a thousand dollars a month, but after a year he stopped the money and I was broke. That hurt a lot because it showed he didn't really care what happened to me. I had to pawn my own belongings to survive. For eighteen months I tramped around trying to find a job. I was emotionally unable to resume my singing career. It was too late to pick up the threads. I would have taken any job, but no one would employ me. They were all afraid that Lee would get mad and make trouble. Men were wary of dating me after one stuntman at a party remarked... 'You'll always be Lee's old lady.'"

Michelle sought counsel with the renowned and shrewd lawyer Marvin Mitchelson who persuaded her to fight her case in court demanding a half share of the $3.6 million that Marvin had earned from his films during their relationship.

The Californian court rejected the claim but awarded Michelle $104,000 in alimony. But this award was later quashed by the Court of Appeal and as a result she received no money from Marvin.

Needless to say Michelle was inconsolable when I called her. I did not want to take sides, knowing that journalists have to remain neutral. It was now essential for me to get to talk to Lee.

He was angered by the court proceedings and the prolonged years it had taken to settle the case which he had no desire to go into. "It's a dead part of my life," he told me dismissively.

Things had calmed a little in 1976 when I caught up with Marvin filming in South Africa. The granite jawed actor was not going to get bogged down in the past.

By then I had learned that Michelle had found a new partner in her life — Dick van Dyke — a Hollywood star with a milder reputation than that of the notorious hard-drinker that was Lee Marvin. But no mention was made of Michelle in our conversation. As Lee remarked: "We all move on."

A Nightmare in the Bush

The Hollywood star had joined Roger Moore to lead the cast in a World War I adventure 'Shout At The Devil' based on the blockbuster Wilbur Smith novel.

Marvin was now happily settled in his marriage with Pat who had flown with him to Africa for the film shoot.

The Oscar winning actor who was awarded a Purple Heart medal for bravery as a serving Marine fighting the Japanese in World War II, was in top form heading into the movie like a swashbuckling pioneer. The film contained all the ingredients that whetted his appetite for the big outdoors, like how he prospected for gold at his own mine in the Tucson desert, and how he buckled with the sea on his regular marlin fishing expeditions.

"It's the same sort of thing goin' on here," he said, relishing the wild location of Africa's Transkei.

Some observers might have believed mistakenly that he regarded film-making as more of a hobby than a career and he managed a smile as he told me: "It's better than working."

Marvin spoke about the film industry at large and singled out investors who were always ready to back a movie. "It's called culture buying," said Marvin. "Those dull guys love all that. It gives them something to talk about over dinner... it gives them some glamour they can bask in."

For his wife Pat, the actor was making a pledge to cut back on booze.

"There are moments when an old-timer has got to play cautious," says Marvin, his snow-white thatch of hair falling back into place like rye grass after a gale.

"I've cut down on it all. Hangovers are not hangovers anymore. They're hangers on..."

Cast and crew were relieved but I suspected when I left the set that characters like Lee Marvin would always break the rules on a whim. And true to form Lee Marvin took me aside and winked: "Don, have you got time for a farewell drink?" How could I have refused?

****

There are times in life when we all do foolish things. None more so on my part than when Oliver Reed, another notorious star of the screen and a master of great fun, duped me into accepting his challenge to a drinking contest.

In readiness for my arrival, two bottles of brandy and glass tumblers were laid out on the coffee table in Ollie's hotel suite in Madrid where he was taking a break from filming 'The Three Musketeers.'

My intended mission was to talk to Ollie about the film, but the actor shook his head insisting we should all loosen up before we got down to the nitty gritty.

Then he threw down the gauntlet.

"Here — there's a bottle of brandy for you and one for me. First one to finish wins," he said.

His younger brother Simon and Ollie's friend and film stuntman Reg Prince were to be the referees. I tried to abstain but a bellowing Ollie refused to listen. He opened the bottle, pushed it closer to me and filled the glass to the brim. Then, he repeated the motion to fill his own glass. He looked at Simon and Reg and nodded his head.

"Right, away we go," he stormed, demolishing his first glass of the fearsome brandy in one gulp. I picked up my own glass and sipped it tentatively.

One hour later, just as Ollie looked as though he was going to be the clear winner of this ludicrous match, he slumped back on the couch where he was sitting, appearing completely inebriated.

Reg smiled: "That was Ollie's second bottle of the day. He drunk a bottle of brandy before you arrived!"

My hangover the next morning was near to a total eclipse of mind and body. I imagined I had only drunk half of the bottle of brandy.

"Your trouble is," Ollie hissed to heighten my headache, "you don't know when you've had enough."

I couldn't help but feel that was a little hypocritical on Mr Reed's part. Wasn't he the one who dived into the goldfish tank at the Hilton? Didn't he utter that immortal explanation, "I am Athos — you can't arrest me," when police were summoned to a drunken downtown brawl?

"Maybe," he growled. "But there is a time and a place for everything. Just look at yourself. Please don't embarrass me by dying on the plane."

I phoned my colleague newsman, Roy Rutter, who operated out of Madrid to say goodbye as I was about to catch the plane home. He rasped: "Make sure you get the plane. I don't want you to snuff it on my patch."

I caught the plane but I needed to inhale a few shots of oxygen from the drop-down mask above my head.

It took another couple of days to recover. I could only blame myself. I should have been prepared for Ollie's antics.

I remembered how our previous drink together had ended in such chaos at Wimbledon. We were entrenched at one of his favourite lunchtime pubs and, on the stroke of closing time, he purchased several kegs of beer and announced to the customers that he was throwing a picnic on the Common.

Mr Reed marched like a massive Pied Piper on to the Common, his followers at the rear. Once encamped, he handed me what appeared to be a ham sandwich from a basket he had bought en route at a delicatessen.

Until my first bite, I did not realise he had substituted the ham for peppers. His sullen eyes danced with delight as my mouth almost broke into flames.

Ollie's intoxicating parlour games were well known in the film industry. One of his favourite rituals was to challenge opponents to bouts of arm-wrestling — a contest he rarely lost having been a boxer in earlier years. The actor had also been in booze raddled appearances on the Johnny Carson show in America, when actress Shelley Winters poured a glass of whisky over his head after he made derogatory remarks about women. Ollie also appeared worse for wear on Michael Parkinson's television show in London.

Remarkably, his rise to fame as an actor contradicted his alcohol-fuelled lifestyle.

When he played Bill Sykes in the 1968 movie 'Oliver!' he won wide acclaim and other stellar performances came with movies like 'Women In Love', 'Tomorrow Never Comes', 'The Big Sleep' and the Musketeer films.

It was inevitable I would meet with Ollie again on the circuit. I made sure I laid down my own terms, although he disbelieved my assertion that I was on the wagon. Well, that was the case I made as far as Ollie was concerned.

CHAPTER TEN

FACE TO FACE WITH FRANK SINATRA

My friend Eddie Fisher invited me to an elite cocktail party at Caesars Palace in Las Vegas.

"Every Hollywood star in the business will be there," said Eddie. "You'll get to know a lot of new people."

Sure enough, I recognised many of the faces. Dean Martin was in an animated conversation with a producer on one side of the room and I spotted Sammy Davis Jnr a shoulder or two away. So, I assumed, members of the infamous Rat Pack were likely to be here in force.

Mingling as inconspicuously as I could among the guests, I saw Frank Sinatra chatting to a blonde woman who was sipping a glass of champagne.

In a friendly gesture Eddie tapped Sinatra on the shoulder and intervened, unwisely as it happened: "Frank, I'd like to introduce you to a friend — Don Short a journalist from London."

I was ready to shake Frank Sinatra's hand but he ignored my own extended hand and just scowled back at me.

"A journalist? Fuck off" said Sinatra turning his back on me.

"I'm sorry Frank," stammered Eddie, in an alarmed voice that he may have upset Sinatra, a man never to be disturbed. "But Don is a friend and you can trust him."

Sinatra wasn't listening and resumed his conversation.

Eddie steered me away to another part of the room, passing friendlier guests as we threaded through.

Said Eddie later: "I didn't think Frank would react that way. He really must hate newspapermen."

No truer word was spoken. Over the years Sinatra refused to give interviews and newspaper people were the enemy. As Eddie consoled me: "It wasn't personal."

He may not have wanted to talk to newspapermen, but I knew first-hand that he had been pleased to meet royalty.

In 1962, Sinatra had organised a party for ninety guests to see a preview of his latest film, 'The Manchurian Candidate,' some of whom gathered in his hotel suite at the Savoy in London for cocktails. Princess Alexandra slipped secretly into the hotel and was greeted with a "Hiya honey!" from Sinatra. The Princess, in a summer dress, stayed for half an hour in Sinatra's suite, chatting with him and other members of his Clan, including Fisher, and his agent Kurt Frings. When Princess Alex left with her lady-in-waiting, Sinatra put a pile of his records into her hands and she smiled with gratitude.

But there was one personal friend of Sinatra's that I could rely on and I flew to Paris to meet him. April in Paris 1971 was the kind of romantic interlude that the Canadian-American singer and songwriter Paul Anka had secretly arranged as a surprise holiday for Anne, his lovely wife.

Paul invited me to share some time with them and I took a room close to their suite at the elegant George V hotel — a favourite sanctuary of the stars through the years. Paul had composed one of Tom Jones's chart busters 'She's A Lady' and delivered the English lyrics to a French song that gave Frank Sinatra his greatest hit 'My Way.'

I dined with Paul and his wife Anne in a typically Parisian restaurant on the Left Bank. We had got over the business end of the deal: Paul apparently holding no regrets that he had given Sinatra the song that would have been his own all-time legacy if he had chosen to record 'My Way' himself.

"Frank is a close friend and I knew that this song was made for him," insisted Paul, although I remained a little unconvinced by such loyalty.

We were nearing the end of our enjoyable and relaxing lunch, when a gypsy dressed in shawl and Bohemian garb appeared in the restaurant with a straw trug of roses which she was feathering out to the diners. She was also offering the diners the opportunity to have their fortunes read. At first, Paul refused with a polite smile and said: "No, never. I don't want to hear any bad news." But the gypsy managed to persuade him to extend the palm of his hand for her to see. Paul bought a rose for Anne and then motioned for the woman to sit down on a spare chair at our table and proceeded to read his fortune and that of a curious Anne. The fortune teller flattered the singer's handsome looks, his many talents and was equally rapturous when she came to read Anne's extended palm.

"You are so in love with one another. You will always be together," she cooed. My two friends glowed with happiness in all that she recited.

With another smile, Paul gave her some money, and suggested that I should also show her the palm of my hand. She nodded and I held out my hand in the innocent thought that it was all in a day's fun and I could go along with all the hokum-pokum anyway.

She carefully scrutinised my lifelines and then, to the horror of all the diners in the restaurant and to my own personal alarm, she screamed hysterically to her feet, dropped her basket and fled from the restaurant. Everyone was aghast in disbelief as the tables echoed with the clatter of fallen cutlery. I was the unwelcome focus of all and sundry.

My mind searched for an explanation. Was it a dramatic piece of theatrics? Perhaps she was hoping that Paul might give her role in his next film. Wearing a credulous expression, L'Patron shrugged in astonishment. As the hubbub died down, he picked up the gypsy's fallen basket and its strewn flowers and placed it behind a nearby counter.

"This has never happened before. I imagine she will be back here tomorrow to collect her basket. Maybe then we will know what is wrong Monsieur," he said, apologising for her disappearance.

Both Paul and Anne shared their thoughts on the episode. "They don't always get it right," placated Paul, worried I might have been shocked by the gypsy's foreboding.

But whatever the theories I never got an answer to the mystery of the fortune teller's wild reactions. What alarming visions she might have seen haunted me for several days until I had expunged any superstitions from my mind. Besides, from the start I had viewed it all as nonsense and as it happened, the gypsy had not got Paul and Anne's future entirely accurate. They divorced in 2001 after nearly forty years of marriage. As Paul mentioned at the time... fortune tellers don't always get it right.

****

At home Cliff Richard was very much in the thick of things. He had been a big part of the Swinging Sixties fare with a succession of chart-topping hits. But he was something of an enigma among the pop fraternity having distanced himself from the scene's darker habits when he became a Christian. His deep faith saw him conduct his life with impenetrable standards of dignity and decency. His fans respected him for it and voted him as their favourite pop idol.

Cliff may well have frowned on the depraved lifestyles of many of his contemporaries. Certainly, he viewed the social revolution as being tarnished by drug addiction, misbehaviour and promiscuity. At the same time, he admired the musical creativity of his rivals and was happy to appear on concert stages with many of the stars whose morals and attitudes were at odds with his own.

There was one frustrating pitfall in Cliff's booming career. He just could not crack the American market. In most parts of the world, he was the ultimate clean-cut idol. His devout fans asked then and still today why America turned its back on him.

But the theory I was given in 1968 may still provide the most valid answer. Cliff's career was then guided by his candid talking Australian manager Peter Gormley — and the theory he advanced to me ticked all the right boxes.

"It's a long story," acknowledged Peter. "And goes right back to the beginning of the rock 'n' roll era. In those days the American studio producers tried to put Cliff across as the new Elvis Presley — or Britain's answer to him, anyway." Peter shook his head. "To say the least it was a deadly mistake. They just refused to see Cliff in any other light as an entirely different talent with an entirely different appeal."

I shared his view that it was an undeserved tag that Cliff still can't shake free from. Cliff's great catalogue of records which have conquered hit parades at home and across almost every other land on the planet, have all failed to scratch the U.S. charts. Only 'Living Doll' managed to tweak the thirty mark. Even critically-acclaimed tracks like 'The Young Ones' 'Bachelor Boy' and 'Congratulations' — all of them gold disc winners — didn't gel across the pond.

Cliff split away from his backing group, The Shadows, in the spring of 1967. It was a friendly parting of ways with Cliff explaining that he needed to give more time to his faith. But I suspected at the time that Cliff might also have felt that by going solo, he just might win the American fans over.

Cliff dated many women through the sixties. His name was later linked with tennis star Sue Barker and subsequently the dancer

Jackie Irving who later married another singer Adam Faith. They were thought to be platonic relationships — but Cliff called them "false alarms" if they were purveyed to be on track to marriage. He said that he believed his bachelor state was God's will: "If it is not God's wish for me to marry then it is something I must accept. He may feel that my work can be achieved more purposefully by remaining single."

During the heady days of the sixties, there was one memorable luncheon with Cliff when over his meal he drank two Bloody Marys and a half bottle of hock, which at the time, struck me as being slightly at odds with his personality. But as we left the smart West End restaurant Cliff had an answer for it. He declared: "The greatest Christian that ever lived was a sinner." Cliff hasn't ever pretended to be an exception.

****

For David Bowie the turn to religion came late in his career. First, there was Buddhism and then a fascination for other forms of spirituality. Unlike Cliff, the pop scene's anti-hero Bowie had indulged experimentally with the seedy blandishments of the music world. Cocaine, acid, pot, torrid relationships and band bust-ups — Bowie experienced them all. He also experimented with gender and sexuality. Through his career he alternately stated that he was heterosexual, gay and bi-sexual.

His play with gender rode in tandem with whatever his career persona demanded. He was creating new identities in the glam rock field. His previous transformations were all but forgotten, however, in the eyes of his adoring fans when he stepped out onto the stage as 'Ziggy Stardust.' It was a theatrically costumed role that catapulted him to stardom.

When, unannounced, I visited the twenty-four-year-old David Bowie at his Beckenham home in the Spring of 1971, he opened the front door wearing a dress.

His wife Angie, only two weeks away from expecting their first baby, was thrilled by the way her husband looked. "I rather fancy him that way. He looks so lovely in a dress," she said. They both invited me in to stay for lunch.

Bowie's long shoulder-length blond hair hung over the flowing pink and blue dress which he wore with knee-length calf boots. David said he liked the 'Mr. Fish' dress so much that he had already ordered six more at £150 a throw.

"I get all sorts of abuse showered on me. But it doesn't worry me anymore what people say. I get called a queer and all sorts of things."

But in America only a few weeks earlier where David had been plugging his new album 'The Man Who Sold The World', he had reason to worry. He told me that when he landed up in Texas, he found himself staring down the barrel of a gun and a huge rancher snarling at him: "If it wasn't against the law I'd blow your brains out you fag. Quit town!" David, a natural pacifist, beat a hasty retreat and decided "The World" could sell itself.

Pouring himself a vodka-tonic, David Bowie reclined into a chair. Angie reappeared from the kitchen having rustled up a delicious chicken lunch.

I glanced across at Bowie. "Oh, do take your eyes off him," Angie rebuked me. "You're making me jealous."

My eyes went instead to the apartment, which occupied the ground floor of a rambling mansion. It seemed more like a curio market with guitars, saxophones, a grand piano, an ironing board, a bookcase, a television, and ornaments and lampshades cluttered around a king-size bed in the centre of the floor.

Angie went on: "Fashion should be fun. You should wear whatever you feel like wearing."

David added: "I cannot breathe in the atmosphere of convention. I find freedom only in the realms of my own eccentricity."

His eccentricity was evident in the huge lounge of the couple's apartment where Bowie liked to work. He had hit the jackpot with his record 'Space Oddity' released just a few days before Houston's launch of Apollo 11.

Only a few weeks later, I was able to congratulate the couple on the birth of their son Duncan, who they liked to call Zowie, and they were pictured wheeling him out in his pram with David wearing Oxford bags, a blouse and floppy hat while Angie wore a lumberjack coat, velvet trousers and suede boots.

It was many years later that I got a call from Angie to help her with her memoirs. She and David had divorced and she felt she had never got the credit she deserved for the way she had helped to steer David to stardom. She had helped him create the 'Ziggy Stardust' image and she had played a vigorous part in mapping out his career. She was to make numerous revelations in her book, many of which made the headlines.

Face to Face with Frank Sinatra

Bowie dallied with Buddhism and then converted to the Anglican religion which was very much part of his mind-set in 1992 when he married his second wife, the Somali-American model known as Iman. Earlier that year he had knelt on stage at the Freddie Mercury tribute concert and recited the Lord's Prayer. David Bowie's life as a musician, artist and avid art collector had been truly transformed.

****

The Kinks' hit song 'Lola' was at No.2 in the charts in July 1970. Ray Davies, the Kinks lead singer, told me that the experience related in the song actually happened.

The lyric explains: 'She walked like a woman and talked like a man,' and Davies said to me: "Five years ago I went to one of those Soho cellar clubs under a Chinese restaurant and danced with a girl. But it wasn't until afterwards that I realised it must have been a boy dressed as a girl. At the time I was shocked but today blokes in drag are something you accept. It's a facet of life. But I didn't think it would make a hit record."

I wondered what Danny La Rue must have thought of it.

****

When Richard Nixon announced from the White House that The Carpenters "Represent all that is true and best in America" it was an accolade that Richard and Karen Carpenter did not welcome. In fact, they believed it did them a lot of harm. They faced a backlash as they were variously described as square, vitamin-swallowing, shower-fresh, squeaky clean babies with toothpaste smiles. It was an image that had to be thrown overboard. The brother and sister act did it in style.

They made their own announcement to counter Nixon's view of them. They said that neither of them was a virgin, that they believed in pre-marital sex and, while they didn't smoke pot, they didn't object if others did.

"It had to be done," Karen told me when I caught up with them as they set out on a European tour. "We had to shed the goody-two-shoes image. People must have been dumb to believe we were that good."

Karen said she didn't drink because she didn't enjoy it. She admitted that she and Richard had spoken out about drugs. "When we said that we thought pot should be legalised — in came a shoal of letters saying we were drug addicts!"

Richard nodded. "We know that no one in their right minds would screw up their lives by taking drugs," he said. "Sure we said a few words about pot. We said we didn't know whether it was more harmful than alcohol."

Karen shook her head. "We had to speak out and tell the truth about us as it is. It's hell living like a pair of angels."

I told Richard and Karen that they should not get too het-up about their image, because I was sure the only thing that mattered for their millions of fans was their incredible music — great hits from Richard's pen such as 'Close To You' and 'Goodbye to Love.'

Looking back over their career they said they were very grateful to their parents. They helped them to break into the music scene. Their father worked a double shift as a printer and their mother took a job in an aircraft factory.

"We have a lot to be grateful to them for," said Karen, who had played in her college band.

One day she slid in behind the drum kit on the rostrum, picked up the sticks, "And from that moment on I became a girl drummer. I never stopped to think it was not a 'girl's instrument'," she told me. "In certain fields I'm every bit as good as any of the male drummers, but maybe in sheer power I can't compete."

Karen's magnetic voice captivated fans. Yet Richard insisted that he had to push his sister into singing.

"It was like pulling teeth," he told me. "We couldn't get her away from the drums. Now her voice has developed into one of the greatest in the world."

Karen was equally complimentary about her brother.

"The trouble is he doesn't push himself. But I can tell you that all our super hits are his. I want to strangle people who come up and ask who writes our hits for us. Richard is too modest to say so... I wouldn't have anything to sing if it wasn't for him."

That's how The Carpenters will be remembered. As the world's most loved brother and sister act of all time.

****

Sonny and Cher were similarly keen to shake off their sweet image. They were once the most dandy and sugar-coated act in showbusiness. They trailed the world in gaudy silks and colours and scent-sprayed, shaggy furs, and they were a huge success.

Face to Face with Frank Sinatra

Until the morning they woke to hate themselves for it.

"We shuddered when we realised what it all meant. We were the confectionery and we no longer liked the wrapping or the taste," Sonny told me in his hotel suite in April 1969.

"To us it was a form of prostitution. There we were, earning £250,000 a year for concerts and tours and making records. If someone said: 'Jump on those milk churns, wave and laugh.' Oh boy, we did it because it meant another picture somewhere. It was a false life and we could no longer stay married to it."

Sonny's candid and sometimes brutal self-appraisal provided ample explanation of why the American couple had ghosted out of the pop scene where three years before they were a forceful factor.

Another reason, of course, was that Cher had just had their child, called Chastity. The wonder of motherhood was reflected in Cher's voice as she told me: "She's seven weeks old, twenty-one inches long, weighs ten pounds and sits up already. I've just bought her a pram in Harrods and they're going to ship it home. There are no prams like English prams anywhere in the world."

Sonny smiled. He wanted to tell me about their records. In America, they could count ten golden discs to their credit and, of these, 'I Got You Babe' was the biggest seller in this country. But it was a success they had since failed to match.

Said Sonny: "There have been other records and it's true, they've flopped. We're not disputing that. But here's the answer. It was lack of enthusiasm and interest on our part because we were growing sick of the scene. The day we saw ourselves for what we were, we had to become real. We had to look for a new dimension. To be more creative."

And that, precisely, was where Chastity came in. She took her name from the title of the most recent screen-play Sonny had written for a picture in which his wife would star. 'Chastity' was the story of a girl in the current promiscuous world who goes round in one big circle.

Sonny did not know that the film was going to flop badly. He summarised its plot and told me it was about "a girl who sets out hitch-hiking and ends hitch-hiking."

Sonny was concerned about his wife appearing nude in the film, but she said, "I didn't really object. Look, if you can't undress for your husband, who can you undress for?"

Another problem was money. Said Sonny, "Hollywood has an established tradition for making movies. They like to do things on a mighty scale with mighty stars and budgets even though they may have found the plot in a phone directory. I only wanted 500,000 dollars for my picture. I should have asked for four million because I would have got it easier. As it was, I had to beg, scrape, and put all our own bread into it. But now the picture is done and we sink or swim with it."

They were in London for a Tom Jones television show and were set to fly home after that for Cher to star in a play on Broadway.

"She is going to be a big star," predicted Sonny, "And my role from now on is going to be more in the background, producing and directly, but essentially being creative. We'll make records again too. Only they will be more vital. Because now we know where we are going and that old adrenalin is pumping again."

Sadly, it was not to be, their marriage broke up.

****

Touring with Engelbert Humperdinck had its tricky moments. He was on stage in a swanky New York night spot when an anonymous caller informed the police that a bomb had been planted there.

Dozens of police descended on the club, but to avoid any panic among the audience no announcement was made from the stage where Engelbert was in the middle of his act.

As quietly and as systematically as possible, the evening dress clad guests were led out onto the street to safety, while Engelbert, totally unaware of the drama around him, went on singing. He ignored the frantic signals from the wings to close the show, and finally an official had to stride on stage and tug him away from the microphone and spotlight.

"Why would anyone want to do this?" the singer asked afterwards.

Fortunately, after searching every corner in the club, the police found no trace of a bomb. It was a hoax.

"What can you do in such circumstances? Cranks are capable of doing anything. It's frightening," said the singer.

Spurned and jealous lovers also provided some disconcerting problems. None more so than an incident in Oklahoma when Engelbert and his party, after the show was over, were invited by the management of the Hilton Inn to a nightcap drink in their club-restaurant. Engelbert wanted to catch up on his sleep and declined and I went to my room to file some copy to London.

Face to Face with Frank Sinatra

But road manager Tony Cartwright and musical composer Laurie Holloway went along. Apparently, three girls were sat on the table that had been reserved for our party and suddenly into the club came a young man yelling hysterically that his fiancée had left him for Engelbert Humperdinck. In the affray, Holloway had two ribs broken and Cartwright's face was slashed, leaving a wound which necessitated twelve stitches in hospital. In the dimly lit club Cartwright had been mistaken by the assailant for Engelbert.

Cartwright told me: "I was rushed to hospital but when I got there it was to find there was no doctor immediately available. I was about to complain when the doctor came in from the adjoining surgery and said: 'What are you worrying about with a scratch on your face? I've got a patient in there with two bullets to remove from under his heart.'"

Cartwright's 'scratch' fortunately healed in time without any visible scarring. I shared his view when he said: "So who wants to become a star?"

Engelbert sympathised with his two friends and asked how such an incident could happen. Crime in New York at that time was manifest. "But these kinds of things can happen at home," he said. "We've got cranks too."

He told me how he had once received a letter in a batch of fan mail that carried a real threat. It read "Dear Pretty Face, my girl has left me as a result of you. We will see what your pretty face looks like after a bottle of acid. Watch out for the acid — or a knife in your back!" The police traced the youth who sent the letter and gave him a severe warning.

Engelbert was proving as much as a heart throb in America as his stable mate Tom Jones, but it was clear that there was always an undercurrent of rivalry between them.

One female fan got Engelbert's attention at the end of another concert when she asked him "Just how sexy is Tom Jones?" Showing his irritation with the girl, Engelbert retorted: "How the hell should I know?"

I admired the way in which showbusiness manager Gordon Mills was able to look after his two stars without showing greater favour to one more than the other.

"They are on top of the world. I am proud of them both," Mills affirmed.

Mills had seen Tom Jones conquer Las Vegas and now he was engineering the same feat for Engelbert.

Until 1967, Vegas was virtually an exclusive American show business fortress. Then came the coup masterminded by Mills as he placed Tom Jones into their midst and the American fans went wild. Now Engelbert was to step out onto that same stage.

I stood in one of the aisles of the Riviera Hotel as Engelbert, in a black tuxedo and dress trousers, made his entry to a deafening reaction from the American fans as he broke into his big British hit 'Release Me.' His velvet voice and smouldering looks won them over in an instant and they showered him with a colourful array of underwear that fell at his feet. Some fans had even scrawled their telephone numbers on the garments. Engelbert Humperdinck had arrived.

****

Joe Cocker was proud of his name. It was Yorkshire to the core. That was why he got a bit cross when recording bosses at EMI suggested that he change it to a slicker sign-off, such as 'Whiplash.'

In anger, Cocker exploded. "What's wrong with an honest-to-goodness name like mine?"

He caught the EMI rank off guard. No one could explain. There was just an uncomfortable silence.

So, twenty-two-year-old Cocker won his point and down to the printing works went his name, unchanged.

He was still seething from his exchange when I met him. "There was the bloke behind a big desk saying 'Come, come Cocker, you can't have a name like that for the Hit Parade. I said 'Why not? Even my best friends call me Cocker.'"

He tugged his pink cravat over his brilliant blue velvet jacket as he went on: "I'm not going to sing better whether my name's Whiplash or Cocker."

Young Cocker, with matted hair and a bulging belly, was not likely to challenge any established pop stars in the sex symbol stakes.

But he had a colourful character and was talented too, with an earthy gravel voice and ability to play drums and harmonica. At the time, he had made his second onslaught on the pop world. "I flopped first time," he admitted, "and almost landed in a dole queue." But he shouldn't have worried. He had hit after hit and enjoyed great success.

CHAPTER ELEVEN

ON TRAGEDY AND TRIUMPH

Few stars could have experienced as much tragedy in their lives as the American singer Roy Orbison. I met Orbison in 1967, nine months after he had lost his loving wife Claudette in a road crash in Tennessee.

"Since my wife Claudette died, I've been the loneliest person in the world. It's no good pretending any longer," he told me.

"I've gone into deep states of depression. The world has been good to me — but nothing can make up for the loss of the woman in your life."

Orbison was on a six-week tour and trying to come to terms with his loss when we met just before he went on stage. Life had to move on, he said, then adding: "It's all right to be a swinger. To be with the in-crowd and on the scene. But there comes a time when the party is over, when you are all on your own."

Roy was anxious about the upbringing of his three children and had arranged for a nanny to care for them at their Nashville home while he was on tour. "But it is really a mother they need to see in their home," reflected Roy.

Roy's bleakest days were sorrowfully not over. Just two years after the loss of Claudette, when he was playing at a concert in Bournemouth, he received the news that his house had burned down and he had lost two of his eldest sons in the fire.

I believed, like many others, that Roy would quit his career as his life appeared truly broken. How could any man face the future? But he looked to the therapy he had applied before. He sensed the need to work in the hope of blotting out this fresh tragedy.

Roy told me bravely: "These tragedies happen. You must accept what life brings."

The showbusiness industry rallied round him and Orbison in his traditional dark sunglasses — it was said he wore them to calm his stage nerves — was back in the spotlight performing medleys of his greatest hits including his best known works 'Pretty Woman' and 'Only The Lonely.'

He also began touring with other iconic groups –The Beach Boys, The Beatles and The Rolling Stones.

All were stunned by his motionless stance on stage as he sang. No gyrations, no twists and turns. No gimmicks. His tenor voice also earned him the nickname of 'The Caruso of Rock' although the fans just called him 'The Big O.'

It seemed that his fortunes were changing and in the spring of 1969 he married Barbara Wellhoner Jakobs, the eighteen-year-old daughter of a German diplomat. They had met at the Batley Variety Club where Roy had been performing on yet another UK tour. It proved a happy marriage, despite the fourteen-year age gap between them and they were to have two sons. Barbara devoted her life to the singer, managing his career and setting up a new record company.

Roy was a close friend of George Harrison and Bob Dylan and in April 1988 they formed a new supergroup naming themselves the 'Traveling Wilburys' together with Jeff Lynne who played with the Electric Light Orchestra and Tom Petty. It was a line-up like no other. Anticipation gripped the record industry.

But tragedy struck again. It was as though Roy Orbison was cursed. He did not live to see the triumphs of the new supergroup. He died from a heart attack at the end of that year. He was only fifty-two.

****

Judy Garland was another legendary American star whose life was scarred by ill-fortune which tended to overshadow her triumphs on stage and on screen.

My column greeted her warmly when she flew into London to appear for a season at the Talk of the Town close to Christmas in 1968. 'The Magic That Makes Garland' was the big headline.

Often I was asked about the secret behind her success. Four times married, probably more lawsuits than any other star, hotel rows and punch-ups, bad bills and the rest. The turbulent life of a turbulent girl. But Judy survived everything. She was still a success. Was that strange? Not really. The answer was so simple: the secret was in a little something called nostalgia. It resonated whenever she rendered her greatest hit 'Somewhere over the Rainbow.' Judy ignited a magic between her audience and the stage. Warm hearts reached out for her remembering the good she had done.

When I had last seen Judy Garland, she was in her flat in The Boltons in Kensington where she discussed her divorce from Sid Luft. An American judge had just ruled that, for the time being, she must share the custody of two of her children with Luft. She said, "In spite of everything that was said back there I am a very good mother."

But now, after an absence of four years, it seemed that she had come through the difficulties of the past. She was planning to marry her fifth husband Micky Deans, a thirty-five-year-old New York discotheque manager.

"I am putting all the bad times behind me," Judy assured me. "My life is moving on and I am so much happier now."

Judy never let us down. The mix was the same, but when you rode a rainbow as Judy had done, it was all colours.

When I wrote the words that closed the article, 'Welcome back and good luck, Miss Garland,' I could not have known the terrible tragedy that was to befall her only six months later when she died aged forty-seven. Fans all over the world mourned her loss.

A few years later, her daughter Liza Minnelli, now emulating her mother's stardom, revealed to me that she had been secretly paying off Judy's debts. Liza, talking to me over breakfast at the Savoy in London, didn't want to say just how much her mother's debts had been. But a close source told me that the debts were estimated at £100,000.

She said: "I'm doing this because I want to, not because I want people to think what a good little daughter I am. Now all that's left to clear is a fifty-seven dollar bill due to a New York hotel and I'm going to settle that too."

Liza was twenty-seven-years-old and in sparkling form, giving an impromptu cabaret in London's Park Lane. She bubbled about in a trouser suit and diamante-studded shoes — "My happy hooker shoes" — and an orange rosebud in a tiny silver vase worn on a chain around her neck. She dazzled, just like her mother.

The Beatles and Beyond

****

My column was exploding as it recorded the activity of many stars over time. According to one kind reader, it created its own hall of fame which featured the chart busting calibre such as Elton John, The Carpenters, The Who, Cilla Black, Dusty Springfield, and Gene Pitney. A new era dawned with the arrival of Swedish super troupers Abba but also of Freddie Mercury and his group Queen. I lunched with Freddie and he explained: "Our music has its own concept." It certainly proved so.

But in 1968, there was a shock new entry that relegated the leading stars to lower slots on the hit parade charts. Few people recognised the intruder's name and were left asking "Who is this newcomer?" They didn't have to wait long before they got the answer.

Noel Harrison, son of legendary stage and screen actor Rex Harrison, was hitting the top spots with his recording of the romantic ballad 'The Windmills of Your Mind' composed by the French music director Michel Legrand and given English lyrics by Marilyn and Alan Bergman. It was adopted as the theme tune of the acclaimed film 'The Thomas Crown Affair' and it won an Academy Award for being judged the best original song of that year. By sheer coincidence his father Rex had won an Oscar the previous year for his rendition of 'Talk to the Animals' which he sang in his hit movie 'Doctor Dolittle.' Noel joined me for drinks in a Fleet Street pub the morning after he performed the song 'The Windmills of Your Mind' on television to rapturous applause.

The bar was pretty quiet as it was only around midday. Two printers walked in, both wearing bib and brace denims. The more heavily built man of the two came over to us and interrupted our conversation.

"Mr. Harrison," he interjected. "I saw you on television last night." Noel beamed back at him anticipating some praise for his performance.

"Oh yes," he said. "I am pleased you enjoyed it."

The big man shook his head, "No," he retorted. "You were fucking awful."

I spluttered my drink, horror-stricken. I looked at Noel to catch his reaction. But Noel gazed calmly back at the hefty print worker and said, "Thank you for your constructive criticism."

Few artists could have conjured such a subtle putdown, which left the printer lost for words. He retreated hurriedly to a far corner of the room. More temperamental stars would have probably thrown a punch at the disgruntled man or poured their drink over his head, I suggested.

Noel shook his head and smiled, "No I don't think so." And, casting a glance across the room, he added: "Besides he is a lot bigger than me."

Noel was a former British ski champion who went on to star in many television shows and perform concerts in America and elsewhere, but wherever he went his audience demanded a reprise of 'The Windmills Of Your Mind.' It became a life-long dedication.

Dusty Springfield also loved the song and she produced a cover version released many years later. The American polls in the early sixties named her as the best ever UK artist of all time. Another trade poll went a step further and voted her the best female singer in the world.

The fashionable Dusty with her soulful, mezzo soprano voice, her striking blonde bouffant hairstyle and glam rock 'panda-eye' make-up was a cultural figure of the age, produced one hit after another from one of her earliest releases 'I Only Want To Be With You' to her later cut 'Son Of A Preacher Man' which found its way onto the soundtrack of the movie 'Pulp Fiction.' She was another star I asked to write my column for me as a guest while I was away on holiday.

In the sixties, newspapers were adverse to running stories about gay and lesbian artists, as they were concerned that they would lose readers. Up until 1967 in the UK, gay or bisexual men could face going to prison. The big record companies were also disdainful, not wishing to lose sales if any of their gay artists were publicly identified.

Dusty Springfield was fearful of coming out. She spent hours agonising over the fraught situation and she called me to discuss her dilemma.

"I have heard from one of my friends that you have been told I am a lesbian. You are not going to publish it, are you?" she said.

I allayed her concerns. She sounded relieved. "It's true I have girlfriends but I am not going to say that I wouldn't go out with a boy if one invited me," she said.

It was not until the early nineties that Dusty came out into the open about her sexuality. She was applauded on both sides of the Atlantic. She embarked on a string of same sex relationships before going through an invalid 'marriage' ceremony in 1983 with American actress Teda Bracci which ended a year later in a fist fight between the couple. Dusty, who lost some of her teeth in the tussle, had to undergo plastic surgery. I was pleased to record that both Dusty and her career survived.

****

From being a hat check girl at the Liverpool Cavern to being hailed as a national treasure of the UK, Cilla Black leapt to stardom. John Lennon and the Beatles discovered her and persuaded Brian Epstein to sign her. A nervous Cilla failed her first audition and Eppy was on the verge of giving her up. He played me an acetate of a song that Paul Mcartney had written for her.

"I'm not sure," I told Eppy, but we were more convinced by the more promising and confident result of Cilla's second audition. The man who was quite certain about her potential from the start was the Beatles very own record producer George Martin. How right he was, producing her great hits 'You're My World', 'Anyone Who Had A Heart' and 'Step Inside Love.' She also recorded 'What's It All About?' for the Michael Caine film 'Alfie'.

When Brian Epstein died, Cilla appointed her boyfriend Bobby Willis to be her new manager and I felt honoured when her parents invited me to the couple's wedding in 1969. Her career was still on the rise and she won over new audiences with 'Blind Date', 'Surprise, Surprise' and other television shows. Cilla without a blemish to her name brought cheer and joy to the UK and many other countries. They all loved her.

****

Cutting a romantic image and singing as a duo were the Israeli husband and wife Esther and Abi Ofarim. Stardom came with their international hit 'Cinderella Rockefella.' They were on course to surpass those other world-famous husband and wife teams Nina and Frederik and Sonny and Cher whose marriages in both cases eventually failed.

When it seemed that Esther and Abi had a clear field, their marriage also fell apart. Husbands and wives singing together night-in night-out were vulnerable to suffocation.

Esther was deeply saddened by the breakup and was still very emotional when I flew to Sweden to see her.

"I'll never sing with Abi again," she told me. "My career is now totally solo. I do not need anyone else. When I sing, I forget the world and I am utterly alone."

Suddenly, as we dined in one of Stockholm's most fashionable restaurants, Esther's big, brown saucer-like eyes filled with distress. She scanned the table. Something had gone missing.

"My diamond ring!" she cried in anguish, "it has gone. I put it down on the bread plate and the waiters must have taken it away. I must have it back. It was a gift from Abi."

There followed a great flurry of action and concern, and waiters and managers were scurrying around searching for it in all directions. Four kitchen hands were detailed to go below and churn through the slop palls at the foot of the waste chute to find the missing diamond-studded, gold signet ring.

"Abi gave it to me for my birthday," sighed Esther. "I would not like to lose it."

Only a few minutes earlier, in true folklore tradition, Esther had been demonstrating the mystical powers of the ring suspended from a thread of cotton.

"Look I can make the ring swing in any direction by just thinking about it," she said.

Esther was in Sweden to film a television show. She talked about her childhood growing up in a small, humble home in Haifa where her father worked as a stonemason.

"I was unhappy as a child. In fact I was never a child. I can't remember playing with dolls or even with other kids. I lived in my own dream world and I was its princess."

When she married Abi six years earlier it meant she served only two months as a conscript in Israel's armed forces.

"I didn't deliberately marry Abi to get out of my time in the forces," she said "Although I would not have been happy in uniform. I hate war and I hate Jews killing Arabs and Arabs killing Jews. No I married because I was in love and that was the only reason."

But she and Abi were very different people. Esther loved her own home while Abi liked to explore the bright lights. Esther confessed they were incompatible in so many ways. She laughed: "I like fish and he doesn't."

But she could not hide the joy in her face when a triumphant waiter returned with the ring which he was wiping with a cloth.

"Here it is madam," he said. "It was under thirty kilos of garbage, but we found it and it is all right."

Esther expressed her gratitude as she slipped the ring back on her finger. "Thank you," she said to the waiter "It makes me very happy. I would not have like to have lost it. It means so much to me."

Esther's ring was saved. But not her marriage. The couple were divorced just one year later. I met with her in London in 1972 when she was picking up her career as a soloist. "Ours wasn't an ordinary marriage. We didn't live normal lives like Mr and Mrs Brown," she told me. "I didn't cook — because I didn't have any idea how to — I never saw the washing up or took on household chores. Abi didn't come home on office hours; we didn't have children. So how can I say I miss marriage?"

****

It was a story I felt that would intrigue pop fans and classical music devotees in equal measure when, at the start of 1969, an American guitarist of Cherokee-Indian descent moved into the London house where the great composer Händel lived and died more than two centuries earlier.

I went along to see the new occupant, the wild man of pop Jimi Hendrix, acclaimed by many as rock's greatest ever guitarist.

I admired Jimi Hendrix for his honesty as he didn't pretend to know much about the old tenant.

"I didn't even know this was his pad, man, until after I got in," he said. "And to tell you the God's honest truth I haven't heard much of the fella's stuff. But I dig a bit of Bach now and again."

Luckily, Jimi's words didn't fall on the ears of some of the students who had gathered in the street below to gaze at the blue-coloured plaque in memory of the old master. It was in this house in Mayfair's fashionable Brook Street that Händel is said to have composed 'Messiah' and the 'Water Music.'

Hendrix, dressed in a yellow shirt and scarlet trousers, promised not to let tradition down and said he too would compose here. Music, he defined as being "twenty first century" and "that sort of scene."

Words, perhaps, to make Händel turn in his grave if Hendrix's reputation could be believed. "I guess I'll never need a blue plaque outside the front door for folks to remember me by," Jimi laughed.

When Hendrix played on stage, he set his guitar on fire, or smashed it to the floor or even played it with his teeth. He admitted he had been in all sorts of trouble and had known what it was like to be in gaol. "Spent seven days in the cooler for taking a ride in a stolen car. But I never knew it was."

He also confessed he smashed up a hotel room in Gothenburg when he was drunk and got fined £250. An American moral society also banned him because they rejected his act as "too erotic."

We talked in the singer-musician's favourite room of this famous house — the attic. It was furnished with all sorts of bric-a-brac, and a Victorian shawl hung from the ceiling like a canopy over his bed.

His girlfriend was from the North and shared the flat. Jimi looked over at her and said, "My girlfriend, my past girlfriend and probably my next girlfriend. My mother and my sister and all that bit. My Yoko Ono."

At two o'clock in the afternoon, Hendrix was making the bed, neatly folding back the black sheets and straightening the colourful Persian bedspread.

As he did so he said: "One day I wanna become a parent. Now that is what the world is all about. Having kids. Like planting flowers."

Hendrix reached out to the cluttered mantelpiece to retrieve a copy of his new album 'Electric Lady Land' the sleeve of which featured twenty-one naked girls. Many shops refused to display it. "Man, I don't blame them," said Hendrix, "I wouldn't have put this picture on the sleeve myself. But it wasn't my decision."

Our conversation moved on like a confessional. The guitarist wanted to own up to his erratic lifestyle — involving girls, pot and hooch. Hendrix pleaded guilty on all counts — or to the experience of such happenings.

"That's how I got the name of my group — The Jimi Hendrix Experience," he said. "I would describe my music as electric church music — church meaning religion and not meaning God, that is. Many folk are blocked up but I hope they will come to understand my music soon."

What of his wild reputation? I asked him. "No. I'm just natural all the time. What others think or say doesn't worry me man."

His next words were to be tragically prophetic: "People still mourn when people die. That's self-sympathy. The person who is dead ain't cryin'. When I die I want my people to play my music, go wild and freak out an' do anything they wanna do..."

In September 1970, the music world was mourning the death of Jimi at the age of twenty-seven. It was recorded he had died from asphyxia after taking too many sleeping tablets while lying in bed with his girlfriend Monika Danneman, a former German ice-skating champion.

An open verdict was recorded at his inquest. For the heartbroken Monika there was only a sense of woe. She wasn't going to freak out... all she wanted to do was to paint a picture of the real Jimi Hendrix when he had been free of the glare of the spotlights and the public adoration.

Only a few days after his death, Monika expressed her grief. Holding back tears she went back on their last hours together. They had dinner and went to bed but Jimi could not sleep. So he took some of Monika's sleeping pills. Far too many as it transpired and in the morning she could not wake him.

She told me: "Much has been recorded of the last four days in Jimi's life. I shall always remember our last night together. When I cooked Jimi spaghetti bolognaise and we drank a bottle of wine over dinner. It was our last moment of happiness."

Monika and Jimi had been in a relationship for eighteen months, having met in Dusseldorf where Jimi had been giving a concert. She told me: "Like the rest I was almost fooled by the wild stories about him. Wild? Jimi was the most sweet and tender man anyone could meet. Everyone took advantage of him because he was so kind. I soon realised how sincere Jimi was. Of course he had been around and had other affairs. The pop world is like that. Perhaps it was because I was not a groupie who was pursuing him, but I managed to find the real Jimi Hendrix and his heart, the heart that no one seems to have discovered. Jimi lived for his music — and he was sick of all the rest of it. He told me many times how groupies would get into his hotel room and wait for him in his bed until he arrived. Jimi would get his road managers to throw them out."

Monika said, "I am certain that he was not a drug addict, nor an alcoholic, nor a sex maniac. The real Jimi behind the stage façade was a very sensitive, compassionate and shy person who genuinely believed in the message of love, peace, freedom and brotherhood that he tried to give the world." It was a message that Monika hoped the world would come to follow.

****

There was news buzzing along the grapevine in the summer of 1969 that Bob Dylan would be coming to England to headline the Isle of

On Tragedy and Triumph

Wight festival. Such news caused a stir in the News Room and I flew to New York to get to the truth. Little had been heard of Dylan for three years as he convalesced from a gruesome road crash.

As the cool morning mist hung over his country house just an hour's drive out of the city, Dylan's first words as he greeted me into his home were intended to mark the end of his long hibernation from the scene.

"I can't wait to get back. What's happening out there?" he asked me. He looked fit and well, wearing a stubble beard to the face and clothed in a white shirt and denims.

It would have taken some hours to go over the ground, but I knew Dylan was more than aware of what was happening out there. Nevertheless, intrigue and curiosity had grown in all quarters by his absence. Dylan had carefully avoided direct communication with the outside world.

Now the American singer-poet-songwriter felt able to talk about the crash on his motorbike and its aftermath. He had been riding his 500cc Triumph motor bike when he lost control, possibly blinded by the sun or a skid on an oil patch. He could never be sure. But luckily his wife Sarah was driving behind him and got him into her car. Dylan suffered a serious neck injury.

"I still get some effects from the crash, like when I move suddenly, or at odd times when the weather is cold," he told me. "But I'm very happy with the way I've progressed and I like to think my voice is better now than ever before. I like my new songs too."

Thinking ahead of his comeback, Dylan admitted: "Gee I'm nervous. I have been so long out of it."

Dylan was faintly amused that he had, to the outrage of top American and British impresarios, chosen the Isle of Wight festival as his comeback venue.

"I always wanted to go to the Isle of Wight," he chuckled. "In three weeks' time you'll see me there."

Indeed, I did see him there, along with 150,000 hysterical fans — a huge crowd, the equivalent of half as many again as had watched a Cup Final. Also paying homage in the wings of the arena were key members of the pop scene's hierarchy — John Lennon, George Harrison and Ringo Starr, Mick Jagger, Keith Richards and many other stars all of whom had been inspired by Bob Dylan's work and ethos over the years.

They were all keen to sing Bob Dylan's praise. George Harrison could have been identified as Dylan's number one fan. He told me: "I could go on talking about Dylan for eight hours. He's unlimited in what he is doing. And I think ninety-nine per cent of the people out here know his potential."

Keith Richards of the Stones said: "I love his eyes, man. But I really came to see Alfred Lord Tennyson's grave!" He gave a wry smile before he disappeared.

Terence Stamp was among the dedicated: "I think he's fantastic, this man Dylan," he said.

The magic was there for the music devotees switched on by Dylan's brand of music embracing poetry, peace and protest in his lyrics. Certainly, Dylan did not disappoint the fans with his repertoire which included his hit songs 'Blowin' In The Wind,' 'Mr Tambourine Man,' and 'The Times They Are a-Changin'.' But those true music lovers may have been dwarfed in numbers by others who descended on the Festival with a different motive in mind.

The images of the Isle of Wight that year make the exploits of the Glastonbury and Reading festivals of today look rather tame in comparison. Teenagers were out for fun and freedom, seeking a free-loving, free-living society. There was a frenzy of nude dancing; a teenage couple made love in a field full of foam and were watched by an enormous audience; a bearded fellow who, on an 'acid trip' clobbered a friend with a beer-bottle and then kissed a security man's Alsatian dog. I interviewed several teenagers, many of whom were unashamedly there not for the music, but to live and love as they wished, without parental discipline.

These scenes were not in the eyeline of Bob Dylan and the artists who took to the stage. Their only focus was on the impact of their music and Dylan departed triumphant with his comeback performance.

Some dream! That's me auditioning for Ringo's vacant drum-set; And here I am chatting with Paul McCartney.

Who wouldn't miss a birthday celebration with Olivia Newton-John and Cliff Richard? And I meet up with the mighty Barry White at an evening bash in London.

Enrolled as a bodyguard at Mick Jagger's tumultuous wedding to
Bianca. (Mirrorpix)

ELVIS with the
Daily Mirror's
DON SHORT, during
the meeting at
the star's Bel
Air home, which
Short reports here.

Finally getting to meet Elvis in Bel Air.

With Princess Ira in Venice before their assault on the paparazzi.
(Mirrorpix)

Enjoying a hot tub splash with Engelbert Humperdinck after
completing his biography.

Stevie Wonder lets his views known to me at the San Remo Song Festival in 1969.

Enjoying the nightclubs with Richard Harris in New Orleans.

David Niven (in sunglasses) lunches with his film crew in Malaysia on the set of 'Paper Tiger.'

Catching up with singing duo Abi and Esther Ofarim and their manager at a London record gathering.

Louis Armstrong and his wife Lucille strike a happy pose with me in San Remo 1968. (Mirrorpix)

Muhammad Ali encourages his pet cockatoo to perch on my arm at his Chicago home. (Picture: Terry Fincher)

A long way from Phoenix – it's Glen Campbell and showbusiness agent Jimmy Henney enjoying a relaxing break with me at a London party.

Film producer John Marshall, author Mario Puzo ('The Godfather'), hellraiser Richard Harris and two heavy negotiators after cutting a new movie deal in California.

Me with songwriter Bill Martin, England football captain Bobby Moore and star player Geoff Hurst at a record company reception.

Dining out with Queen's Freddie Mercury as manager John Reid drops in on our table with some cordial words.

Roger Moore with Luisa Mattiolo.
(Photo: Terry Fincher)

Elizabeth Taylor leaving London Clinic in 1960 with Eddie Fisher.
(Trinity Mirror / Mirrorpix / Alamy Stock Photo)

I'm a conscripted RAF cameraman photographing Princess Elizabeth in Nairobi just five days before she became Queen on the death of King George VI.

Me with photographer Terry Fincher on a windswept assignment in the Balkans.

Me, in the office of my literary and syndication company, Solo.

Good journalistic friends Vic Davis (left) and Donald Zec (right) at my retirement party at Simpson's in the Strand in 1998.

CHAPTER TWELVE

FROM SAN REMO TO RIO

L ong before the days of the Isle of Wight and the mud fields of Reading and Glastonbury, the age of music festivals was already well established.

The one festival which has stood the test of time, having been launched in 1951, is the San Remo Song Festival and I regularly attended to report on the activity. In its early years it consistently boasted the appearance of some of the world's top stars. For writers from across Europe and more distant lands, it had become a yearly pilgrimage to the Italian resort. International artists queued to perform there. The San Remo affair was always elegant and sophisticated with bow-tie audiences and conducted in an atmosphere of refinement.

I had to ask whether it was all that it seemed. Behind the scenes existed suspicions that the whole show was really controlled by the Mafia.

I had a rather sobering experience while I was there in 1966. A big, swarthy man in dark glasses was sitting at the end of the row of seats. Someone nudged me and suggested I should clap the singer on the stage. So I clapped — like the rest of the audience — and looked out of the corner of my eye at the man on the end of the row. He nodded his head and smiled with pleasure.

My nudging neighbour explained: "You see the singer is very special and this man wants him to win. He comes from some organisation in Naples. It's a Mafia. Oh yes, they're all here. But they're alright. It's only when they don't like your face that they kill you."

Of course, the organisers were always ready to dispel such slurs. An official raged at me when I raised the rumours a few years later:

"How can our contest be 'rigged' when we have nearly six hundred people on the jury in twenty one cities and towns all over the country?"

Later, meeting surreptitiously with a man from Naples — his formidable frame always in evidence at the yearly festival — cast further doubt in my mind. But he was ready to tell me: "Anything can be arranged — for a price." If they could not fix a winner then they might influence the gambling stakes.

But these were the days when any event in Italy was rumoured to be 'run by the Mafia' and it was prudent to put the matter aside as the music was all that mattered.

The Sixties were to make little change on San Remo other than the music becoming more commercial in its appeal.

One of Dusty Springfield's most enduring hits evolved from the San Remo festival. Dusty competed in the 1965 competition and reached the semi-finals with her song 'What Do You Know' but it was another composition being performed at the festival that arrested her attention. Her friend Vicki Wickham and future manager Simon Napier-Bell agreed with Dusty and saw its instant appeal, giving the song its English lyrics and title 'You Don't Have To Say You Love Me.' It became a world-wide success.

San Remo was not without tragedy. In 1967 one of the Italian singers Luigi Tenco shot himself after his song in the competition was voted a miss. One year later, the organisers thought again about the concept of the festival which was founded primarily as a competition for invited artists.

In 1968 the San Remo festival organisers suddenly felt shockwaves. They were made aware of the threat of a rival new festival being organised in nearby Cannes. There was one expensive remedy. San Remo voted to lift the lid on its coffers. The organisers decided to showcase the performances of guest stars who did not have to participate in the competition. The organisers attracted a mass of international stars for the event that year. It was a bonus beyond belief for the hacks and the paparazzi. Festival officials said that the invited stars all dropped in as a goodwill gesture, but I was reliably informed that the 'gesture' had cost nearly £200,000.

Some stars on the billing were legendary. None more so than Louis Armstrong — the great Satchmo — whose gravel throated voice still haunts us today with the nostalgic 'Hello Dolly' and 'What a Wonderful World.'

Satchmo performed at the 1968 festival and brought his devoted wife Lucille with him. I was fortunate in being able to meet them ahead of the pack.

I went to their hotel suite and immediately saw Satchmo in the bathroom giving his golden trumpet a clean before the night's performance. It was a curious sight as he was flushing the trumpet under the bath taps.

I could not help but ask: "Are you sure that's the right thing to do? It won't rust?"

Lucille standing behind me laughed. "He treats his trumpet like a baby. There's not a day when that cat doesn't clean it."

Satchmo had no qualms or nerves performing that night. He was then nearing sixty-eight years old and was pledging to play on across the world for as long as he lived.

"I'll go on blowing for as long as I can. Only today I do it all in my own time. I don't have to bat my brains out any more for a dollar. Some people never let up. Then they drop dead. Never live to enjoy the bread they worked for."

Satchmo shook his head. "Not me, my friend," he said. "There was a time when I worked 365 days a year. Now I work when I wanna work. If you're asking why I don't retire, I'll let you into the secret: I always live by a code and it's this, friend: 'You can't have bread — and loaf.'"

With white handkerchiefs wrapped round his head and neck to prevent sweat soiling a new white shirt he had just changed into, he played his trumpet for a bit.

"I've been playing since 1913 and I've seen a lot come and go. Today they all wanna be way-out, but way-out means they wanna be original. When we were blowin' the blues, we were as way-out as they are now. It doesn't matter how way-out you are, in the end a note is still a note you've gotta hit."

The Beatles, he declared, were top cats.

"So many followed 'em and got lost on the way."

Satchmo gave his trumpet another shine with a cloth while the friendly Lucille, a former Gaiety Girl dancer, told me: "There's one way Louis is different from most artists. He is free from temperament. He doesn't get het up or let things get him down. He has simple tastes and has never lived the big life. Although people tell me he's a legend, I'm sure he never realises it. What he cherishes most in life are his friends."

Satchmo's fingers hit the trumpet buttons and he played the opening bars of 'What a Wonderful World.'

I was enchanted by it. "That is going to be a big hit," I told him, the tune still in my head.

He looked at me and laughed: "I shan't worry too much. When I started out there was no hit parade or radio. And I wasn't worryin' then."

I remembered earlier in the week, he had told me: "If a man starts worrying whether he's gonna win or lose when he's sixty-seven, then he's got real problems."

Words of wisdom, I felt, for all future wannabes.

I was in Athens in 1971 covering the Olympiad of Song when I heard the sad news that Louis Armstrong had died. I met the American lyricist Sammy Cahn who had written many of Satchmo's hits. He reminisced about his friend's one big failing — his refusal to learn the words of his songs. Lucille used to plaster them up everywhere. If he went into the bathroom to have a shave, they would be pasted upon the mirror. When he climbed into bed at night they would be lying on the pillow. Cahn once asked Louis Armstrong what was wrong with a mutual friend who'd died. Said Satchmo: "When you're dead, everything's wrong." It was certainly all wrong with Louis gone.

San Remo in 1968 was a vintage year. Not only Satchmo but another legendary star Eartha Kitt was billed to appear. It was a night in which I was to suffer some of the consequences.

Eartha was known for her staccato singing style, resonant of her huge hit recording of 'Just an Old Fashioned Girl.' But she had just been given a new Italian ballad to perform.

Come the time of the rehearsal, Eartha waved away the intended orchestration of the ballad and replaced it with her own, catchy interpretation, very similar to that of her big hit.

Ironically, the English title given to the song was 'What's Good For Me' which bemused the singer. Those watching the rehearsal gave her courteous applause. Leaving the stage, she invited me and two or three other friends to join her dinner table within the arena's restaurant.

Eartha, who was born on a cotton plantation in South Carolina, was known in the showbusiness world as something of a tigress. She was often outspoken and controversial but she knew how to enjoy life. She chose her friends carefully.

Uninvited guests were not welcome into her circle as I was to witness first hand when, suddenly, without any announcement, a portly Italian figure strode to our dinner table. He was the composer of the ballad that the American singer had just performed. It was not difficult to see that he was a trifle angry. In fact, he was more like a raging bull.

Leaning discourteously over Eartha he bellowed: "Miss Kitt, I implore you. Please do not sing my song in the festival. You ruin it for me because it's not your style. This isn't the way it should be."

There was stunned silence in the restaurant. Other diners gazed across to our table at the commotion. For one tense second, I feared Eartha was going to claw out his eyes.

Somewhat aghast, I jumped to the singer's side and led her out of the arena in tears. Ignoring her stress, the Italian composer marched away still fuming.

There was time to recover the next day and by the evening when the festival was live Eartha, with a determined cat-like glare in her eyes strutted out on stage and delivered the ballad in precisely the same way, deliberately taking revenge on her would-be assailant.

"Now if he had been polite to me, I would have listened," she said.

She thanked me for coming to her rescue by giving a playful tug on my frilly fronted evening dress shirt and ripping it away from my chest in the process. My bow tie was discarded with it. Needless to say, I could not help but feel a little self-conscious. I was left sat wearing just a white cotton vest beneath my evening dress suit for the rest of the night.

An act of romantic passion? Hardly. More likely she did not know her own strength. Eartha and the table guests reeled with laughter at me. I mused: the work of a showbiz journalist is not only giving the shirt off your own back, but having it torn off you, by a star, before a crowd! High jinks were clearly going to be top of the menu that night.

Shirley Bassey was another spectacular star of the night. She was also performing a new Italian composition which, once given English lyrics, would become one of her greatest international hits and titled, 'This Is My Life.'

"I love the song," Shirley told me. "Particularly because it is the story of my own life. So often I've forgotten the breaks in my life and when I've been lonely put too much emphasis on the mistakes... I'd much rather look at the things I should be grateful for. Like success. To be able to go anywhere without fear. To be free."

Barefoot singer Sandie Shaw was invited to compete in the 1970 event. Sandie, who had won the Eurovision Song Contest in 1967 with the Bill Martin and Phil Coulter composition 'Puppet On A String', was a hot favourite to win. But the judges were not easily swayed and she was only placed ninth with her entry 'You're Affecting My Mind.'

I commiserated with her off-stage but Sandie wasn't going to allow the setback ruin her day. She still went out to celebrate — it was her birthday after all. In later years Sandie developed a dual career. She qualified as a psychotherapist and set up a clinic to provide advice and health care for those working in the creative arts who were in need of such help. No one could say it wasn't a worthy cause.

I witnessed one of the most emotional scenes in San Remo in 1971. José Feliciano, the blind Puerto Rican musician, was mobbed by the audience after he performed 'Che Sara' ('Shake That Hand.') Some broke down and wept knowing his story, while others stood in tribute.

José put down his rise to stardom and the success of his world-wide hit 'Light My Fire,' to the affinity he had with his dog.

He told me: "I owe it all to my best friend... my dog."

He halted his career when his collie guide dog Trudy died in the United States leaving him heartbroken and "without his eyes." The faithful collie had always been by his side.

José's wife Hilda added: "There have been moments when I thought that José would never get over the heartache. So I decided to bring him away. Trudy went with him everywhere. She even led him out on stage and would sit at his feet in the floodlights."

There was only one time in eight years together that they had parted, and that was in 1967 when Feliciano visited Britain and Trudy was taken into quarantine on arrival.

"It is the most inhuman law I know of," the twenty-four-year-old José said. "Isn't it time your laws were changed for blind people who rely on guide dogs for their sight? Somehow I would liked to have met your Queen. She is a dog lover and would have understood."

I could not apologise to José for our archaic laws but he had certainly made a justifiable case.

Feliciano said he never regarded lack of sight as a handicap, "I was born blind so I don't know what handicap it is."

José left me feeling as humble as another pop idol had done so in San Remo a couple of years earlier.

When I met Stevie Wonder, there was no self-pity in his voice as he talked to me. "What is sight, man! It doesn't bother me to have been born blind. People who can see can't always see things as clearly as I do."

He was eighteen years old and he was fulfilling the genius predicted in him when he was only ten.

He added: "I live only to sing and play. I believe God gave me this talent in exchange for my sight and I am happy with it. Even without a smash record I would still say the same."

He laughed as he talked. I imagined his life being hard, but he gave me the opposite impression.

"I've enjoyed every moment I've lived," he assured me, and talked about his music. "Soul music can be any kind of music as long as it's sung with feeling and emotion. I'm a Rhythm and Blues singer, but as I sing from my heart it means I sing with soul. And don't Frank Sinatra and Tom Jones sing with soul, too? That's what soul is all about."

No one had any more soul than Stevie Wonder. Both he and José were worthy of all the admiration of their fans and the music world at large.

Another day, another festival. Only on this occasion it promised to be a little more exotic than the sophistication of San Remo. My destination was the iconic carnival land of Rio de Janeiro. It was going to be my first visit to Brazil and from my window seat on the plane I was awe struck by the spectacular scenery of the Rio coastline as we came into land.

The routine through Customs went smoothly and, to my pleasant surprise, a limousine was already waiting, ready to whisk me to the sports stadium where I assumed the very first concert of the festival was being staged. I was impressed. Incredible timing — impeccable organisation. Or so I thought.

Some officials greeted me warmly and quickly ushered me to my seat in the vast stadium which was packed to capacity. With a courteous exchange of handshakes, I was then introduced to the occupant I was to sit next to. I was startled: it was Pelé. I didn't have to be a football fan to recognise him, one of the world's greatest soccer stars.

To my absolute disbelief, I was about to witness not a pop concert but a Brazilian football match between two rival national sides, and Pelé was present as a guest of honour. What was I doing here?

Then the truth emerged. I learned that the driver and officials had misidentified me as a sports journalist who had also been heading to Rio and I now occupied his place.

But it was too late to rectify things as the two teams were already spilling out onto the pitch and the flag waving fans were in vocal crescendo.

Pelé was amused by the slip-up and he took the opportunity at half time to quiz me about Britain's rock 'n' roll fever and tales of the Beatles and the Rolling Stones. It was a classic case of a role reversal! Pelé was the interrogator and I was the interviewee. It was just as well. Pelé certainly knew more about music than I could have proffered on football.

Sports writers at home were amused when I related my story to them. One editor shook his head in dismay and said: "For Pete's sake. What were you doing? Why didn't you interview Pelé? We've been waiting months to get an interview with him! We just can't find him."

"Well," I suggested. "Let me get you tickets to the next Rio festival. You might find Pelé there."

The Rio festival may have been expecting America's top duo Simon and Garfunkel to appear. But only Paul Simon arrived and he broke the news to me that he and Art Garfunkel had separated as a duo. They now intended to pursue their own individual careers.

Paul, whose role in Rio was now to be a member of the judging panel, was philosophical about the split. He had not announced the break-up officially, but he said he had to face up to the situation. He told me as we lunched in a Rio de Janeiro restaurant in 1970:

"You can't just kill a friendship that's lasted sixteen years. Who can say what will happen? We are not as close as we were and with Arthur gone off to do another film I've decided to go ahead and cut an album on my own rather than just wait around."

As we talked, Art Garfunkel was already in Canada filming 'Carnal Knowledge' with Candice Bergen and Mike Nichols, the creative director who made 'The Graduate.'

But Paul, the music writing genius of the pair having composed all their major hits including 'Bridge Over Troubled Water' wasn't going to say much about the Hollywood dream for which Garfunkel had forsaken their partnership. But I got the impression that he frowned on it.

"I never want to become a star myself in that sense," he told me. "I am happy to stay with my music as it is. There's no world with Hollywood in it, as far as I can see," he confided.

He then recalled his earlier days. "For a long period I was on my own in London. I stayed with an English family in Brentwood, Essex, where they had tons of cats, dogs and kids. They adopted me like one of their own and I shan't ever forget them. They were wonderful."

At night, Paul and his guitar haunted clubs and pubs, venturing as far north as Warrington and Widnes. He cut a long playing record and it sold 100,000 copies, but the big break didn't come and he returned to New York to renew his friendship and partnership with Art Garfunkel. They had known each other since they were twelve and had grown up in the same neighbourhood and had always been singing together.

Then success came. Turning professional, the duo had an early chart-maker with 'Homeward Bound.'

Paul avoided the glamour of showbusiness and gave no indication of being a rich man.

"What do I do with my money? Well, I have a lot of things happening and there are one or two causes I like to help."

Looking ahead to the future, Paul tried to be realistic: "I don't say there aren't other singers around who couldn't do my songs just as well as Arthur but I don't think I could ever take on another partner."

****

A new age of jazz was dawning in London in 1970. Ronnie Scott believed that the scene had gone full cycle and thought perhaps more people would realise that pop owed everything to jazz, anyway.

"Pop has poached on jazz without apology," Ronnie Scott told me in his living-room-style office behind the stage of his Soho club. "That may irritate many jazzmen, but not me. I would never lose any sleep over it. It's for the fans to choose the music they want to hear. I play. I don't attempt to convert. But many young people are discovering just how hip jazz is."

He was quietly spoken, silver hair running to grey sideburns and gaunt, sallow-faced. Behind him there was a montage of jazz giants, including Louis Armstrong, Tubby Hayes and Stan Getz. From the opposite wall bounced the blare of jazz as that week's guest star, Roland Kirk, took the stage. Scott listened and gently nodded his head in approval. "That's some music to dig," he said.

Many popularity polls had placed Ronnie Scott as Britain's No.1 tenor sax player, and it was said that the veteran saxophonist, well-known for his gambling instincts, had often laid bets against himself in the poll results. But the man who, in his early days, once blew his band's £200 wages on a horse, laughed and said: "That would be too easy. Too many polls are too easy to rig, and maybe that is why I have not won anything lately."

He grew up in London's East End. His father was a saxophonist too. His first break was with Ted Heath's band; his first setback was being sacked from the same band three years later because "They thought I wasn't good enough." He went on to play with Bert Ambrose and Jack Parnell.

At that point in time, he had run his club in Soho's Frith Street for four years. Before that the club was in Gerrard Street but the premises were too small. Scott set out with the policy of playing pure jazz only. "You would have thought that in a city of ten million people we would have found enough fans to fill the club," he said. "But we had trouble finding a hundred." There was urgent thinking to adopt a new policy. The pop boom was having its effect, so, with the move to Frith Street, it was decided to open the top floor as a disco and invite pop groups along to widen the scope. "If I had to rely on pure jazz, I knew we would not have been able to keep the doors open," confessed Scott.

The Ronnie Scott's Club was growing slowly and its popularity was accelerated by a BBC television series which caught the eye of the masses. The club was regarded as Europe's No.1 jazz centre, and it still holds that accolade today.

Scott, although not irritated by contemporary pop music ("Some of it I like, The Beatles and Co,") he was sometimes hotter under the collar when he saw guitarists like Jimi Hendrix and Eric Clapton described as the best in the world.

"Personally, I can understand it because of the pop idiom and its sex connotations," he said. "But it makes jazz musicians choke."

Scott, at the age of 42, remained a bachelor. "I've seen too many marriages in this business break up. I enjoy being free," said the jazzman who had a flat in the "poor" end of Chelsea.

There was never a night when he was not at the club. The box office was beginning to show signs of a jazz revival. "More young people are coming in than ever before," he told me.

Many offers were made to lure Scott into a more commercial bag, but he remained true and dedicated to his music. "I couldn't debase jazz or myself by deliberately making the hit parade my objective," he said.

Scott and the sound of Soho were quite, quite pure.

CHAPTER THIRTEEN

TOM JONES, MISS WORLD, AND WOMEN'S LIB

Maybe I should have felt some guilt. But when I introduced American beauty queen Marjorie Wallace to the heart throb Tom Jones how could I have foreseen the consequences? Or was I being overly naïve?

Such was the depth of their love affair that within weeks Marjorie was stripped of her Miss World crown and Tom's sixteen year marriage to his loyal wife was rocked to the core.

It was not as though it was the first time that Tom had strayed from the straight and narrow. But he maintained his one-night stands and casual affairs didn't mean a thing: just fun and games, in his way of thinking. He declared that there was only one woman who meant anything in his life and that was his wife Linda, the girl he met when they played as teenagers in Wales. He once told me, "I have no regrets about being married at all. In fact, I am forever glad I married before I became famous." Instead of sharing in Tom's glitzy lifestyle, Linda chose to stay at home and raise their young son Mark.

"There was a time when I was jealous," Linda told me. "You see I didn't feel I was good enough to be Tom's wife. Well just seeing him in the papers surrounded by all those more glamorous girls was something I found hard to accept. Tom knew my fears and helped me to come through it. Now I never worry, because I always know that Tom is coming home... I am sure of him."

But Linda spoke too soon. Suddenly into the frame stepped the nineteen-year-old American Marjorie Wallace who had just become the reigning Miss World. Linda's instincts sensed immediate danger the moment she saw the morning papers. Her thirty-three-year-old husband was pictured in romantic clinches with the American blonde.

She realised that this was not a one-off fling. Conflict was afoot and I found myself uncomfortably locked in the middle of the situation as it unfolded.

Torn apart by the growing scandal Linda confronted Tom and threw punches at him when he arrived home one night. Tom consoled her and said he deserved it. He said he understood Linda's reactions and she was still the only woman he loved.

Looking back, it had all begun so innocently. Marji had made a friend of me just a few days after she was crowned Miss World in November 1973.

She needed an escort and one evening she entreated me to see the West End and its night time glamour. But the fashionable night clubs we slipped into were too quiet so early in the evening. Where next to go? A thought occurred to me.

Maybe Marji would like to meet Tom Jones who was appearing on stage at the nearby London Palladium? Marji was aware of Tom Jones but she had grown up with the music of Elvis Presley, Frank Sinatra and Andy Williams.

When we arrived at the theatre, Tom's performance had just ended to the echoes of his big hit 'It's Not Unusual.' We had to weave our way through a mesh of fans to reach his dressing room. I managed to introduce Tom to Marji through a maze of arms, faces and champagne filled glasses. It was so crowded that we stayed for just a few minutes and as we departed Tom waved to us from across the room and gave Marji a big wink in the process.

Outside the Palladium stage door, there was the usual throng of fans who wait through the night to intercept their emerging idols for autographs. No-one recognised Marjorie, the collar of her white trouser suit turned up against the cold. We stepped into the street to hail a passing cab and decided to take a late drink at Trader Vic's.

Marji ordered an exotic cocktail with a white gardenia floating on its frothy surface. She pored over the drink wistfully.

"He's quite down to earth when you meet him, isn't he?" she said, her thoughts running back to Tom. "It's so strange. You go backstage and meet a star and they are so different from what you imagine them to be. Why do they build up stars like that? They are really human beings just like the rest of us when you get to know them."

A smile lit up her face. One of Tom's aides had asked for her telephone number. "I hope that was not intended for Tom. He is not really the kind of guy I fancy."

"No?" I questioned.

She shook her head. "Oh don't get me wrong. He is a terrific singer. You want to see how they go for him in the States. He really turns them on. But for me he lacks some essential qualities."

"Like what?" I asked.

She shrugged. "Elegance, mainly I guess. Do you think he is the kind of man who would open a car door for a lady to get in?" She bit her tongue. "But I guess he's got a chauffeur so he would have no need to."

Marji could not conceal her curiosity about him. "Is he really a miner's son?" she asked coyly. But then came the question I had anticipated much earlier in our conversation.

"Is he married?" she finally put to me searching my face for an answer. And so I told her of Linda and how in the early days of his career his manager and agent had deliberately kept his marriage secret in the widely held belief that fans only idolised stars who were single — and available.

It soon became clear to me that Marji could not dismiss Tom from her mind as she chatted on.

Just a few days later she got a call from the BBC inviting her to play a role in a projected Tom Jones television 'special' to be shot on a £60,000 budget in Barbados.

Marji, who had set her own sights on stardom, was over the moon with delight.

"I did not think that Tom Jones would remember me!" she argued.

Stewart Morris, a formidable BBC producer of the day, was aglow with the prospect of a screen encounter between Tom and Marji in her role as Miss World.

He did not have to wait long into the shoot on the sun-drenched beach before his two young stars came together for the cameras. But it was a lingering kiss between them that ignited the romance rumours and caused a furious backlash.

Mrs. Julia Morley, co-organiser with her husband Eric Morley of the Miss World pageant, had flown with the American beauty queen to Barbados and demanded that the kiss should be censored because it was not mentioned in the original screenplay.

Some harsh words were exchanged between Mrs. Morley and

her newly crowned Miss World, causing a detectable tension for the rest of the filming.

At 3:00am a note was pushed under the door of Mrs. Morley's hotel room. It disturbed her and she switched on her bedside light to discover it. Written in a scrawled hand were the words: "Go home you bum — go home."

Marji pleaded innocence. "I have no idea who wrote the note," she said. She apologised to the Miss World organiser but the ill-feeling between them hardly subsided. Marji in one outburst accused Mrs. Morley of being narrow-minded and pedantic.

Mrs. Morley had heard enough. She flew back to London suffering from nervous exhaustion leaving Marji to her own devices. Now the romance rumours really ran wild. Tom was telling friends: "This girl is different from any others I have met."

Marji called me on her return.

"I would like to telephone Tom's wife Linda and assure her that there isn't anything going on. There is nothing in it..."

I advised her not to. "I don't think that is such a good idea. It will only cause more pain and suspicion."

Marji thought about the situation for a few minutes and then deliberated: "Goodness. I imagine she must be used to this kind of thing. Look — if Tom had been filming with Raquel Welch I have no doubt the same kind of thing would have happened. In Hollywood they always try to create a romance between two co-stars. It helps with the publicity." It was an argument that I could not dispute.

I suggested to Marji that she should keep a low profile for a few days and let things settle down.

Quietly, if reluctantly, Marji got back to her round of Miss World duties. She had come a long way from her home in Indianapolis. There she had worked as a model and as a promotional hostess at trade fairs and exhibitions. Her parents had split up. Her father Dell Wallace ran a general supply company with one of her uncles. Her mother Mrs. Alice Wallace went to live in Las Vegas.

Marji was a very bright student at Broad Ripple High School and came through with eight academic certificates. But early in her teens Marji felt she should explore the world at large. She fell in love with a boy named Jeff Myers, a guitarist with a local pop group and they shared a flat together.

"It was my first love," related Marji, brooding over her past. "You know how it is. It all means so much and you think it will last forever. We spun it out for two years before it blew."

Marji took a camping caravette style holiday in Florida with a girl friend to get over the break-up. They threw some wild parties, smoked grass and sampled the big outdoor life.

"You have got to feel your own way through life. No one can preach to you on how you should live," reflected Marji philosophically. "Besides, if I hadn't done all of that, would I be here in London now? I doubt it."

Jeff Myers may have been her first love, but before she left America she had formed a liaison with racetrack driver Peter Revson. She had been in Indianapolis and out on a shopping spree when she heard on her car radio the resident DJ announce that Revson, the glamour-boy of the track, was about to race in the famous Indianapolis Five Hundred, but first he would be signing autographs in a downtown store for his legion of fans.

Marji spun the car round and motored there on the spur of the moment.

"When I got downtown I thought I was too late," she recited. "But I caught him just as he was leaving the store. He swept me along with his party to a coffee shop and I just found myself with him at the end."

They appeared ideally suited, although Marji recognised that Peter's first love was motor racing. "He lived and breathed it. I could not ever have stopped him from racing."

Marji shrugged. So much of the past to mull over but now she had to face the future and her committed Miss World programme that lay ahead of her. It was a daily round of fashion and charity shows, mayoral tea parties, supermarket openings and modelling engagements. She toured nationwide and eventually reached Manchester — and football star George Best.

She had never heard of George Best before, or even seen a game of English football. But she was booked to make a brief personal appearance in his Slack Alice nighterie.

"I was told he was very famous," said Marji. "And in my own mind I identified him with someone like Joe Namath who is one of America's top footballers."

The bearded George Best was besotted at first sight by Marji's beauty.

"He asked to date me the same night, but I couldn't stay that evening," Marji recalled.

It was not long before George pursued her to London and rang her persuading her to go to Tramp, the fashionable, celebrity studded night haunt in the West End. Outside, close to dawn, they faced a barrage of paparazzi and once more Marji was on the front pages. The next day she dined with George at Rags.

"George was such a screwball," Marji later conveyed. "One minute he acted the perfect gentleman. The next minute he would fly off the handle and do something that just would not add up. Within minutes of meeting me he told me he was in love with me. Then over a meal he was talking of marrying me and I just sat there amazed. Not saying a word. How could I? Anything I said would have hurt his feelings."

Their whirlwind affair lasted precisely two days and it ended as explosively as it began. George, who had looked in on Marji at her rented Marylebone home, flew into a jealous rage when she had to depart hurriedly to go to the BBC Studios for another segment to be shot for the Tom Jones television show. It was the last time she saw George.

"I could not believe that any man could act so childishly as George did," Marji reflected.

Some days later, events took a dramatic twist. Marji was on the brink of hysteria when she discovered her flat had been burgled. Champagne soaked the carpets from bottles that the intruder had uncorked and sprayed around the living room. The champagne had been given to Marji by well-wishers.

Her newspaper cuttings had gone, so had a photograph of Peter Revson. Her Miss World tiara was missing along with the £2,000 mink coat she had gained as one of the prizes for winning the earlier Miss USA beauty queen contest. But it was not the missing mink so much that worried Marji. It was the disappearance of her diary — the one that I had suggested she should keep to record her year as Miss World.

"Gee, I wish I knew where it has gone," she sighed nervously. "Oh it doesn't contain anything that will hang me," she reasoned, trying to calm her own fears, "But there are some things that girls write in diaries that men should not see."

One satirical magazine ran a story saying that Miss Wallace had not only named her lovers in her stolen diary, but gave them star ratings on their sexual prowess. George Best was accorded three points and Tom Jones nine points. Marji saw no humour in it. She was filled with anger. "A girl would not do that... I would not write down who I slept with in a diary. But the diary does contain some notes I would like to keep private to myself."

It was a period when Marji was wearing a gold ring embossed with a lion's head which was noticed by an observant photographer but she denied it was a gift from Tom Jones who wore an identical one. "I collect costume jewellery. I've got over a hundred antique rings," she answered defensively.

Dark clouds were now rolling in and Marji was in a tangle. Behind Miss World's HQ doors there fears were that her high-living exploits would leave the pristine Miss World title in bad odour. Marji went to the Morley's home in Dulwich where she was given a code of conduct by Eric Morley.

Later, Mr. Morley recalled the interview to me: "I remember I sat talking to her in the drawing room, while my wife was doing things in the kitchen. I felt it was necessary for Marji not to see George Best or Tom Jones again and pointed out to her that she was losing the opportunity of earning a great deal of money. There was £30,000 to £40,000 at stake. Marji understood and she looked at me and said: 'Mr. Morley, I realise how wrong I have been and I do not want to let you and Julia down. I have been a fool. I shall never see either of them again.'"

Two hours after that showdown, Marji by her own admission, met Tom Jones at the Churchill Hotel but the Morleys were not told.

But now other dark events were accelerating. Soccer star George Best was arrested by the police and accused of stealing Marji's things. Once more the headlines hit the front pages.

Suddenly, anonymous and frightening phone calls were made to Marji and the Morleys. One caller threatened to disfigure Marji for life and another told Mrs. Morley she would be dead by three o'clock the next day. Police believed the calls were made by disgruntled soccer fans angered by George Best's arrest.

The final showdown was not far away. Marji was summoned to the Miss World HQ in Blackfriars and the decision to strip her of the title was delivered by Eric Morley.

"I asked her whether she thought we had been fair in view of all the circumstances and she said we had," said Morley. "She showed no emotion and there were no tears," he recounted.

Marji looked pallid when she left Blackfriars but told me resignedly: "I am not bitter about it at all. Frankly, it is just as well. The strain was getting too much to bear. I could not have taken any more. They expected to run my life for me — without any will of my own."

The Beatles and Beyond

Her reign as Miss World had lasted one hundred and four days. Julia Morley was also upset by the decision to sack Marji but admitted: "We had no alternative. We do not expect Miss World to live like an angel. We've all got skeletons in the cupboard and none of us is infallible. But it is essential that when a girl becomes Miss World she should act with decorum. Miss World is a figurehead and she is always in focus of the camera."

The dejected Marji turned once more to Peter Revson and flew to Florida to recover from the shock of her dethronement. At one stage she had not been sure whether she loved him or not. But in that moment she was sure.

"The reason I haven't married him," she told me earlier, "Is that he has never asked me. But now if he does then I will not hesitate... Yes I do love him, very much."

A day or two later the couple became engaged. They holidayed together in Florida. On their return home, Revson had to pack his things for a race meeting in South Africa. Marji had planned, after a few days at home with her mother, to catch up with him when he left for the airport. She saw Peter off, not realising that it was the last time she would ever see him.

In London I called Peter Revson just after he had arrived in South Africa to see whether he would talk of their wedding plans. But I just missed him by seconds. The hotel receptionist told me that he had just walked out of the entrance hall on his way to the Kyalami circuit in Johannesburg. Five hours later my rebooked call was to discover that Revson had been killed on a practice lap. Around his neck was the gold medallion given to him by Marji a few weeks earlier and inscribed with the words: 'Ifs are not for you.'

The news was broken to Marji in New York where she was making a stopover to collect her air ticket to join him in South Africa. There is little doubt they would have married.

Marji returned to Indianapolis in a shocked trance. She was still too shattered to fly to London some weeks later to give evidence against George Best and she said she didn't want to pillory him. The case was withdrawn against the Northern Ireland star footballer, who was told by the magistrate that he left the court without a stain on his character.

Through the ensuing days Marji grew more morose and in June she was rushed to hospital, in a coma, having taken an overdose of barbiturates. She was placed on the critical list for several days. It took several months for her to recover before Marji was seen back

Tom Jones, Miss World, and Women's Lib

in the warm circle of her friends and once more in high spirits.

She spent a happy if ill-advised reunion with Tom Jones who was performing in Las Vegas. It did not meet with the approval of Peter Revson's sister Jennifer who thought that Marji had been 'disloyal' to the memory of her brother.

But Marji was ready with an answer. She said she would never forget Peter Revson, "but life must go on."

Her name soon became romantically linked with Berry Gordy, the boss of the giant Motown record company and then tennis star Jimmy Connors, whom she accompanied to Wimbledon. When in London, just a year or two later, she admitted: "I regret the mistakes of the past but from my experiences I have had in life I shall now build my future."

Certainly she was not the kind of person who was going to allow life to slip by without being noticed. She relished fame — and the famous. Her career flourished as an actress and television presenter. She also appeared in many high-profile television commercials.

In 1978 she married film producer Michael Klein and they had a son Adam. But the marriage did not last and in 1996 she married real estate developer Donald Soffer but were divorced two years later.

Over the years Linda Jones, who moved to Los Angeles, was close to becoming a recluse but she had not lost her love for her husband.

Tom's stardom had never faded. As a judge on the television programme 'The Voice' and global concert tours he attracted a new generation of fans guided by his later-day manager — his son Mark. But their lives were devastated when together in the Philippines on another tour, they were to hear of Linda's death at the age of 75 after a short battle with cancer. They cancelled the rest of the tour and flew home in sorrow and grief. When Tom came to reflect on his life it was not without feelings of guilt. To this day he maintains that Linda was the only girl he loved. "And I will never find such love again," he said recently as he lamented over Linda's loss.

He contemplated quitting the big stage. "But that is not something that Linda would have wanted me to do," said Tom.

Women's lib activists first targeted the Miss World contest in 1970 — and they could not have chosen a better night to have registered their dissent of a contest they labelled as a cattle market.

Some twenty-four million viewers switched on their television sets to see the line-up of the fifty-eight contestants competing for the title and the winner to be crowned by the legendary Hollywood comedian Bob Hope who had flown in from America. Outside the Royal Albert Hall the activists gathered displaying hostile placards reading 'End exploitation of women,' 'End This Cattle Market,' 'Women Against Beauty Contests,' aimed at the contestants themselves with the clear message: "You Poor Cows." Two protestors even dressed as a cow in theatrical costume.

At this stage, there was no indication of what would happen next, but halfway through the programme with the beauty queens lined up on stage and Bob Hope humouring the audience, a torrent of flour and smoke bombs was thrown from the upper balconies along with a downpour of protest leaflets.

The liberation mantra was loud and clear: "We're not beautiful. We're not ugly — we're angry. Ban this disgraceful cattle market."

Bob Hope felt it would be wiser to leave the stage, but as he headed to the staircase, he was stopped in the wings by Julia Morley who grabbed one of his ankles. Police and security guards moved in and Bob Hope returned to the microphone to condemn the activists.

"Anybody who tries to break up an affair as wonderful as this with such wonderful girls from all around the world have got to be on some kind of dope — believe me."

He went on to crown the night's winner: Jennifer Hosten from Grenada the first black girl to have won the title. It was not the organisers' smoothest of nights as many believed that the voting was rigged because Grenada's prime minister Sir Eric Gairy was sitting on the judge's panel. The Morleys were persuaded to display the judge's voting papers to prove that Jennifer had come out on top in the marking system.

Unbeknown to the audience and television viewers there had been another protest aimed at the Miss World contest that day that got little mention in the morning papers. In the early hours a homemade bomb was planted beneath a BBC Outside Broadcast lorry parked alongside the Royal Albert Hall. It instantly exploded and residents saw a group of youths running away from the scene. They were later identified as members of the 'Angry Brigade' who for their own motives didn't want the contest to be broadcast. Fortunately the bomb did little damage.

Several of the feminist demonstrators appeared in court and were summarily dealt with but they had formed a new movement known as the Women's Liberation Movement. Other protests were motivated and the uprising grew. Many famous figures joined the battle. Actress Glenda Jackson appeared on the Michael Parkinson television show two years later. Glenda did not agree with the idea of beauty contests and put her case.

But there was another guest on the show that night — Marji Wallace — just into her reign as Miss World. After the programme she told me: "Maybe Glenda Jackson is one of those frustrated ladies. How can she differentiate between a beauty contest and an audition for a stage play? You get so many girls queuing at auditions that I would say that is just as much a cattle market."

The feminist movement gained momentum and in 1980 the BBC dropped its contract to screen the Miss World event. Many believed that the show had become too old fashioned in its format. The corporation had listened to the protestations and recognised the need for women's equality. Not to be beaten, the Morleys quickly restaged the yearly show in other capitals around the world and it continues to attract millions of viewers on other television channels.

But now as I write and recall the flour bomb attack on the Miss World contest forty eight years ago, a movie based on the happenings that night is being made. Titled 'Misbehaviour' it stars actress Keeley Hawes playing the role of Julia Morley and Keira Knightley cast as one of the formidable protestors. The fight for women's equality is still very much on the agenda.

****

Helen Mirren had an idea that she wanted to put to Equity, the actor's union: when an actress is filmed in a nude scene, everyone in the studio should strip. She told me over lunch in London, "Why should the producer, director, and the whole film crew get away with it?" The twenty-six-year-old actress was a member of the Royal Shakespeare Company and asked me: "How would you feel if you had to strip in front of forty fully-clothed women? People are sensitive about their naked bodies. They think of their ugly features first."

One of the most influential liberalists at the time was Vanessa Redgrave. I first met Redgrave in 1967 at a reception in London announcing her new film 'Isadora' — the film version of the life story of a famous dancer. She had to play many nude scenes in the £2 million picture and summed up her feelings about appearing nude with one simple word: 'Smashing.' She went on: "There are some actresses who make pompous statements that they appear in the nude scenes for the sake of art. I play them because I just want to play in them."

Vanessa Redgrave campaigned for a square deal for acting's 'serfs.' She urged radical changes for Equity whose "uninspired" policies she blamed for poor pay and bad conditions, and she was touring studios and theatres canvassing support. She called for the nationalisation of all Britain's studios and theatres without compensation.

"They should be handed over to the workers," she said. "Everyone in the acting profession is entitled to a fair bite of the cherry. There should be no golden carpet for a precious few."

It was perhaps this strength of character and willingness to speak out for what she believed in that kindled the friendship between Vanessa Redgrave and Jane Fonda. Indeed, Jane Fonda even named her daughter Vanessa after the actress.

Jane Fonda herself was considered a crusader. In 1974, millions of people in America shunned her for her actions against war and against injustice. She was branded a traitor for having flown to Hanoi for preaching peace from a Communist platform. Two congressmen wanted her prosecuted for treason. She even had eggs and paint thrown at her, and she was regarded as "box office poison."

"She is like a Joan of Arc," said her former husband, French film director Roger Vadim. "She wants to save the world."

Fonda's opponents dismissed her as being the puppet of political extremists who manipulated her whenever they wished. Her father, the legendary Henry Fonda, once said in despair: "My daughter is being used."

But Henry Fonda, like many Americans, had time to think again. One of the many questions that lingered after Watergate and Nixon's downfall was: "Just how right is Jane Fonda?"

Jane filed a £1 million lawsuit against Nixon and his administrators in October 1973, alleging they tried to intimidate her because of her anti-war views. Her name was listed under the Nixon regime as 'enemies of the State.'

After Nixon was swept from office, that shadow vanished. Sceptics pondered on whether Jane Fonda's crusades made a worthy contribution to the American society.

One Southern Senator told me in Texas at the time: "If that girl has nothing else, she's got guts. She's done a lot to break down our hypocrisies."

Years before, while still thought of as a successful and popular actress, Jane Fonda rejected the "star life" as totally synthetic. Her career was sparkling. She had starred in 'Barbarella' and 'Barefoot in the Park,' and was hailed as Hollywood's answer to Brigitte Bardot.

Jane protested. "That's not how I want the world to remember me... a sex symbol. What gratification is there in that?" she told friends.

Beverley Hills, the home to many celebrity stars, was losing a resident. Jane Fonda sold her belongings, her jewellery and everything that mattered to her.

She said: "What comfort can one feel from material things when the world is full of suffering and want?"

She moved into a humble home in Santa Monica where she lived with her husband and two children.

Their house was plain with little furniture and bare boards with only the odd piece of matting. The coveted Hollywood Oscar that the actress won for her performance in 'Klute' was used as a doorstop. Any other star would perhaps place their Oscar in a glass cabinet. Not Jane.

I expressed the hope at the time that Jane Fonda would keep on fighting her revolution. Her motives were not of treason, but of truth.

Fonda's political views differed to those of the entertainer Sammy Davis Jr.

He was in London in 1973, making a documentary on the Watergate affair when I met him. At the time, he had been on television with his arms around President Nixon and he had been one of the leading celebrities supporting Nixon in the election campaign. I wanted to know what he thought of his friend after Watergate in the midst of the almost daily revelations of furtive deeds in high places?

"Goddam it. It's unfortunate, it's disgraceful and it's a tragedy. But you can bet your bottom dollar that this kind of thing could happen, and does happen, in other governmental establishments across the world. Phone bugging is a gremlin of our times. But the way I see it, most premiers and rulers in other countries still have faith in President Nixon, and I'm sure he is going to get the benefit of the doubt."

Sammy Davis Jr had been quoted on television as saying: "There's an honesty about the man I love."

Did he still feel that way?

"Sure I do," Sammy told me. "I didn't change camps. What I did was to back the man I thought was best for the job. I haven't changed that opinion."

Said Soapbox Sammy: "With the world as it is today you've got to get off the fence and commit yourself. That's why I dig the youth of today. When they've got something on their minds, they say it."

At the age of forty-seven, Sammy still had ambitions that reached beyond the realms of entertainment. "My one aim is to help create better understanding between all people — and through the United Nations and UNICEF I'm trying to make some impression. I couldn't be content to sing 'Mister Wonderful' and 'What Kind of Fool Am I' and think that's all the meaning I had in life."

Although Sammy worried about the world's problems, he was happy himself, since he had married his wife, Altovise (the name is Indian for High Vision).

"She's been gone two days on a shopping spree in Paris, and that's the longest time we've been parted since our marriage two and a half years ago," Sammy said.

There wasn't time for Sammy to give a live concert on this particular trip. "But when I do come back and sing, it will be down to charity. Britain has been good to me and I believe you can't go on taking all of the time. You've got to give some of it back."

While in London, Sammy had been talking about a possible film with Roger Moore.

"Roger looks like ice cream and cake — that's an American expression meaning the cat looks super," he said.

CHAPTER FOURTEEN

MISSION: 007

Going to the aid of the future James Bond was not something I had ever envisaged.

Roger Moore's predicament was not to be found in any of his film scripts. It was something more personal. Simply, it was an affair of the heart.

Roger had fallen in love with the Italian actress Luisa Mattioli who he had met months earlier on a film location in Italy. But he was already married, to the Welsh born singer Dorothy Squires, who was refusing to give him a divorce.

I had known Dorothy for several years while on the showbusiness beat. She had been a superstar with great chart-busting hits like 'If You Love Me' and 'Till' which had brought her international fame.

Roger and Dorothy had married in 1953. She was thirty-eight and Roger, who, as a student, had been briefly married to an ice skater, was twelve years younger.

It was a high-octane-temper-fuelled marriage that had reached crisis point in 1961 when Roger left the singer to move in with Luisa. For him, there was no turning back.

The more the actor pushed for a divorce the more resolute Dorothy became. There were turbulent scenes between them. Dot's frustration at the situation escalated. She once smashed a guitar over his head in one altercation, and on another occasion, she resorted to throwing stones through the windows of the new home he shared with Luisa. Roger ran out of the house to calm her and saw that her hand was bleeding from a fragment of broken glass, but she did not want sympathy.

She stammered: "It's not my hand that's bleeding — it's my

heart."

Roger tried to obtain the divorce. Believing it might break the stalemate, he and Luisa decided to go ahead with their wish to have children. Their daughter Deborah was born in 1963 and three years later they had their son Geoffrey.

Dorothy was unmoved. She brought lawsuits against Roger for loss of conjugal rights and against actor Kenneth More for referring to Luisa on a television show as "Mrs. Roger Moore." Ultimately, she did not want to let Roger go.

Roger Moore was ready to make a public statement about his marriage and relationship with Luisa. They had been silent on the matter until that point. It was to be an exclusive story for me, so I visited Roger and Luisa at their home.

"So you see Don it's just an impossible situation," Roger lamented as he finished. "She is not going to give in."

I sensed that Roger Moore wanted me to do something to help. My feeling was proved right when I read in his later published memoirs that he stated: "Don Short from the Daily Mirror came out to the house. We discussed it and when he left I sat back relieved to feel that at last a bit of stability was just around the corner."[1] But what could I do?

Two nights later, I called on Dorothy at her Bexley mansion home. At first, we discussed another concert tour she was planning and we went over the ground for some time. I tentatively moved the conversation forward to talk about Roger and her reluctance to grant him a divorce.

She exploded with rage at the mention of his name and the atmosphere became super-charged at the suggestion of a possible divorce.

"Why in the hell should I?" she asked. "I made him a star! I took him to Hollywood. Got him to meet the right people. He was just a knitwear fashion model when I got hold of him. And what does he do to me in return? He treats me like dirt."

She continued: "You say he didn't love me?"

She went over to a drawer and produced a bundle of Roger's love letters for me to read. I shook my head and discreetly put them aside.

"I am sure he did love you," I agreed, as diplomatically as I could.

"You do not know the heartbreak this has caused me," she said.

She picked up the letters and clasped them in her hand. "When

I read these letters, I thought I could never forgive or forget. There was a P.S. on one which told me I had lost my husband forever. It was as though someone had poured tar over the years we had spent so happily together."

Dorothy gazed forlornly at me. "Why haven't I given Roger a divorce? Well my feelings were those of a woman whose soul and pride had been grievously injured. I know the public saw me as a dragon, the flint-hearted bitch who refused to give her husband a divorce. Yes, I know... and don't you think that has been hell to live with? The public imagine that showbusiness folk have no feelings or personal life. That the eternal triangle is something stars only get involved with on the screen. But that isn't so. Oh, I didn't pretend that a husband could be absolutely faithful. I told myself that as long as I didn't know — I didn't mind. And when I saw the girls pursuing Roger, I prepared myself for the fact that one day my husband might go off the track... But I didn't ever dream he would fall in love."

She sighed. "We wanted children desperately, but we could not have them. I lost four in early pregnancy." She paused for a moment. "But I do not think they would have saved our marriage."

I mentioned Roger's youngsters with Luisa and their future, and how the present quandary might be affecting their lives. I reminded her of the unnecessary lawyer's bills as I was aware her finances were running low. Wasn't it all so futile? I cautiously put to her.

As the night wore on, I thought I was beginning to talk Dorothy round to the fact that it might be less stressful to simply divorce Roger Moore instead of dragging it out and potentially incurring costly legal fees. I didn't want to think of Dorothy suffering even more heartbreak.

She stayed silent for several minutes. Finally, she gesticulated in a mode of surrender and took a long deep breath. I could visibly see in her face that the anger of the past five years were dissolving from her state of mind.

"Alright. I will instruct my solicitor tomorrow and let the divorce go ahead," she said wearily. It was 3:00am but I felt relieved for her.

I couldn't believe that she had been so easily persuaded by my suggestions. I checked with Dorothy's lawyers during the course of the day and found that she had kept her word.

That evening, I caught up with Roger and Luisa attending the Royal Variety Show at the London Palladium and broke the news to them that their initial story about their relationship going public was not going to be used, as I had better news.

Roger recalled the moment: "Don Short came down the aisle looking for me at the interval. He beckoned me out to one of the foyers. 'Dorothy's lawyers have said that she has decided to divorce you'. I was delighted and told Luisa the moment I got back to my seat."[2]

Their faces were filled with happiness.

After all the years of bitter wrangling, the wheels were now put in motion for the rocky marriage to be dissolved. It took almost two years for the legal complexities to be settled, until in 1969 the actor married Luisa and they had their second son Christian in 1973.

****

Roger Moore was the clear choice when the role of James Bond fell vacant in 1972. Everything pointed to him. He had triumphed in the television series 'The Saint' and 'The Persuaders,' and had become hot property in showbusiness terms. There had been no pressure on him to wipe out the image of Sean Connery as 007, although Roger admitted: "He is a hard act to follow."

After he had completed his first Bond film in 'Live and Let Die', Roger suggested I might like to join him in Thailand where he was taking on his second 007 blockbuster 'The Man With The Golden Gun' with Swedish actress Britt Ekland and American actress Maud Adams as his co-stars. His wife Luisa had created her own role as an on-set photographer.

So I set out for Bangkok and for six weeks I was given privileged access to experience the daily inner workings of the Bond film-making processes. It was like being given a seat in a front row seat to watch a play unfold in a West End theatre.

Only here it was panoramic. Scenery and stunts blitzed the mind in their sheer size and ingenious concepts. The filming schedules were ambitious. One could detect pressure in every corner. But the cast and crew coordinated like a well-oiled machine. To break the tension, spontaneous nights of revelry erupted too.

My mind casts back to one riotous party in particular. I had joined the Bond clan of actors and crew dining happily on the hotel terrace. A delicious Thai dinner was being served by a team of waiters directly from a huge charcoal barbecue. It was a hot and humid night with a rainbow coloured haze surrounding the moon.

There was lots of noisy banter through the evening and it wasn't until 2:00am before the party began to drift away, much to the relief of the exhausted waiters.

I found myself escorting Britt and Maud towards the hotel veranda. We passed the swimming pool, its still surface reflecting the starry night sky. Suddenly, without warning, Britt tossed down the chain link belt of her evening gown, while the more casually dressed Maud kicked off her moccasin shoes across the terrace. Together they plunged fully clothed into the pool — tugging me in with them.

Roger and the rest of the crew, a few yards ahead, spun round. Soon everyone was in the pool. Roger, in a sleek blue cotton shirt and cord trousers, was dragged to the pool's edge. He clutched a bamboo to try to save himself, but the man who played Bond with such cool demeanour hit the water with a lighted cigar still intact between his teeth.

Already thrashing there like a benevolent hippo was the seventeen-stone Bond film producer Cubby Broccoli, his Savile Row suit clinging to him. "I thought this could only happen in Hollywood," he roared.

Maud Adams, once counted by Henry Kissinger as one of his jetset, lost two gold bracelets and willing hands had to work hard to retrieve them from the bottom of the pool.

Lights blinked in the hotel. Guests complained about the noise. One angry resident threatened to call the police.

We all adjourned to Maud's suite, our dripping figures leaving puddles along the carpeted hotel foyer. Upstairs, Maud, completely soaked with trousers stuck to her like glue, handed round towels and dressing gowns. She poured drinks, then went off to change.

Cubby Broccoli recovered a sheaf of soaked dollar notes from his wallet and ironed them out on a table using a bottle of Martini as a rolling pin.

"It's all the money I've got to get back to my own hotel. How else can I pay for the cab?" he joked.

It was a humorous sight to behold as Cubby was a multi-millionaire, not that anyone would ever guess from his lifestyle.

He stayed in a downtown hotel in Bangkok with his production staff and crew and refused to move with his stars into our luxurious hotel. Broccoli travelled economy class when he flew and explained: "I like to keep in close liaison with the boys." But he worked hard for his wealth: every morning he was on set at first light and stayed until the last scene had been shot.

It was dawn when the party finally broke up. Broccoli and six of his production team, in a colourful variety of towels and dressing gowns, departed like a dishevelled spa party to take taxis back to their own hotels.

The morning after, Roger Moore was suffering from an acute hangover. He wasn't alone. I offered him some of my Alka Seltzer for which he was grateful.

"I can't remember Bond ever having a hangover," I taunted him.

The star shook his aching head. "Bond isn't human!" he countered, "but Roger Moore is."

Luisa kindly poured us our morning coffees and her husband recovered at a remarkable rate. An hour or two later James Bond was ready for action.

Later in the afternoon, he was to film with four Thai handmaidens named Wandee, Srireun, Raweewan and Prakakaew. But first, there were some drawbacks to overcome.

Roger, coached by an expert instructor, had to do Thai-boxing with villains for a scene. It left him bruised and battered, and the ball of his right foot injured. In another sequence, he decided to abandon his out-of-control speedboat as it leaped over a riverbank and crashed into the other side.

"My backside is aching," moaned Mr. Moore who was instantly attended by a medic and given three jabs to protect him from typhoid, dysentery and similarly frightening illnesses. That night he couldn't sit down comfortably for dinner. The cast were helpless with laughter at his expense. Cubby Broccoli basked in the revelry. Again, it helped to break the tension on location where the heat, mosquitos and tropical rainstorms had played havoc with the filming schedule.

When the Bond outfit first arrived, local students were not happy. The ninety-strong unit pitched a tent near the isle of Phuket (pronounced 'Poo-ket' although the Bond crew had another way of saying it) and scene-makers had innocently covered a beach plaque to eliminate it from camera range, not realising that the plaque bore the signature of the King of Thailand. The students were outraged and said it was an act of discourtesy. They staged angry protests, waving banners screaming 'Go Home — Capitalist Movie Makers.' It gave Cubby and the production bosses additional moments of anxiety.

However, it was not long before the local community saw an opportunity to help their situation. Numerous boat excursions were organised promising tourists a front-line view of the Bond filming. What's more, the Bond unit needed food and water and extras for crowd scenes. The locals happily obliged. Thailand, the land of smiles, was glowing again. But it didn't solve all of Broccoli's problems.

Outside our plush five-star hotel was parked a black Mercedes limousine — one of Bond's supercharged cars. It cost £12,000 at the time and was fitted with guns and a whole range of other technical gadgets in true James Bond style plus a floor-level harness for cameras. But when it came to filming, it was discovered that someone had forgotten to install a vital accessory — a clutch.

"Just how can that happen?" Broccoli exploded in a rare black mood.

Meanwhile, I learned that one technician had quit and gone home while others had to ride out the rows.

Britt Ekland (the former wife of Peter Sellers), dined with me downtown in a Thai restaurant. We left our shoes at the door, in accordance with Buddhist custom. I soon found out about Britt's fondness for shoes: she told me that although she had hundreds of shoes at home, she was reluctant to leave her expensive snakeskin pair at the door.

We ordered our food. She insisted it should not be cooked in garlic.

"I couldn't do that to Roger. That's how Diana Rigg fell out with George Lazenby when he played Bond in 'On His Majesty's Service'. Diana kept upsetting him by eating garlic..."

Britt held some admiration for Roger. She appeared amused rather than annoyed that he often referred to her as Miss Impact because she threatened to upstage Bond.

One day on the set, however, she was far from amused. Assistant director Derek Cracknell ticked her off for chatting while filming was in progress.

"No one talks when you are filming," he remonstrated with her. "So keep quiet when others are." Miss Ekland flushed like a school-girl who had just had a rap on the knuckles. But she did not argue.

If any real hostility was evident, Britt couldn't conceal it in sharp exchanges with Luisa. Britt was convinced that Luisa had a jealous streak: "I wish Luisa would calm down," she remarked. "Anyone would think I was going to eat her man alive."

Luisa, I noticed, was usually on set when Roger was filming, and temperaments often flared.

Luisa joked when I asked her if she was the jealous type. "Look darling, I let my husband go to bed with any of these girls. But if he makes love to them for real I would kill him." She laughed: "Why should I worry? I know that Roger does not like thin girls."

Later chatting with Roger, the actor made light of it all. "James Bond may fancy his leading ladies, but Roger Moore daren't. He is married to an Italian spitfire whose arm is like a sword."

As if to prove she was not as possessive as others may have thought, the camera-equipped Luisa planted Roger aboard a boat on the river and snapped him with Britt and Maud, one on each arm.

"There darling!" she told me. "Would a jealous woman photograph her husband like that?"

It was apparently suspected earlier on that the real conflict on the film set might ignite between Britt and Maud. Leading ladies have been known to clash in the past, although such conflict was sometimes staged for publicity purposes.

"I had heard so much about Britt that I was pretty apprehensive," Maud admitted to me. "I was told that Britt was self-centred and I wouldn't get a look in. That's the danger of forming an opinion based on what others say. But that hasn't happened at all. We've turned out to be great pals."

Cubby Broccoli christened Britt and Maud as the 'Swedish au pairs' while others described them as the 'Siamese twins' as they stayed so close to one another.

The avuncular Broccoli was clearly quite a character. It was no secret that he did not see eye to eye with his co-producer Harry Saltzman who remained back in England. But Broccoli insisted there was no split in their partnership.

Hollywood superstar Jane Russell was one of Cubby's early discoveries when he was on the legendary Howard Hughes's payroll.

One morning, missing breakfast, Cubby was tempted to try a banana cooked on a charcoal grill at a nearby market stall. "How much?" he asked the Thai stallholder.

A production assistant came running across.

"Mr. Broccoli — we've bought the whole stall. It's yours. It's going to be part of the background scenery."

Broccoli grunted — and still paid the young stallholder.

Between scenes, he played backgammon with Roger Moore. Sometimes there was as much as £1,200 at stake on the throw of the dice. Roger won one big session and allowed himself a smile.

"Roger Moo — you're a gloater," Broccoli muttered.

Broccoli always called his star Roger Moo. He had nicknames for most of the cast. Hervé Villechaize who played Nick Nack the manservant to Bond's towering, would-be assassin Scaramanga portrayed by Christopher Lee, was referred to as the 'Mighty Mouse' as he stood at three foot ten inches tall. But despite his lack of height, French-born Hervé was the playboy of the Bond group.

"Let James Bond have his beautiful birds," he said. "They're all artificial. You can't make love to plastic dolls."

So Hervé found his own girls after several forays on Bangkok's night life. Eventually, however, he was summoned by director Guy Hamilton to get a good telling off for his wild nocturnal adventures.

"Stars don't act the way you do," snapped Hamilton. "How can you work when you haven't had any sleep and you've got bags under your eyes?"

Hervé was repentant. But as he left the production office he shrugged, clutching onto the positives from their exchange: "Remember he did call me a star!"

It was difficult to leave the Bond crew but the curtain had come down on my stay and I had to return to London.

It went without saying that I would be seeing Roger on many other movie sets and we remained friends throughout his life.

Nevertheless, it was something of a shock to learn from afar that after some thirty years of marriage he had left Luisa to marry one of her best friends Swedish socialite Kristina "Kiki" Tholstrup. I was told that his marriage to Luisa had descended into stormy, bitter feuds. Like Dorothy Squires before her, Luisa kept Roger on tenterhooks before giving him a divorce. It was said she finally agreed after being offered a settlement of £10 million.

Roger, knighted in 2003 for his charity work as a UNICEF ambassador said after marrying Kiki: "At last I have found peace in my life."

Despite suffering from prostate cancer, Roger lived out the rest of his life to the age of 89 with the kind of tranquillity he had perhaps always sought.

[1] The Roger Moore Story. 1972. TV Times Extra, Independent Publications Limited.

[2] The Roger Moore Story. 1972. TV Times Extra, Independent Publications Limited.

CHAPTER FIFTEEN

PLAYGROUNDS OF A PRINCESS
AND THE PAPARAZZI

The paparazzi have been the bane of the Royal family and movie stars, ruthlessly stalking their celebrity prey until they have cornered their quarry and secured that one rare picture to sell for a lot of money to global newspapers and magazines. Federico Fellini, the director of the landmark 1960 film 'La Dolce Vita', provided the origins of the word 'paparazzi' in his character, Paparazzo, a photographer in the film.

Armed with their telephoto lens, the paparazzi will hang out of helicopters and pose in disguise with hidden cameras to get that one precious shot they know could be worth a fortune.

Many countries have introduced new privacy laws that restrict the paparazzi from their activities, and a number of celebrities have won court injunctions to prevent the renegade camera pack from pursuing them. Some newspapers have also banned paparazzi pictures if there is any suggestion that the new laws have been breached.

But in 1966, the paparazzi were rampant, with no rules or regulations to abide by, and they descended in droves on the Venice Film Festival.

I was made aware of their threat when visiting the very glamorous Princess Ira von Furstenberg at her lovely canal-facing villa. We had made plans to go out for dinner but there were three or four members of the paparazzi awaiting her emergence, staking her home.

I asked the German princess what it was like to be perpetually hounded by the paparazzi as she gazed out of the window at the cluster of photographers. She said: "They never leave you alone." Then she smiled. "But if we are going to risk going out then you are about to find out for yourself."

The Princess, radiant in a beige coat over a light blue dress, wasn't going to be deterred from exploring the Venetian night life. Ira was ready to throw caution to the wind and run the gauntlet of the paparazzi. She told me before we ventured out that the photographers would question us. "Tell them we are just good friends. Otherwise the paparazzi get a little excited."

In some ways, I liked the idea of seeing how it felt to be one of their targets just for one brief moment. It was an initiation by fire.

As we stepped out of the villa, we got through the first wave of flashbulbs without too much trouble at first. We walked through the narrow streets towards San Marco Square when suddenly an exuberant cry filled the air. Instinctively, we paused as we heard the heavy drumming of feet bearing down on us. Cries of delight echoed around the square as the paparazzi closed in on us and threw an unbroken cordon around us. The main squad had found their quarry. Flashbulbs popped, loud Italian voices demanded my identity, while photographers on the edge of the posse were tussling one another for space.

Princess Ira was always an A-list figure for photographers. She was a European socialite, her first husband was Prince Alfonso, and she was a big screen actress. The demure Princess had experienced many altercations with the paparazzi in the past. Most of the camera clad crowd lurked on the Via Veneto — their ancestral base in Rome — but the lure of the stars arriving in Venice for the film festival was too good an opportunity for them to miss.

Amongst the throng of the paparazzi, I held her hand protectively and said: "Perhaps they will go away soon."

The Princess smiled back at me. "They'll have us here until dawn. They always want one more picture."

One photographer wanted us to take out a gondola so they could picture us in a more romantic setting. As luck would have it, the gondola boatmen were on strike.

We made a dash for the Chez Vous night club but when we got to our table, it seemed the whole world had joined us.

Camera lenses brushed our eyelashes. One beefy, perspiring photographer grabbed my arm to pull me into focus. He motioned me to look at him while some of his compatriots wanted me to look the opposite way in their direction.

Playgrounds of a Princess and Paparazzi

Then, amid the confusion and chaos, flaying arms pushed me aside as Ira (who had recently appeared on the cover of Vogue) was tugged across the floor for a spontaneous and involuntary fashion shoot.

An Italian journalist stepped to my side. "Who are you? Inglese?" she questioned.

"Yes," I conceded.

"You are friends?" she asked nodding towards the Princess.

"Yes."

"Romantici?"

"No, no. Just good friends," I replied, just as the Princess had wished me to say.

I didn't know whether she believed me, but the reporter left with the rest of the paparazzi to chase down another celebrity in a neighbouring restaurant.

At last, we were able to dine in welcome peace. The Princess talked of her love of Venice, of her recovery from two broken marriages and her bourgeoning film career. At the end of the evening, we headed for the jetty where Ira had arranged for a motor launch to collect her to take her back home. A helmsman greeted us and switched on the boat's motor as Ira climbed aboard thanking me for dinner.

"It's time to go home. Now you know what it is like to have the paparazzi constantly on your tail."

I understood her sentiments. It was an invasive and intimidating experience. The intrusion over our dinner table alone was enough to convince me she had a point.

"Yes. I wouldn't like to live with them myself," I told her as I wished her goodnight.

Our romance-that-wasn't had ended.

The labyrinth of streets was pretty empty as I strolled back to my hotel. I suspected that the paparazzi were now holding siege elsewhere pinning down some other unfortunate victim.

In a doorway, a little Italian boy who had seen the mob pursuing us in San Marco square stopped me. In good English, he told me: "Signor, the paparazzi not happy. You did not kiss her once."

****

Of all film festivals across the world, The Cannes Film Festival is the one that Hollywood and the global film industry cannot afford to miss. It is still the ultimate marketplace for movie makers to peddle their wares internationally.

Out pour the superstars to tread the hallowed red carpet, photographer hordes battle with each other to snatch their pictures, champagne parties noisily erupt along the esplanade, while VIPs covertly board the polished decks of the magically lit yachts moored in the harbour for their own celebrations.

Every year at Cannes there has to be at least one sensation. But in 1971, something much more sinister happened. It was the screening of 'Gimme Shelter,' a frightening documentary of the Rolling Stones' tour of the U.S. eighteen months earlier when they played at the Altamont Free Concert in the Californian desert to hundreds of thousands of fans wildly spread out before them. Its content made the travails of Woodstock look like a kid's picnic party.

Harrowing scenes unfolded on the screen: a young black man was stabbed to death by a Hell's Angel guarding the stage; other Hell's Angels hired for security were seen mercilessly bludgeoning pop fans; tripped-out music fans formed a sea in the audience.

The Stones' guitarist Keith Richards arrived in Cannes to face the uneasy restlessness the film was likely to provoke. He tried to explain the whole unedifying episode to me.

"We've still got it on our minds," he confessed. "You can put it all down on us and everyone will. It was our show, but we didn't organise it. We went along with the idea of giving a free concert to our fans. We believed it would be properly organised, but it wasn't. The Hell's Angels were brought in to look after security, and we thought they would be cool, but they freaked out and went berserk. Then this Negro cat flashed a gun, was stabbed to bits, ten or twelve lines from the front. We didn't see it happen. When you are on stage doing your number, you don't see anything, there is just a wall of faces, and at this concert the wall seemed to stretch for miles."

Keith accepted that the Rolling Stones felt some responsibility for the outcome.

"As I said, man, everyone is gonna put it on us. But it was not our fault. We went along with good intentions. We can't act as marshals as well. People have been killed at our concerts before. A cop got crushed a few years back, but this one has put a seal on it for us."

The alarming documentary did just that. Audiences seeing the movie were left in a shaken state of shock and revulsion.

Another sensation erupted just one year later with the premiere of 'Last Tango In Paris' — a film that would go down in the annals of film history as being the most erotic movie ever made for the big screen.

Marlon Brando, at the age of forty-eight, and the nineteen-year-old French newcomer Maria Schneider, were involved in explicit nude sex scenes, which many believed were gratuitous, played out to satisfy the fantasies of the Italian director Bernardo Bertolucci.

Arriving in Cannes for the torrid premiere and its aftermath, I was just one of hundreds of reporters chasing the story.

Caught up in such a media mob, it can be more effective to combine forces with one of your competitors to pull the rug on the rest of the pack and the paparazzi. I decided to collaborate with my friend (but normally fierce rival) Victor Davis of the Daily Express.

Every reporter and photographer in town was frantically searching for the two stars. We had to move fast if we were to find them.

It was evident that Brando and Schneider had gone to ground rather than face any kind of backlash. Every hotel along the sea front was turned over by the eagle-eyed press but they could find no trace of the couple.

Wandering along one of the jetties I struck lucky. I got a tip-off from an unlikely source — a boatman who seemed to be in the know and sent us in the direction of a cove closer to Antibes. We got a taxi straight there.

In the bay was anchored another of the luxury yachts, similar to the kind moored in Cannes. If the boatman was right, then this was where our two missing stars were in hiding.

We persuaded a fisherman untangling his nets on the shoreline to get us out to the yacht. We boarded his little boat with an outboard motor and quietly ran alongside the yacht. Stealthily (and more than a little nervously) we clambered aboard to be immediately confronted on the deck by the unmistakable figure of Kirk Kerkorian, head of Hollywood's biggest empire MGM Pictures.

"Well, well," he exclaimed as he recognised us. "So what are you here for?" Then he laughed: "But of course. You are looking for our two stars."

Kirk admired our audacity and rewarded us by revealing that Maria was below deck, but Brando was still in America. "Having got this far, I will see if Maria will talk to you," said Kirk disappearing to the saloon. A few minutes later he returned. The news was good. "Yes," said Kirk. "Maria will see you — but just one of you."

Vic and I exchanged glances and tossed a coin to see which one of us would conduct the interview. Vic made the right call, while I was left to interrogate Kerkorian about the moral issues of the movie.

Eventually, with our interviews intact, we returned to Cannes having exchanged notes and filed our copy. We could not help but feel a sense of triumph.

We were both confident we had a world scoop on our hands. Indeed, that is how it transpired for my paper as it was splashed all over the front page and centre spread of the Daily Mirror. But not a single word or picture appeared in the Daily Express. Vic, flicking over every page in search for his missing story, was horror-stricken. What had happened? Choking in rage he got on to his Editor — a devout Presbyterian editor no less — who told him bluntly: "Stop wasting your time laddie. We'll not have nude sex scenes appearing in my paper."

Victor took weeks to recover.

The aftermath of 'Last Tango In Paris' caused widespread controversy. Art lovers described it as 'liberating' and free of the shackles of censorship, but others condemned it as the most shameful picture ever made. Maria Schneider had a nervous breakdown and felt she had been used by Brando and Bertolucci, while Brando tried to soothe her by reminding her that it was only a movie. Many countries banned the film and Italian court actions were taken against Bertolucci and early copies of the film destroyed.

Cannes thrives on controversy. It evokes publicity not only for the festival but for its movies and the stars, and it was not the first time that such scandal had evolved.

The legendary mastermind of suspense was in town in 1972. Alfred Hitchcock had arrived for the premiere of what was to be his penultimate movie as a producer. 'Frenzy' (a grisly story about a serial killer who tore through London raping women and strangling them with a tie) caused shock amongst even the most fervent Hitchcock film-goers. They were left nerve-shattered and on the edge of their seats, precisely the reaction that Hitchcock aimed for, as he acknowledged when he greeted me in his hotel suite.

There was a vase of red roses and white lilies on the mantelpiece and the rotund Hitchcock, in a black suit and black tie, managed to emanate an aura of suspense in his being.

He had been on record for saying that screen nudity was something he would never contemplate. But it seemed that he had identified the modern trends and the arrival of the permissive age.

"It was just the same in Victorian England," he said. "They all had their clothes off then. Look at the size of the families they had. We know more about permissiveness today because of films and other forms of communication."

Hitchcock was dwelling on the subject because 'Frenzy' had broken with his own traditions and featured a nude sequence. The two lead actresses, Barbara Leigh-Hunt and Anna Massey, refused to do the scenes and models were used instead.

The Old Master defended the nature of his movie and denied he had capitulated to the popular theory that a film must have a nude scene if it was to become a box office success.

"Nonsense," he thundered. "I sell my films on suspense — not sex. People get sick to death of sex but will always pay money to be scared out of their wits."

Hitchcock, famed for his mantra 'Always make the audience suffer as much as possible', was already plotting the depths of suspense for his next big movie 'Family Plot' about a fraudulent spiritualist. At seventy-two he had no plans to retire.

"I am ready to face any challenge. If I retired what on earth would I do? I say to hell with croquet."

At a star-studded party across the bay, I bumped into another Hollywood legend, Gregory Peck. He was a bewildered man as he watched the anti-American sequences at the Film Festival which had brought outbursts of cheers from the audiences. And he had seen many Americans join in wildly.

"I cannot understand," said Peck, "The American who goes abroad and stabs his country in the back. In England or France you can walk down a street freely without fear of violence. But no country in the world has such massive social problems as the United States. It is going through an intricate period of adjustment and one day it will surely restore itself to sanity."

Peck had come to the festival as the producer of a film — the true story of 'The Trial of the Catonsville Nine.' The film cost Peck only £200,000 to make. "In the Hollywood days we would have spent that on the trailer," he said.

As an actor, Peck's career marked time. He told me, "I have vowed not to appear in any pot boilers just for the sake of it. I will wait until I've found a part I really want to do."

Peck, at fifty-six, still cut a distinguished, elegant figure as film fans always knew him to be. He said the one philosophy he had derived from life is: "To enjoy the good times and endure the bad."

It seemed the festival had entered choppy waters.

There was just one redeeming feature to the whole programme. It was the screening of a documentary of the previous summer's New York all-star concert conceived and organised by George Harrison through which was raised £6 million for the child victims of the Bangladesh war. George, like the other Beatles, had already been awarded an MBE but as I wrote in my Mirror column, did he not deserve higher recognition?

When I returned to Cannes one year later, scandal pursued actress Sarah Miles who, only three months earlier in Arizona, found herself implicated in the mysterious death of her business manager and screenwriter David Whiting.

They had been in a relationship while Miles was filming 'The Man Who Loved Cat Dancing' and Whiting's body was found in her motel room. She had vacated the room earlier that night after an affray with Whiting which left her nursing a bloody nose, bruised forehead and cut lip. She stayed for protection in neighbouring co-star Burt Reynolds' apartment. When she returned to her room, she found Whiting had taken an overdose of barbiturates with loose pills strewn over the floor. An inquest cleared Sarah of culpability in his death. A devastated Sarah had said of the ordeal as suspicions circulated about her role in her lover's death "I already saved him from three suicides so why would I want to murder him?"[1]

When we met in Cannes, the actress was still coming to terms with the trauma. She told me: "I cannot cower or run away from the past. Of course, what happened was a tragedy. But my conscience is clear. I still feel numb and scarred and I don't think I will ever recover from it. But you cannot live your life in the past."

I asked Sarah what she thought of the rumour that the adverse publicity had made her a hot box office star. Sarah nodded.

"That is the sickness of the society we live in," she said. "I find it deplorable. I lie in bed thinking it over for hours. But all I can say is that the engagements I am undertaking over the next year or so were arranged long before this trouble occurred."

Sarah talked of the love and trust of her famed playwright husband Robert Bolt, the screenplay writer of 'Lawrence of Arabia' and 'Doctor Zhivago' — and how the Arizona scandal had not destroyed their marriage.

"I do not know of another man like him," she said. "Unlike myself, he thinks before he takes a decision. I do something and say 'Christ, what a mistake!' Nothing will ever change him. There is something about me, however zany I may appear, that fascinates him."

Sarah, who said she had to keep her chin up and carry on, was in Cannes for the premiere of her new film 'The Hireling' that told the story of a lady's scorn for her chauffeur. It won rave reviews, shared the best picture award, and, for her, helped to soothe the torments of recent months. More importantly, she had proved that she had not lost her grip on stardom achieved through her award-winning films 'Ryan's Daughter' and 'White Mischief.' Two years after we spoke, Sarah and Bolt split and divorced. She became romantically involved with Sir Laurence Olivier. But in 1988 she remarried Bolt who admitted: "I cannot live without her."

One evening, I was chatting with Peter Ustinov, widely regarded as a marvellous raconteur on the circuit of superstars. He suggested we should escape from the razzmatazz of Cannes to have a drink in a night club he had been recommended to by a friend. We took a taxi to the club a few miles out of town.

Ustinov was thrilled when we stepped in. I wasn't quite so sure of the place, but as long as Ustinov was happy then that was all that mattered. In my view, it was probably one of the sleaziest clubs on the French Riviera. A clutch of hostesses scantily dressed occupied the dimly lit tables which were all numbered, and a telephone placed on each one. The club's rules were clear: if you wanted one of the hostesses to join your table you merely had to dial her number. Some of the tables were situated on a gallery above us. I suspected that for an additional fee one might have been able to escort a girl home for the night.

I could see the club manager keeping an alert eye on our table and seemed mesmerised when he saw a sequence of telephone lights on the hostesses' tables light up. Ustinov was providing the action, making one call after another. I didn't know what to say. I thought we were going to be overrun by the number of girls he was dialling. There were French girls, Italian girls, Moroccan girls, German girls and many more. They were all laughing at something Ustinov was telling them. Ustinov, sipping his cocktail from time to time, was entertaining them all — and in their own languages.

I didn't know how to proceed: the strange 'dial-a-girl' set up of the club, all of the people in there... I thought I could at least comfortably talk about Ustinov's linguistic skills.

I asked the actor: "Just what have you been saying to them?"

Ustinov shook his head. "Now that would be telling my friend," he said. "But I will tell you one thing. We were not discussing the weather!"

****

Two top stars who fell out of love with the Hollywood star Raquel Welch were keen to express their displeasure of her 'prima donna' stance when filming 'The Last of Sheila' which was being screened for Cannes's 1973 event.

Raquel may have had many fans. But her co-star, actor Ian McShane, was not one of them. He related the true extent of the discord when the movie was being filmed on the Riviera.

Disruption and anger broke out explosively during the scenes leading to a fierce row between Raquel and the movie's director Herbert Ross. Amid a shower of tears and tantrums Raquel swept back to London.

Raquel left her other co-star James Mason to bristle: "She is the most selfish, ill-mannered, inconsiderate actress that I have ever had the displeasure of working with."

Ian McShane, who played the part of the American beauty's husband in the film, nodded in agreement with Mason's blistering appraisal.

"She isn't the most friendly creature. She seems to set out with the impression that no one is going to like her," he told me.

In the film, a thriller set on the Mediterranean, Raquel was cast as an actress caught up in murder and intrigue aboard a Hollywood producer's yacht.

Some aspects of the plot seemed to have a parallel with her own life. McShane coincidently played Raquel's manager as well as her husband which used to be the joint real-life role of Patrick Curtis before their marriage was dissolved.

"Even Raquel assumed I was Patrick for a time," said Ian. "Once or twice when we were playing a scene she would say things like: 'Pat would always do this or that.' I had to remind her that I wasn't Patrick. Being Raquel's screen husband wasn't so very romantic. We didn't even kiss and after the day's filming, we split. Socially we didn't mix at all. To me Raquel isn't the kind of woman who turns men on. She has to live constantly around her sex symbol image and she is always conscious of what she must wear and how you must look. Frankly I feel sorry for her."

Playgrounds of a Princess and Paparazzi

The actor's wife, the former fashion model Ruth Post wasn't at all jealous of her husband filming with the Hollywood star. "It didn't worry me a bit," she told me. "I don't think she is Ian's kind of girl. He is likely to go for someone more subtle."

****

Into Cannes harbour one morning sailed the sleek white hulled yacht the Mamy Blue and aboard was an unexpected guest that I had been unable to contact in London before his hasty exit from the Beatles boardroom. Allen Klein, often regarded as the toughest promoter in the film and record industries, was on a cruise of the Cote d'Azur and intending to sample some of the movies being screened at the festival.

Only a year earlier, Klein had been the powerhouse behind the Beatles empire Apple Corps but they severed their links with him amid financial squabbles. Now, I was to learn Klein's side of the argument when he made me welcome aboard deck.

I remember his first words: "I can live without the Beatles," and, as if to justify his comment, he gave me a snapshot of his vast wealth: two Rolls Royces, two yachts, homes in London, New York and Los Angeles and his multi-million pound ABKCO film and entertainments company.

"So do I need them?" he gestured.

Klein's appointment as business manager at Apple had been favoured by three of the Beatles, but Paul McCartney said he didn't trust the American whizz kid. As it materialised, Paul's views were not without some foundation.

Klein, a stocky compact figure with grey flecked hair and perceptive eyes, was ready to talk about his dubious image.

"If people say I'm a crook then I haven't found one who's had the guts to say it to my face. Am I a crook?" Klein's eyes narrowed. "Don't crooks go to gaol? I may have told lies in the context of negotiation but I don't ever steal. I know I've got this kind of image that the only thing that counts in my life is money — that isn't true because more than anything else I think of my wife and our three children and I think too of the people around me. But I am not going to argue about it. Of course I'm tough. I've got to be. Clients send for me when they're in a jam because they know I can tie up a deal better than anyone else around. I'm the champion and like a boxer I don't set foot in a ring to lose. You wouldn't have expected that of

Henry Cooper in his day, would you?"

Klein outlined his strategy for me. "At the negotiating table I let the other side dictate the pace, the odds and the mood — and then I weigh in at the end. The trouble is that there is no contract I've yet seen that hasn't got two different meanings."

I could not resist asking him just how much money he made for The Beatles in the four years he was with them? Klein was happy to oblige.

"Apple was worth £900,000 when I was brought in," he replied. "Today it is around £5 million so you can draw your own conclusions."

At one stage in his career, Klein had been financial adviser to the Rolling Stones but that association ended in familiar waves of litigation and lawsuits over finances.

Klein came ashore with me. He had a letter to post. It was addressed to the Beatles and contained his bill for £2 million. Nothing more. "That's the money they owe me and it is still outstanding," he claimed. "I hope they just pay up like the good fellas they are. Oh God, it will be sad if that doesn't happen and I have to fight them for the cash," he said, dropping the letter into a mailbox.

No doubt, I construed in my own mind, that it would all come down to negotiation. But in 1980, I couldn't help but recall Klein's fatalistic words "Don't crooks go to gaol?" when Klein went to gaol for three months for tax evasion.

My friend Victor Davis suggested a nostalgic visit to Cannes at a period when we were both freelancing. Once more we were in luck. We each secured a rare interview with Hollywood idol Robert Redford. Once back in London, Vic sold his story to Woman's Own and I placed my copy with its renowned rival Woman magazine.

On publication day just a few weeks later, anyone looking at the newsstands may have been forgiven for becoming confused as to which of the two magazines to buy.

Robert Redford was plastered on the cover of both magazines. There was just one difference. Vic's story was headlined: 'Why I Will Never Marry Again,' while my own story was labelled: 'This Is The Girl I Am Going To Marry.' We were both reduced to tears of laughter when we caught sight of the two magazines and heaven knows what the respective editors must have thought.

But it all came back to the canny Robert Redford. He knew precisely how to give each of us an exclusive story!

Playgrounds of a Princess and Paparazzi

Flying to the Philippines for the Manila Film Festival with my colleague Terry Fincher, we became embroiled in a head-to-head squabble with Jeremy Irons. Terry shot some casual pictures of him, but the English actor demanded that he should vet the photographs before we distributed them. Terry refused point blank, regarding Jeremy's demand as a slur on his professional abilities.

Attrition erupted between the two and I had to step in and prise them apart as they were on the verge of exchanging blows with one another. Jeremy finally retreated in a huff realising that Terry was not going to hand over the roll of film from his camera.

In today's world journalists sometimes have to acquiesce to such demands. Not only photographers having to give picture control to the artists and their publicists but reporters being refused an interview with a star unless they submit a set list of questions in advance and even remit their copy for sanction. Thankfully we did not adhere to those restrictions in the past!

---

[1] Barry Egan "I Can't Wait To Get Off This Planet" The Independent, 16 September 2007.

CHAPTER SIXTEEN

THE REWARDS AND PERILS
OF STARDOM

Major lawsuits were threatening the production of the big budget movie 'The Greek Tycoon.' But granite faced actor Anthony Quinn wasn't the slightest bit worried. All around him, controversy raged about the movie which remarkably resembled the life story of Aristotle Onassis, a Greek shipping tycoon who had passed away in 1975. His widow, the former Mrs. Jacqueline Kennedy, and his daughter Christina, were incensed by the resemblances to them and their family and were threatening to sue the producers and the Mexican-born Quinn.

It was not too difficult to detect the uneasy climate on the film set when I arrived in Corfu in 1977 to make sense of the perplexities.

Anthony Quinn told me he felt comfortable in playing the title role because if it came to a legal show down, he would tell the courts that Onassis actually asked him to play his double.

Quinn had already triumphed as 'Zorba The Greek,' but after that his career went into a dive. "For five or six years I had a dry spell and I was desperately trying to find another Zorba. But there wasn't one. I began to think I was a misfit. The secret is learning to live with your hang-ups and with each season of your life."

Now, Quinn was adamant that there could not be any obstacle to portraying Onassis.

He told me: "Six months before Mr. Onassis died he called me and suggested I should play him in a film. He said to me: 'Somebody is going to do it someday Tony, why not you? I'd be very happy about it — because I know you will be kind to me.' Another reason

Mr. Onassis asked me to play him was because he thought I looked like him. 'Tony,' he said. 'We're so much alike and we have one thing in common. We're both Zorbas.'"

The actor nodded wistfully. "Yes. Onassis was a Zorba. He never lost touch with his people even though he possessed such wealth. So on this issue my conscience is clear."

His words were unlikely to sooth Jackie O or Christina who were apparently ready to proceed with their legal action if the story got too close.

But how close is close? I asked around the film set.

Quinn's role was that of a Greek shipping tycoon named Theo Tomasis who just happened to own a private island, a fabulous yacht and who married the widow of an assassinated American president. He even had a beloved son who is killed... just like Onassis. Actress Jacqueline Bisset, his bride, was named Liz Cassidy in the script but might well be mistaken for a lady who once lived in the White House. I found that also in the cast was a 'fiery opera singer' who would remind everyone of Maria Callas.

I questioned the producers Allen Klein and Nico Mastorakis but they refuted the suggestion that it was a movie about Onassis.

"This all comes from a novel," Nico told me, although I was not convinced. My suspicions deepened when I saw Quinn appear on set wearing a wig to thicken his thinning grey hair and donning heavy-rimmed spectacles that accentuated his likeness to the late Mr. Onassis.

In the saloon of the magnificent La Belle Simone, the yacht owned by Theo Tomasis in the film, Quinn told me simply, "There are elements of his life here — yes. That's inevitable. How can a dramatist omit Onassis when he writes about a Greek tycoon?"

Director Lee Thompson must have read my doubts. He told me that the story line was more of a fable loosely based on Onassis's life.

"It is the story of a man who loved four women all at the same time with equal passion."

It was a theme that rang true for Quinn.

The star overheard our conversation and he related to me: "It is not only possible for a man to love four women at once — I have experienced it myself. I don't know where nature says that you should only love one woman. That's a law imposed on us by man."

He went on: "I am not the kind of man who washes up the dishes or puts his slippers by the fireside."

The Rewards and Perils of Stardom

Was he not upsetting women's rights by holding these views?

He laughed at my suggestion: "The only way to fight a woman is to grab your hat and run."

Filming continued despite the threat of lawsuits and I left Anthony Quinn optimistic that Onassis would have approved this 'fabled' version of his life. The likeness was unmistakable and it was thought that at the end of the day Jackie O and Christina may also have approved Quinn's exacting portrayal. No writs were served.

****

Brigitte Bardot came to London in 1963 to film 'The Adorable Idiot.' There was a frenzy on the streets as fever-struck fans relentlessly trailed her night and day while she was filming. The police had to be called to contain the riot that occurred in Hampstead where one of the movie scenes was being shot. Brigitte, portraying an English spy, was to be seen stepping from a house into a waiting armoured car. But the French film unit could not get the shots they needed as a five-hundred-strong crowd surged forward to block their cameras. Two attempts were made to capture the scene but, finally, police had to order the film unit to quit the site because of the obstruction the crowd was causing. For the producers, the loss of a day's shoot cost thousands of pounds in lost money.

Brigitte, in a sweater and jeans, was running late for her Press conference at the Westbury Hotel in London. Her plane had been delayed and she was behind schedule.

I was among a throng of hacks who took their seats in a rather congested conference room.

Hemmed in by the crowd and looking dazed, she went straight to her suite — for a bath. And the crowd waited another eighty minutes.

At long last, she reappeared at the door of the conference room and, sipping a glass of champagne, asked: "Why did they do this to me? Why all this fuss?"

Brigitte had to inch her way into the room passing through a battery of elbow-pushing cameramen.

There was nowhere for her to sit so I offered her my seat. But she motioned me to sit back down. To my surprise, she curled herself down on the carpet to squat between my knees to answer all the questions fired at her by the journo posse gathered around her.

The Beatles and Beyond

I had some questions that I would have liked to have asked her about the film, but in order to do so, I realised that I would have to lean rather awkwardly over her head to get her attention. I knew I would have to wait my turn.

Fortunately, I did manage to get a chat with Brigitte in her suite later. Over a Scotch, she told me that she could not understand the impact she was making and why so many people were interested in her.

"Wherever I have gone in London it has been the same. I am pursued everywhere. Why is it happening to me?"

Brigitte Bardot was frequently in the headlines. There were to be many relationships and marriages in Brigitte's future life. In the Mirror newsroom it was a recurring question on who Brigitte might marry next. She had a much-publicised romance with heart throb French singer Sacha Distel but when it ended he told me: "I'm glad I didn't marry Brigitte. I just didn't want to become Mr Bardot."

For Brigitte there were four consecutive husbands who agreed to live with such a label.

One of them, her first husband and film producer Roger Vadim, made contact with her sixteen years after their divorce. He wanted her to star in his new screen movie 'Don Juan' in a love scene.

But then Roger revealed something very different and persuaded Brigitte to go along with it. She would be appearing in a same-sex love scene with the English actress Jane Birkin.

Jane told me: "I play the dominated wife of a nouveau rich man who is befriended by Brigitte, a female Don Juan and man-slayer. Suddenly the cameras switch to a scene where we are in bed together and everyone is left to guess whether Brigitte has changed her attitudes about the opposite sex."

Jane went on: "There were fifty cameramen and technicians in the studio when we shot the sequence. The jealousy it caused!" She smiled and added, "I think that the only reason this particular sequence was possible was because Brigitte and I are so physically opposite. She has big boobs and no hips — my dimensions are in reverse. Against Brigitte I was like a mouse. Brigitte really is a star. She has tremendous panache."

Another scene between the sheets sparked a very different reaction when it was filmed in Madrid in 1973. I arrived to catch the incorrigible Spike Milligan in bed once more, only this time it was with Raquel Welch. Stranger bed partners would have been harder to imagine. The two had been brought together by American director Dick Lester for his big budget version of the Alexandre Dumas classic 'The Three Musketeers.'

Spike, donning white nightgown and floppy bed-cap, reduced the camera crew to hysterics when he climbed into a fourposter bed with Raquel.

"Is this going to be called 'Last Tango in Madrid?'" he asked. "Someone had better warn the censor."

Dick Lester told him to stick to the script. "Spike, this isn't the Goon Show!" he reminded Spike.

Raquel, in a white nightdress, could not contain her laughter over Spike's antics as he edged closer to her on the bed.

Raquel was cast as Mme. Bonancieux the Queen's dressmaker in the court of Louis XIII who is so bound in her duties at the Royal palace that she is only able to sleep with her middle-aged innkeeper husband, played by Spike, once a week.

"Only once a week?" cried Spike in protest. "Then we'd better make the most of it!"

"Cut!" yelled Dick Lester. "Spike! Behave!"

"What no improvisations?" Spike retorted.

"None!" shouted Lester.

Afterwards, Spike remarked: "It's not likely to get an X certificate. And I know what my fellow Goons will say. That I missed my chance! They will think it should have gone to Steve McQueen," he said but then, producing his Goon-like humour, he had his own explanation for winning the part: "Well folks, it was like this... I went along to Finchley Labour Exchange and said: 'Have you got a film with Raquel Welch?' Of course I didn't realise then, in accepting the job, it meant going to bed with the lady. You can't get a job these days without a catch in it."

Spike on a film set? Beware The Three Musketeers. They had a loose cannon to contend with.

****

When I caught up with Charlotte Rampling, she told me she was enjoying a second lifetime. That was how she thought of herself in 1973 after surviving the turbulent, decadent Swinging Sixties. "I was like the leader of a cult," she told me as we talked about her days as the original Chelsea Girl. "It was a wonder I ever emerged alive. Marriage and the baby have totally changed my way of life. I'm far, far happier."

She added, "I came into the film industry when they were searching for young people to identify with the new generation. It was like a tidal wave. From dawn to dusk there were parties, premieres and discos. At times I felt I couldn't cope. But I was determined to prove I could act. It took time to convince people that I was serious about it, but in the end I won them over."

****

Kim Novak talked frankly about the one thing absent from her life: children.

"It's something I have come to terms with," Kim told me. We met at Shepperton studios on the set of the film 'Tales that Witness Madness' in 1972. The actress said, "At least by not having children I've made some positive contribution towards the problem of the world's population explosion!"

She explained, "I love children, really I do — but as long as they belong to someone else. Even if I did have children of my own, who is to say they would be better than any others?"

Kim told me about the family she had acquired. On her clifftop home in California, she kept a menagerie of wild animals. "You should see my house now. It's full of animals."

She delved into her handbag to show me a picture of a raccoon scuttling up one of her bed-posts.

"Does he swing off the chandelier, too?" I joked.

Kim laughed. "All of the animals wander in and out — they have the liberty to do as they please."

Her family included a llama, two goats, three horses and their foals, and dogs and cats, all sheltered in the paradise of her home. "You can talk with animals as you would human beings," she said. "And they've made me a much more honest person. You cannot fake anything — or cheat or deceive an animal. They have incredible perception."

Didn't men have the same kind of perception? Kim smiled. "I don't think they have. After all, women can talk themselves out of any situation!"

****

It was hard to believe that the American star Dustin Hoffman had any problems when he was earning more than £1 million a year.

The Rewards and Perils of Stardom

I was curious to know the root of Dustin's troubles, especially when he confided to me that he was consulting a psychiatrist five times a week at £30 a session. We spoke in London in 1971 as he headed for a holiday across Europe.

"Most people think I am putting them on about the psychiatrist," he told me. "They wonder why someone making as much money as me should need to go for analysis. But money, however much you make, doesn't solve life's tensions and pressures. It may even increase them. I find analysis essential to get me through the day. It helps me break down tension and put everything into perspective. It also helps me make the right decisions."

Hoffman, then thirty-four years old and the star of blockbusters 'The Graduate' and 'Midnight Cowboy', was candid about his insecurities: "I haven't a lot of faith in myself when it comes to decision time. Some artists think they know all the answers but just one mistake can halt their careers. I don't move on an important step until I have consulted my closest friends — and my psychiatrist."

The vision of Dustin stretched out on a psychiatrist's couch got closer to reality when thinking about his most recent film at the time, 'Who Is Harry Kellerman and Why Is He Saying Those Terrible Things About Me?' in which he played a pop star whose mind spins into a neurotic turmoil — until he finishes up in analysis on a sofa.

I ventured to suggest whether his problems stemmed from his million-dollar demands for making a picture and whether he was putting too much pressure on himself.

"Of course I ask for as much as I can get," he agreed. "But I've never turned down a film I wanted to do because of money. If I believe in a film, I'll do it. I have turned down lucrative movies because I haven't gone for the part."

Success, said Dustin, had changed him immensely.

"The best I ever saw myself was a supporting actor at the age of forty. Even when I got 'The Graduate' some voices were raised as to why the director Mike Nichols had cast such an ugly guy like me into a lead role. What I didn't realise was that I really wanted to be adored and loved to become a sex symbol."

The American actor had one ambition left — to be secure in his own mind.

"I've got everything now and I cling to it because I like it. But one day I want to jump off the merry-go-round of success and settle down into an unhindered family life where I can make all the decisions. Myself.''

He laughed as I re-joined: "And just where would that leave your shrink?''

****

It could have been a journey into the past. Nevertheless, I decided to make it, the short hop across to Ireland and County Cork. Few showbusiness writers would have turned down the opportunity of interviewing one of Hollywood's truly greatest legends Fred Astaire. His incredible tap-dancing career may have been over at the age of seventy-seven but he had been dragged out of retirement by the movie moguls to revive his film career.

Fred's straight-acting role in 'The Purple Taxi' was that of an eccentric village doctor trying to cope with a bunch of people who had assembled in Ireland with the idea of burying their past lives.

It seemed a mere coincidence that Fred wanted to bury his past too. He didn't want to talk about the golden days of Hollywood when he was clipping the boards on his way to stardom.

"I can't conjure up old memories," said Fred. "Because I believe people are pretty bored with me talking about those vintage Hollywood days. And my dancing.''

Fred looked fit and well and as lean as he was in in his dancing years. So much so that taking a break on the film set, he was confronted by a jolly-faced Irish woman who sought his autograph and told him her children thought he was wonderful in 'That's Entertainment.'

The fan happily departed with Fred's autograph intact but returned a few minutes later with a group of friends and persuaded the star to pose for a photograph with them all. Again, Fred obliged but was anxious to resume our broken conversation.

"I do hope we've seen the last of this particular lady," muttered Fred.

His words had hardly lost their meaning when the same woman was hovering over him once more.

"Fred!" she cried out, confident that she could regard the Hollywood idol as an old friend. "There's a pianist in the bar opposite. I've told him that you'll come and sing and dance for us all!''

Fred's patience snapped. "That's enough," he retorted, his face flushed. "I'm afraid I'm not going into any bar. And I won't sing and dance for anyone.''

His words were so firm that the woman retreated by a yard and squinted through her glasses.

"Look, I don't mean to be rude," Fred sighed when he saw her hurt expression. "But I am busy here making a film and I just cannot spare any more time."

The woman departed. Fred shrugged and turned to me. "The trouble is they still think of me as they did forty years ago. As though I could get up and sing and dance like I did in those days. I can't sing or dance anymore and I haven't done so for years. You see when you dance it's got to be perfection and you cannot settle for anything less. I didn't ever want to put a toe out of line and I might have done that if I had gone on. I've led a tremendously energetic life and when I danced I expended every bit of energy I had to give. When I reached seventy, then I knew it was time to stop."

In his younger years, Fred and his sister Adele were seen as the most famous dancing partnership on Broadway. When Adele married, Fred took on a succession of new partners — Ginger Rogers, Cyd Charisse, Betty Hutton, Eleanor Powell, Rita Hayworth and Paulette Goddard among them.

"One of the constant questions I get thrown at me is whether I've got a favourite co-star. How could I answer such a question and upset them all? So I always give the fans the same answer. I come up with 'Bing Crosby' and that gets me out of trouble."

Fred Astaire's dancing days were over, but he had already created his legacy, that of an entertainment genius who shone through such colourful and extravagant Hollywood musicals as 'Lady Be Good' 'The Barkeleys of Broadway' and 'Let's Dance.'

****

It was well-known that Sean Connery was a canny negotiator. So it was no surprise when I discovered that Connery had been persuaded back into the role of James Bond that he had previously quit, declaring "I just can't stand it any more."

Even the Queen had asked Connery "Is this really your last Bond film?" at the world premiere of 'You Only Live Twice' at the Odeon in London's Leicester Square in 1967.

"Yes, I'm afraid it is," Connery replied.

The Queen had pressed on with the interrogation: "Did you feel you were being type-cast?"

Connery laughed and confessed: "Yes I think you are right, ma'am."

In fact, by the time he spoke to the Queen, Connery had already shaken off the suave, sophisticated Bond image. He was wearing an impeccable dinner suit but he sported a thick moustache and long hair in preparation for his next film, a Western.

So producer Cubby Broccoli was left to find a new Bond and after an increasingly frantic search finally opted to cast George Lazenby, a little-known Australian actor and former model, to take over the role in 'On Her Majesty's Secret Service.'

However, the voluble Mr. Lazenby's services were not retained and the producers (with another of Ian Fleming novels 'Diamonds Are Forever' ready to start shooting) turned back to Connery in another attempt to lure him back into the role he had made famous. They succeeded — at a price.

But it was not as though that had any bearing on Connery. He was elated by the deal.

"I was really bribed back into it," he grinned, stirring a cup of mint tea at the Dorchester Hotel in 1971. "But it served my purpose."

What had he thought of Lazenby as Bond?

"I felt he had had a fair crack at it, but it was wrong to expect someone with so little experience to cope with a character like Bond. On the screen he looks so easy to play, but there's an art in making things look easy that only comes with professionalism."

I asked him who was next in the follow-up Bond epic 'Live and Let Die' already announced for the following year?

"I don't know. Roger Moore is on the cards, I suppose. But whoever it is I don't envy him. There is a 6-1 chance of making it. Public tastes change. They might say they've stomached enough of Bond. This might happen to 'Diamonds Are Forever.' Who can say?"

Was there one word of advice Connery could pass on to the next 007? He joked: "I'd tell him to have a good look at the small print before he signs the contract."

Connery declined to say precisely how much he got for his film, but insiders speculated that it was well over a million dollars.

"Apart from the money, I got a deal to make two pictures of my own choice. It was too tempting to turn down," said Connery.

So Connery reported back and 'Diamonds Are Forever' was awaiting him on the Pinewood production floor.

The Rewards and Perils of Stardom

In the meantime, George Lazenby was feeling desolate. After being told he was no longer needed as Bond he made a stormy exit out of London for Spain and hit the bottle hard.

"I collapsed one day and friends thought I had died. I didn't breathe for ten minutes. It was terrifying," he told me when we met in 1973.

But, he said on his own admission — he felt he had blown it.

"I thought I was God's gift to the acting profession and I lost my head," George confessed.

"There was a row over fees and I thought I could dictate the odds. I learned I couldn't. The trouble was I lived Bond out of the studio as well as in. I had to have a Rolls to go around in and women just threw themselves at me if I stepped into a night club because they saw me as Bond."

His Bond co-star Diana Rigg said that Lazenby had been almost impossible to work with. Others in the cast felt the same.

George Lazenby nodded. "I remember the parting words of Diana — yes I rowed with her too — on the film set. She said, 'one day we will sit down and talk about it all.' What she meant was when I had grown up. Well, I believe I have at last. I'm not going to play a movie star anymore — unless there's a camera there."

Before being called to play Bond again, Sean Connery was diverting into a different kind of adventure when filming 'The Man Who Would Be King' in the Atlas Mountains of Morocco. He and his co-star Michael Caine were cast as two ex-British Army soldiers who set themselves up as kings in a land known as Kaferistan where no white man had set foot.

Caine and Connery were close friends and so their easy working relationship on set gave famed director John Huston a problem-free task. Michael Caine's wife of two years Shakira, a former Miss World beauty queen, was also cast in the movie in the role of Roxanne. I flew with photographer Joe Bangay to Morocco to cover the story but other than the magnificent scenery we were to leave the film set with very little to report. No tears, no tantrums, no high jinks... what had gone wrong with the film industry?

CHAPTER SEVENTEEN

THE GHOSTWRITER

Britt Ekland was at the wheel of her newly acquired vintage Rolls Royce and I was sat next to her as we drove through Chelsea and Fulham. Britt was an avid collector of art deco antiques and she possessed a shrewd eye for a bargain. But on that particular day, money was not a worry. Just a week earlier I had just given Britt a cheque for £20,000 — the first instalment of her pending memoirs 'True Britt' — which I was ghost writing for the Swedish actress.

At that point in time, my days at the Daily Mirror had come to an end. My showbusiness column had been axed despite the protest of a dozen in-house sub editors and, although in lieu I had been appointed as chief showbusiness correspondent, I could not settle into the new role. One morning a circular letter arrived on the desks of all the editorial staff. The newspaper was looking for redundancies. I put in my application and went ahead with it resisting flattering overtures from the editor's executives to change my mind.

My objective was to start afresh and in journalistic-speak that meant going solo — and so it seemed appropriate that 'Solo' should be the name of my literary and syndication company.

Britt was one of my first clients and driving out with her that sunny day, hopping in and out of antiques and bric-a-brac shops, provided a restful break from the book's preparation. It was a fun day. That is, until I returned to my office in the late afternoon. I got a call from Britt's very irate manager Don Arden.

"What the hell did you give that money to Britt for?" he bellowed. "That money should have gone to me. I look after her financial affairs. Just look at what she has done with it. She has gone out and bought a bloody Rolls Royce with red velvet upholstery and cushions! She is riding around town in it like a high-class hooker from a Parisian boudoir."

I protested, perhaps a little meekly unaware of any contractual arrangements Britt had. "But Don," I felt compelled to clarify, "It's Britt's own book. Surely the money belongs to her..." But Don Arden was not a man to argue with. He had a fearsome reputation in Tin Pan Alley. He was known as The Godfather of the industry — a man never to be crossed. It was a reputation that stemmed from a day in 1966 when, with two heavies, he decided to pay a visit to the fifth floor offices of a rival manager Robert Stigwood who had apparently attempted to entice away a pop group called 'The Small Faces' from Arden's stable of stars. Stigwood (or 'Stiggy' as he was known) was physically grappled with, held by his ankles upside down outside his balcony window and Arden threatened to drop him onto the pavement below if he did not desist from his attempts to steal away the group from his control. Stiggy groaned agreement before he was released. There were other hair-raising stories too of beatings, knee cappings and violent assaults on anyone who stood in Arden's way or anyone brave enough to say he was cooking the books and holding the royalties others were due. Arden enjoyed the notoriety of his fearsome reputation. But in business he was out-manoeuvred by his daughter Sharon, who married Ozzy Osbourne against her father's wishes and finally took over Arden's empire before becoming a television personality in her own right.

However, my problem that day was to try and calm the situation down. I called Britt who dismissed the episode lightly.

"I will talk to Don and straighten things out," she said. And she did. In the interest of keeping the peace, I didn't feel inclined to tell her about Arden's image of her driving through town in her vintage Roll's Royce.

I had known the Swedish actress long before the days she starred in the James Bond film 'The Man With the Golden Gun', as far back as when she first came to London and checked into the Dorchester Hotel and there to meet, and later marry, Peter Sellers. But I did not expect her to remember me and invite me to ghost write her memoirs.

I was in Scotland on holiday with my family when I collected a call from Britt then at her Los Angeles home.

"Would you help me write my book?" she asked.

I took the first available plane. Britt, rarely out of the headlines, wanted to put the record straight about her stormy marriage to Peter Sellers and her relationships with Hollywood's top suitors Warren Beatty, George Hamilton and Rod Stewart. Many dismissed the book 'True Britt' as a "kiss and tell" of classic proportions but for Britt, often maligned through the years, it was a way of restoring sanity to her life. As Britt later observed, "Doing my book was like living my life all over again on a shrink's couch."

When the book came out, Britt appeared on the Michael Parkinson television show and gave the distinct impression that she had written every single word herself. Readers might be forgiven for assuming that the featured authors actually write their own books. In most cases, such painstaking labours have been undertaken by an anonymous ghostwriter — or pen-pusher — adept at immersing their souls and skills into a celebrity mental frame and producing a definitive life story for public consumption. In truth, the rich and famous have rarely got sufficient time on their hands or professional skills to devote to writing their past experiences in book form. It is the ghostwriter who undertakes the research, transcribes endless tapes, checks dates and facts, puts the prose together before delivering the ultimate manuscript on time to the publisher's desk. All of that for a microscopic credit line inside the book jacket!

A well-meaning friend rang me after Britt's appearance on the Michael Parkinson show.

"I thought you had written the book dear boy? Britt seems to be claiming it all. You must feel hurt."

"No," I replied unruffled. "I consider her remarks to be flattering. They say that is the game. You've got to make the celebrity feel that they've done it all themselves."

The one mistake I made was to momentarily bask in Britt's spotlight.

Television presenter Janet Street Porter asked me to appear on her 'Friday Night Saturday Morning' television show and suggested that other actresses might enlist my services as a writer in the wake of 'True Britt'.

"As a matter of fact I've had several calls from other actresses who want me to handle them," I said, swallowing the bait.

Luckily the show was being pre-recorded and I was able to persuade Janet to discard my faux pas to the cutting room floor!

Originally, my initiation into becoming a ghostwriter in 1968 was a baptism by fire. I was invited to write the memoirs of the capricious icon of the fifties, the socialite Lady Docker, known more widely to the world as Naughty Norah. She married three millionaire husbands in succession ("Love? Don't be silly. I married them all for their money.") Norah relished being regarded as the life and soul of an elite society pumping fresh sparkle into the bleak post war years that the Blitz-weary population wanted to leave behind. She was driven around in a gold-plated Daimler and held court for an elite corps of friends aboard the gleaming decks of her yacht the 'Shemara', at that time one of the world's most luxurious privately owned yachts.

But Norah was never less than petulant and confrontational. She managed to get into an unseemly feud with Prince Rainier of Monaco for tearing up a paper Monegasque flag decorating a table at a state banquet and as a result got herself banned from Monte Carlo and its previously welcoming harbour for the Shemara.

Now in London, her lawyer David Jacobs introduced me to her Ladyship and her husband — her third and final husband — the avuncular Sir Bernard Docker, the wealthy but dethroned boss of the Birmingham Small Arms Company (BSA). It was midsummer and we met in the salon aboard the Shemara moored on the Thames downstream from Tower Bridge. Pink champagne — always Norah's trademark tipple — was opened and the meeting got away to a warm and friendly start.

Norah, with a flourish of her hands, said: "How soon can we start this?"

One week later, I caught a plane to Jersey and took a cab to the Spanish-style villa overlooking Rozel Bay where Norah and Sir Bernard had been living for some years. I paid the cabbie off and pressed the front doorbell totally unprepared for the explosive scene that was to unfold.

A butler in a very smart winged collar shirt and traditional uniform opened the door and I told him that her Ladyship was expecting me.

Suddenly, Norah appeared behind him. She was wearing a pearl necklace and a black ensemble.

Inexplicably, she seemed angry at my arrival.

"Oh, it's you," she said venomously, "Well you can go back to London. I'm not going to write my book with you. You write about those dreadful long-haired pop people. They've ruined society and you can tell them that from me. Now be off with you!"

Clearly, she had read some of my Daily Mirror showbusiness

columns, from which I had been granted a four-week sabbatical to make a start on her book. I froze, utterly confounded by her outburst. I glanced down at my suitcase, portable typewriter and tape recorder equipment and gazed forlornly down the long sweeping drive after the disappearing taxi.

"I'm sorry," I stammered. "But could I ask your butler if he would be kind enough to call another taxi for me to get back to the airport?"

Norah sighed. "Well you'd better come in for a minute while you wait."

Once inside the house, incongruously furnished by the relics of past mansions she once owned, Norah thawed a little and invited me to stay onto lunch, having established that the next plane back to Gatwick wasn't until 5:00pm.

Frank the butler was ordered to set another place at the dining table and dispense a glass of her ladyship's customary pink champagne.

I quickly learned that there's nothing like a long and indulgent lunch to tell a life story — and Norah did her best to recount hers in one sitting.

When I gently reminded her that I had to get back to the airport to catch my plane, she snapped, "Oh look here. This story has got to be written. I might end up with someone I really don't like..."

Frank escorted me to an old retainer's room — a palatial bedroom filled with chandeliers and adorned in decadent gold chintz. These were to be my living quarters for the next fortnight.

Unfortunately, my appointment as Norah's ghostwriter was still a verbal one. She had not signed the legal contract which was still in my attaché case and this sad omission on my part was to become an important instrument of blackmail for her over the next couple of weeks.

Every evening, after a day's taping and research, she promised to sign the contract to put things on a more formal footing. But she kept me dangling on a piece of string, like a marionette puppet, and the contract remained unsigned.

Within a matter of days, she threw a dinner party for her Jersey society friends. Bon viveur and pink champagne flowed long into the night. Norah, ever the acerbic and dominant conversationalist, ensured that I was sat next to her like the proverbial and obedient lapdog ready to testify to the authenticity of her past exploits. Poor Bernard was similarly cast, grunting the occasional acknowledgment before nodding off.

The Ghostwriter

In the early hours Norah was still in full cry — and then she dropped her bombshell.

She turned to me and standing to her feet announced: "My friends don't know everything that has happened in my life. Don — let's read my book to them! Let them have a taste of what's to come..."

I hesitated. "But Norah we've only got one chapter complete. The rest are not even prepared".

"I insist!" she cried, "Otherwise I'm not going to sign that damned contract. Is that clear?"

Her friends, including Sir Billy Butlin (the famed entrepreneur who founded Butlins holiday camps) leaned forward to hear more. It is a moment I look back on with great embarrassment but at the time I had to consider the financial implications. I reasoned that, like Norah, most of the guests were pretty pie-eyed. I gathered a first draft chapter on the Monte Carlo affair and read it to the assembled dinner party.

Norah wept after I delivered the third paragraph and sporadic cries of woe punctuated the subsequent passages. When I had finished, Norah dabbed the tears from her face and, with a magnificent flourish, summoned her butler Frank to escort her to retire for the night. Bernard, meanwhile, was still snoozing.

"You see what this book does to me!" she exclaimed to her bewildered guests. "I will send you all a copy. Goodnight!"

Norah signed the contract the next morning and life ever after was to become a hectic helter-skelter of fun, travel and fur flying for her faithful new servant — me, the ghostwriter.

My often-humiliating experiences in writing Norah's book, albeit becoming a best seller, stayed indelibly with me through the years. My added persona as a celebrity ghostwriter imbued me with a far-reaching view of life, where I was a witness to stories of prestige, vanity, tragedy, success and heartbreak.

At times it felt like my job as a ghostwriter had also assumed the role of a therapist, as tolerance, patience and persuasion had to be in unquenchable supply. I had to immerse myself in the very cloak of the subject celebrity and analyse their thoughts, their understanding, their careers and ambitions throughout the good and bad times. Although, fortunately, there was room for the ghostwriter to have some share in the glory, both financially and in terms of gaining a sense of personal achievement. Top professional ghosts were known to seek 50% of the revenue; others settled for 30% or 40%.

Their return depended on whether the work hit the best-sellers lists or if a newspaper bought serialisation rights. Either event meant a five-figure bonus for the ghostwriter, provided amicable agreement existed with the celebrity. Some ghostwriters were very highly regarded for their craft. Ernest Hemingway often sought the advice of my American peer A.E. Hotchner after his brilliant biography of the great man. Not many ghostwriters were as successful as Hotchner, however, who also produced the Doris Day and Sophia Loren autobiographies.

My next assignment concerned one of those pop stars that Norah loathed. I was commissioned to write Sandie Shaw's memoirs at the height of her fame, having won the Eurovision Song Contest with 'Puppet On A String.'

Thanks to Norah's global movements, I was now well accustomed to travelling across the globe to undertake commissions of this kind. Sandie was on holiday in Majorca and I joined her there to start the tapes running. At the time, there was a crippling heat wave on with temperatures soaring above the nineties, which meant that we could only work in the mornings. The afternoons were spent by the pool leisurely sipping long cool drinks until sunset.

The barefoot, waif-like Sandie had come through a turbulent love affair with a married man. It was this particular segment in her life which ultimately 'killed' the book in its tracks.

Her showbusiness agent Eve Taylor explained: "Sandie's family were not happy about the book. They felt that some things are better left unsaid."

They may have been right but at the time I thought "Why the hell didn't they tell me at the beginning?" I knew that a ghostwriter must learn to bury their losses and move on. Some ghosts, even after expending a solid year's labours, can walk away practically empty handed. Thankfully in this particular case Eve sent me a cheque in compensation for my aborted toils.

After that, I found myself in a similarly sunny milieu sprawled opposite Engelbert Humperdinck in a huge hot tub in Germany on one of his concert tours. This was to be an authorised biography and I carefully balanced the tape recorder on the edge of the pool while we sipped the compulsory glass of bubbly. It was a pretty painless and unique approach to getting a life story into print.

Engelbert's paperback book did well — but my next ghostwriting experience found me collaborating on a doctor's book about his years as an abortionist. It didn't work out at all and I felt I had to quit.

But, quite out of the blue, I was invited to write 'Fifty Years With Mountbatten' by the assassinated Earl's loyal valet and butler Charles Smith. It was a welcome relief from all of the other books I had encountered. I spent many days researching at Mountbatten's home 'Broadlands' in Romsey sifting through archives and taping Charles Smith's story at his picturesque staff cottage only a stone's throw away.

The butler was much admired by the Royal family. I dropped a note to Prince Charles asking for permission for certain correspondence to be reproduced and the Prince gave immediate consent.

Charles Smith, to his eternal credit, was loyal to the last. His book wasn't to be a 'tell-all' tome. My research had unearthed some startling facts about Mountbatten and his family. I put these facts to him to validate but his integrity was unflinching.

Was it true that his lordship and the Queen Mother had not always seen eye to eye? I pressed him.

"I can't recall any occasion when that occurred," the faithful servant answered. And what of these stories of Edwina's affair with Nehru? "I cannot comment," said Charles Smith, devotedly unforthcoming.

Charles contributed instead a wealth of warm and amusing anecdotes that gave a side to Mountbatten's character that the public never saw. And he talked in jocular reflection of his own feuds with Mountbatten. Unfortunately the butler died not long after the book appeared but he lived to see it become a best seller and to be published in America.

Finding myself once more in Los Angeles, my new client was David Bowie's ex-wife Angie Bowie. Angie wasn't an aspiring actress although she later pursued ambitions in those areas. I always thought she would be a natural and I came to wonder, when we began work on her first book of memoirs 'Free Spirit', just how much her ex-husband David Bowie owed his fame to her energy and bounce.

Their marriage was a bizarre union with scintillating stories of three-in-a-bed romps and proved to be a fascinating insight into the conception of Bowie's theatrical personas such as 'Ziggy Stardust' and 'Aladdin Sane'.

Angie worked on Bowie's career to possible suffocation point and the marriage may have hit the rocks because of it. When the reality descended and Angie was alone and devastated, I suggested that she should start afresh and channel that insatiable energy into her own career.

Angie gave it her best shot — starting with the book. She had a lot to get off her mind. She wanted to wipe away the bad memories. To help her through the day, as she racked her mind to pull out fresh incidents to record, she would often light a king-size joint, engulfing me in huge clouds of aromatic smoke in the process. There were times when I became more stoned than Angie. Everything that's said about the passive smoker is true!

I recovered from the experience and retreated from Los Angeles to return to London where we successfully completed the book.

All ghostwriters search for a blockbuster and my hopes rose high when the singer Eddie Fisher called me. We had become close friends from the days when he was married to Elizabeth Taylor. Now, Eddie, still bruised from his divorce from Liz, contemplated doing his book and we discussed his plans over dinner in Chelsea.

"There is so much to tell," he said. "How do you think it will go down?"

I smiled: "Eddie your life story would be a blockbuster…"

"Don, you wouldn't be free would you to come over to the States and take it on?"

I didn't have to give it a second thought. "When do we start?" I asked Eddie.

Three weeks later I was booked into the luxury Caesars Palace hotel in Las Vegas where Eddie was renting a house located on the outskirts of the neon lit city. Eddie greeted me warmly and together we went over the preparatory ground for the book and pinpointed some research that had to be done. We thought we would start taping his story on the following Monday as he had to go to Los Angeles for a business meeting. "Don't worry Don," he said. "It will only take a couple of days".

I spent the weekend trying my best not to be tempted by the Vegas gaming tables. Eddie duly called me Monday morning saying he was ready to start work on the book. But the car he promised to send over to collect me did not arrive that morning or afternoon. I phoned him but the line was out of order. I tried the line repeatedly throughout the day and late into the evening before deciding to wait until the following morning to see if I could reach him. But again, I could not get any response. The operator told me the line had been disconnected. I got a cab to the house but to my dismay I found it was locked up and there was no sign of anyone there. It was completely deserted.

I pushed a note through the door hoping that Eddie would get back and urged him to call me. It seemed a complete mystery. What could have possibly happened? Then, at around lunch time, the phone rang in my room. I hastily picked up the receiver with a degree of relief. But nothing had prepared me for the conversation that followed.

"Is that Mr. Don Short?" a distant voice asked.

"Yes?" I replied.

"Well — Mr Short I think I had better warn you that you must cease from writing Eddie Fisher's proposed book. We are the attorneys acting for the New York publishers who have already paid Mr Fisher $100,000 in advance for his memoirs which he has so far failed to deliver. Any contract you have signed with Mr Fisher we will seek to declare as invalid in the court actions we shall immediately commence if you persist in doing this book".

As I put the phone down, I realised then why Eddie had vanished: the lawyers must have already contacted him.

My flight and hotel expenses left me £6,000 out of pocket. I felt as sorrowful as one of the thousands of gamblers who lose their shirts in Las Vegas. To think I didn't risk as much as one nickel in any of the slot machines, but still trudged home a big loser!

I heard nothing more from Eddie Fisher until eighteen months later when he came to London and asked to meet me in his hotel. He wanted to apologise properly, saying he had not understood the complexities of the contract he had signed many years earlier.

"The book is coming out Don but with a writer they had apparently commissioned," he said. "I can only say sorry."

Although smarting with anger and turning over the frustrations I felt at the time, I wished him well. That was the last I saw of him. Close colleagues said I should have billed him to recover my financial losses. I nodded my head ruefully but then another friend remarked that if I made a claim it could all end in litigation. "Lawsuits in America can be a very costly pursuit. And where would that get you?" he said. My feelings exactly.

It was when I was back home that I picked up the call from Britt Ekland, still basking in the success of her career. Her daughter Victoria by her marriage to Peter Sellers was en route to England to see her half-sister Sarah and half-brother Michael, who was considering a biography on his late father Peter Sellers, and the idea was that Victoria and Sarah would help him with it. Could I ghost the book for them? Britt asked. They turned out to be three tremendous personalities and I felt a surge of sympathy for them. Peter Sellers, in one of his rash piques, had seen fit to cut them out of his will and left them a paltry £750 each to survive on. His young wife Lynne Frederick was to inherit his millions, his cars, the Swiss chalet and the continuing royalties from his Pink Panther films as well as other movies.

Just where did it leave the Sellers children? They considered a lawsuit but their father's business affairs were so complex that their lawyers could not agree on where to start proceedings ("in Switzerland or London?"). Eventually they decided to take no action.

I was glad that their book, "P.S. I Love You" hit the charts to put them on their feet again.

But things didn't always pan out the way I wanted them to. I sent a note to Paul McCartney to see if he might consider his autobiography having been pressed by many publishers who were aware of my old Beatle connections. Paul sent me an affectionate reply calling me a lovable old rogue and saying no to the book as "I am up to my elbows in celluloid. Lots of love — Paul, Linda and the kids."

Now I know who I am!

In earlier times, and when he was at the peak of his career, I asked Richard Harris whether he had considered doing his book? Richard shook his head woefully and said, "Giving away 50% would only add another horror story to my life and I have lived enough of them already."

Those words surfaced in my memory and I felt that my days as a ghost had finally been laid to rest. It was time to move on.

CHAPTER EIGHTEEN

GOING SOLO

It was an unexpected letter from an unexpected source, with an unexpected urgency. Jackie Collins, the author of the decade's most daring novels, was writing to ask me to ban a book — a book being written by her own father.

Her father Joe Collins, a theatrical agent of long days past, was writing his autobiography and when news of his intentions reached his daughters Jackie and her famous actress sister Joan they became a little alarmed. I could only surmise from the tone of Jackie's missive that they didn't want any of the family's skeletons pulled out of the closet.

My literary and syndication agency was based in Kensington where I had built a twelve-strong team and we established ourselves as something of a home for celebrity authors and freelancers, as well as looking after the world-wide syndication of the Daily Mail group of newspapers and other global news sheets and magazines.

Our roster of celebrity authors expanded rapidly. Joe Collins made an appointment to see us having decided to write his life story with the help of a former Daily Express entertainment writer Judith Simons whom I knew well.

I did not have to think twice about taking the book on to our listings. I was certain that it would create keen interest among the mainline publishers.

Joe had led a remarkable career having become a theatrical agent as far back as 1931 and had helped luminaries like Peter Sellers, Roger Moore, Harry Secombe, and a host of others along the road to fame.

He was very proud of the achievements of Jackie and Joan and had tried to guide them in the choice of their careers. They didn't always follow his well-meant advice and from many aspects that was fortunate. Notably, he didn't think that the role of Alexis in the Hollywood blockbuster television series 'Dynasty' was right for Joan and tried to dissuade her from accepting the part. He also confessed he didn't read Jackie's books like 'Hollywood Wives' and 'The Stud' as "they're not my cup of tea."

But when I called him to make him aware of Jackie's letter to put a stop to his planned book, Joe was not best pleased.

"What is it they are worried about? If it's skeletons in the closet... well there are none," he retorted. "Leave it to me. I will talk to the girls and see what they are worried about."

Joe presumably smoothed things out with Jackie as I did not hear from her again and his book 'A Touch of Collins' went ahead under the Headline imprint. It was a heart-warming read underlining the pride that Joe had not only for Joan and Jackie but his entire family. It won praise from the critics.

Skeletons in the closet may have been a sharper obstacle for another of my writers Kenneth Passingham, who brought to my desk an unauthorised biography he had completed on singing star Shirley Bassey.

It had taken Ken several years to complete and it had all been a painful process. He lamented that Shirley had refused to cooperate with the book and said that she called all her friends and business associates telling them not to talk to him.

Some writers might well have thrown in the towel but Ken, undeterred, plodded on and with the final page written placed the manuscript down in front of me and asked if I could find a publisher for it.

Warily, I flicked over some of the pages and as I was doing so, Ken had to admit there was just one other snag he felt I should be aware of.

Shirley's lawyers had been in touch with him, saying they would take court action against him and any publisher who might be tempted to print his biography.

"They say it's full of inaccuracies but how can they know that when they haven't read it?" said Ken.

I knew Shirley well from my days on the showbusiness beat. She had a tough, tenuous life with many setbacks and tragedies. She was born and raised in Cardiff's Tiger Bay and the family grew up in poverty. Shirley had to take a job in a local factory before she set out on her career which was to take her to the zenith of the entertainment world. A remarkable feat in light of her impoverished background.

More so, when reaching international stardom, her career was often in recoil from the shock of family grief and tragedy. Two broken marriages, an ex-husband who committed suicide, a scandalous love affair with Australian actor Peter Finch, a daughter found drowned in the River Avon and many other distressing episodes beset her life.

I could understand why, when reading Ken's manuscript which delved deeper into the aspects of many of these sad events, the Welsh singer might have objected to the book's publication.

Reluctantly I returned the manuscript to Ken saying that if any lawsuits were instigated, it would probably cost more than any of the royalties he might have earned from its publication. He was bitterly disappointed.

Ken's next book, another unauthorised biography, was an in-depth profile of Sean Connery but again he ran into troubled waters legally when the book was published. In one of the chapters Ken had mistakenly related that Sean had missed out on a day's filming at Pinewood. It may have been regarded as a trivial error but the James Bond star did not like the implication that he had been unprofessional in his work. So Connery took Passingham to the High Court and was awarded £1,000 in damages which the actor donated to charity.

In the early days, I found the publishing world a difficult one to crack. Unlike the round-the-clock operations of newspapers, book publishers would sit on proposals for many months before making a decision. In the meantime, my office would be deluged with unsolicited manuscripts from writers and non-writers from all over the country. Telephone lines would be jammed with callers seeking advice on how to go about submitting a novel or a true-life story.

In my first year of breaking into the book trade, I trudged with a huge suitcase packed with manuscripts to the Frankfurt Book Fair in the hope of finding publishers who might wish to evaluate them and hopefully make an offer for one or another of them.

Every major publishing house in the world boasts a stand at Frankfurt, but I was soon to discover that their main objective is to sell the foreign rights of their existing books, and those in the pipeline, to other publishing houses in America, Australia and every other country on the planet.

Seeing a forlorn agent attempting to market a manuscript from his overladen suitcase was of no consequence to the actively engaged publishing house bosses.

"If it's as good as you say it is, then send it to me in London... New York... wherever," was the reply I was soon to become familiar with.

I returned to London with my suitcase as heavy as it had been when I set out. I realised just how naïve I was. I could distribute a one-page listing, yes, but that was as much as the publishing fraternity would accept on the hustle and bustle of the Frankfurt floor.

These were early days and I did not launch Solo as a registered company until 1978 after four years of freelancing. I engaged Mike Anderson, the Daily Mirror's retired Night News Editor, as my managing editor. Mike did not relish the idea of retirement and he was more than ready to join me. He was an erudite colleague if a little eccentric in his ways, as it struck me when he went about furnishing our very first office in Crystal Palace. Instead of installing desks, chairs and filing cabinets, Mike had given priority to a second hand temperamental refrigerator which he and his wife Jean had managed to lug up the creaky wooden staircase to the third floor of the tumbledown rooms we agreed to rent above a stationery shop.

Mike was truly a figure of the old school and no-one could have been harder working. I asked him to take charge of one of our first clients, a notorious lady known to the world as Christine Keeler.

She was anxious to write her memoirs and this time, she assured us, she would tell the truth about her torrid affair with Government minister John Profumo when he was the Secretary of State for War. The Profumo Affair, as it became known, rocked the Government and the nation. Profumo, it was suspected, had put national security at risk as one of Keeler's earlier lovers had been a Soviet diplomat. Scandal ensued.

With Mike, I met with Christine at her apartment off the Fulham Road. It was clear she had struck hard times. Curtains, carpets and furnishings all looked worn and threadbare. Her face was gaunt and strained.

At one time she had experienced the high life in fashionable society, having been drawn there like a butterfly from her early days as a model and showgirl in a West End cabaret club. Her potential book carried all the hallmarks of being a bestseller.

Going Solo

Mike began work on the project, but he quickly became victim to Christine's constant beck and call. If she wanted to get some shopping, then she would summon Mike to collect her in his vintage Austin car to carry out such errands.

There was little sight of preparations of the manuscript. I felt we were becoming enmeshed in a time-wasting operation and I called the project to a halt when I went for a drink in Keeler's local pub opposite her block of flats.

The landlord looked at me and said: "Mr. Short?"

Surprised he knew my name, I replied, "Yes, as it happens."

"Ah, good," he smiled. "I've got a bill for you here, sir, of £167."

"A bill of £167? How come?" I asked him quizzically.

"Oh yes," affirmed the landlord. "Christine told me I should give it to you and you would settle it."

To my slight irritation, I learned that Christine had been entertaining friends as well as putting the odd bottle of gin on the slate telling the landlord that we would be settling her account with him.

I sighed, but felt obliged to pay the bill, which left me wondering just how much Mike might have expended on Christine's shopping expeditions. I didn't ask or examine his expenses sheet. Instead, I told him that we should pull out of the project as Christine was just stringing us along with little intention of getting down to the nitty-gritty of her memoirs. Wearily, after all the exhaustive car trips, he agreed.

I just hoped that the next agent Christine approached would have more patience, and plenty of petrol in his tank!

Solo stayed in its rundown Crystal Palace office for nearly two years, but I was anxious to move our operation into our spiritual home of Fleet Street. Mike didn't like the idea as he lived close to the office. We amicably decided to split the agency. Mike formed a new concern he named Duo and I was happy for him to retain many of the forty freelance journalists whose interests we were looking after.

Finding a suitable office in Fleet Street was like playing a game of chess. There were to be so many moves before I could find Solo's right location. Offices in Drury Lane and Exeter Street were tried and tested before I found a spacious and more luxurious office beneath the BBC at Bush House only a short walk from Fleet Street. Solo's team was strengthened with the arrival of John Smallwood another retiree from the Daily Mirror, where he was once Night Editor.

We made good headway but again we were on the move a year or two later when we were offered an ideal office in the heart of Fleet Street. Above our given floor worked the London editorial staff of Rupert Murdoch's group of Australian newspapers and magazines. We were now nestled among our own kind.

We attracted many new writers and authors, bolstering our client list significantly. Celebrity books were becoming a lucrative passion for many publishers and I steered Solo largely on that course. We created a catalogue featuring many celebrity names and the top publishing houses, having disregarded us in the past, were now knocking at our door ready to consider any proposal we put before them.

Tennis legend Fred Perry was one of our first clients, followed by Irish singer Val Doonican, England cricket captain Mike Gatting, snooker player Jimmy White, actress Britt Ekland and a host of others. Most of their books catapulted into the best seller charts.

There were occasions when I felt it was realistic to diversify. As an agency we had to break out occasionally from our customary mould. But I left the office one night believing I had taken on a book and a client that might see us plunge out of our depth.

Gangster Charlie Richardson was brought to me by scriptwriter Bob Long who was helping the reformed prisoner to write his autobiography titled 'My Manor.' Charlie had been head of the infamous racketeering Richardson gang with his younger brother Eddie in the fold along with a pack of East End cutthroats and villains. They had been known as the 'torture gang' carrying out the most sadistic acts of violence on their enemies and rivals. They were said to break kneecaps, chop off fingers and toes with bolt cutters, pull out teeth with pliers and apply electric shocks to their victim's genitals. Charlie's gang were rivals to those run by the equally infamous Kray twins and there were turf wars between them resulting in a long and murderous feud.

Charlie and his gang were finally arrested in a dawn raid by the police and all appeared in the dock at the Old Bailey which was described as the 'Torture Trial' of 1967. Ringleader Charlie was sentenced to twenty-five years in gaol and was freed in 1984 purporting to be a reformed character. Bob Long promised he was but somehow I was feeling sceptical.

Lean, mean Charlie would drive a battered looking Capri to the office and we would sit and discuss his upcoming book for several hours. One afternoon, I had to introduce him to the prospective publishers at Sidgwick and Jackson. He drove me to their offices in Covent Garden and deliberately parked his car on double yellow lines which I alerted to him in passing.

"You could get towed away," I told him.

"Fuck 'em," said Charlie, slamming the door. "They won't dare touch that fucking car when they check it's mine."

After the meeting, the car was intact and there was no glimpse of a parking ticket although I could see two traffic wardens standing on the corner at the end of the narrow street. Charlie drove away at speed as though competing on a racing track.

We finally got the book published and Charlie was happy. Until that is, talk arose about the possibility of a film being made based on his memoirs. Charlie, no doubt eyeing a lucrative deal in the offing, rang me. "Just telling you now Don that I'm pulling out of our contract," he said. "Right. Got it?"

I must have felt meek that morning. I told Charlie: "Fine. I'll cancel the contract. Good luck with the film Charlie."

I did not hear from him again and I felt greatly relieved. I was left asking myself whether there was any proof in the saying that a leopard never changes its spots.

We were back on pristine ground and what a difference a day made. One of the nation's most acclaimed heroes Peter Gurney, regarded as the world's top bomb-disposal expert, brought his completed manuscript to us. It was astutely titled 'Braver Men Walk Away.' Peter Gurney had twice been awarded the George Medal for bravery as well as an MBE for gallantry, having defused hundreds of bombs to save countless lives.

From day to day, Gurney had spent most of his life defying death, ready to step into any emergency where bombs had been planted to cause mass destruction. His courage was beyond description. His fight against terrorism took him from the streets of Belfast to the IRA's mortar attack on No. 10 Downing Street, to the carnage of Lockerbie and to the scene of the bombing of Brighton's Grand Hotel. Yet Peter Gurney remained a modest, unassuming man and someone with a genuine sense of humour. His remarkable story was one that put others in the shade.

Solo continued to syndicate the features and photos of its stable of journalists at home and abroad. We also ran out our own features. Patrick Curtis, ex-husband of Hollywood star Raquel Welch, was ready to reveal the secrets of their marriage, showjumper Harvey Smith was to feature in a three-part series on the equestrian world and from most sources we were getting good feedback on our operations.

One summer I took a call from Sir David English the editor of the Daily Mail asking me if I could act as a consultant to the paper's syndication department. I had no hesitation in accepting the post. At that period, Solo was already handling photos and copy from the redtop tabloid The Sun and Murdoch's newspapers and magazines based in Australia. The Daily Mail was a prestigious account to become involved with. So I juggled my days to sit in most mornings on the Mail's syndication department housed in a dingy isolated office within the paper's Fleet Street headquarters. I could see how things could be improved and new initiatives taken and conveyed my advice to Sir David.

Newspapers at that point were in the throes of cutting costs and outsourcing many of their peripheral activities of which syndication was marked out as one. This brought Sir David to disband his syndication department and to invite Solo to take over the syndication of the paper along with its sister titles The Mail on Sunday and the Evening Standard on the proviso that I absorbed some of his staff into my operations at Solo.

I had no objections and, in any event, concluded that we needed that kind of support. Trevor York was an experienced syndication operator at the Mail and I put him in charge of our output working with two of his old colleagues Danny Howell and Geoff Malyon along with accountant John Appleton.

They were happy to enlist with Solo. It was a twenty-four-hour operation, getting stories and photographs out to global newspapers with their own deadlines to meet on different time zones to our own. We relied on DHL and Federal Express to ship our editorial packages, an exhausting routine which in the years ahead would be replaced with online transmissions.

One observation I made about newspaper 'buy-ups' — the widespread Fleet Street practice of paying celebrities and headline-making individuals for their stories — could be to develop such acquisitions across the board into books, films and television documentaries. It was an oversight that I drew to the attention of Sir David who saw the financial logic in my suggestion and one that we were to implement in the case of the seventeen-year-old South African born athlete Zola Budd.

Because of the apartheid system existing in South Africa at the time, their athletes were banned from running in all international events. The Daily Mail spotted a way round that, having found that Zola's grandfather was British. They brought the athlete to London and persuaded her to apply for British citizenship. Her application was fast tracked, no doubt accelerated by the Daily Mail's involvement, which caused anger to hundreds of other applicants who had been waiting years for British citizenship.

A Surrey hideaway was found for Zola and Mail reporters ensured that rival newspapers were not going to intervene on the paper's exclusive into which some £100,000 had been invested in the enterprise.

Apparently, Sir David English at conference passed an accolade in my direction describing me as 'an entrepreneur.' If I was to live up to such a description, I had to rake back some of the money expended on this major project. So syndication of the story around the world was vital, along with a book and a film.

Zola, who always ran barefoot in her races, began to break track records wherever she appeared and earned her place with the British Olympic team to compete in the 1984 Olympics in Los Angeles. It was there that she was faced with strong competition in the 3,000 metres event with world champion Mary Decker and other star runners in the line-up.

But all the media attention was focused on Zola and Mary. It was labelled the race of the century. Disaster struck. The two athletes collided sprawling Mary off the track with a hip injury and unable to finish the race. Zola, drained physically and emotionally, could only manage to finish in seventh place. Both athletes recovered and no blame was attached to either of them. Clipping legs, elbows and ankles was always considered a track risk.

Zola's story had to be told and I recommended a biography that the Mail's stalwart journo Brian Vine took on, completing the book in rapid time, and which I placed with Stanley Paul publishers. The Mail had also gone ahead with a film and the paper's distinguished sportswriter Ian Wooldridge narrated and interviewed Zola for the cameras.

It was a difficult film to make, with inserts of news reel clips, and there were parts when the quietly spoken Zola was almost inaudible on the big screen.

Nevertheless, I took the tapes to Alan Kean the head of ITC Film Distributors and he called me back within days to say that he would give the film "Zola" its world premiere at the Classic One theatre in London's Haymarket.

Congratulations on the deal came from the paper's hierarchy and the film premiere was billed as a gala occasion. However, the night was also an opportunity for protest from a band of anti-apartheid activists waving placards and noisily invading the Haymarket shouting for Zola to go home.

It was hard not to feel sorry for Zola Budd. Athletics apart, who could blame her for South Africa's apartheid issues?

Ironically in the years ahead Zola did return to her homeland and ran for South Africa in the 1992 Olympics when the international boycott on their athletes had been lifted.

Another South African story of world interest broke in 1987 when the Mail on Sunday signed an exclusive deal with the family of forty-eight-year-old Pat Arnold who was to become the first ever surrogate grandmother to give birth to her own daughter's triplets. Daughter Karen and her husband, who already had a son, were told that they could not have any more children.

Everything was staged managed, even the day and time of the birth. I flew out a camera crew along with a producer to South Africa to film the event by caesarean section which provided the world with its first vitro triplets named David, Jose and Paula. A surrogate grandmother giving birth to her own grandchildren was indeed a world scoop for the Mail on Sunday.

Back in London, we edited the film at Solo and I placed it with ITV to be screened on a peak time viewing slot and a book was to follow.

I was inspired to create two new subsidiaries, Solo Films and Solo Books, and we explored many different avenues. Finding the right vehicle for the television and film world, and raising the necessary budgets, was always going to be a mountain to climb. But Solo Books was the more immediate option. We published the memoirs of holiday camp king Sir Fred Pontin, and then forged ahead on a colourful souvenir book marking the golden wedding of the Queen and Prince Philip boxed with a video showing film clips charting their marriage which was provided by our partners at Pathe News. The Daily Mail commissioned us to publish authorised biographies of Fleet Street giants Sir John Junor former editor of the Sunday Express and Patrick Jackson better known to readers as 'Jak' one of the industry's finest cartoonists. By then, we had surrounded ourselves with layout designers and a team of sub-editors. Distribution deals were signed and we were making fresh impetus in the market.

Syndication, however, remained our main thrust with features and pictures being moved around the world night and day.

I was on holiday in the South of France with my family when I got a call from Bob Edwards the celebrated editor of the Sunday Mirror. Robert Maxwell, new owner of the entire Daily Mirror group, wanted to see me — immediately.

"Can you fly back to London later today?" Bob asked me. "When Maxwell wants to see someone he cannot wait."

I asked Bob what was the cause? Bob told me that it could only be about syndication but he had not been fully briefed. He had only been instructed to find me.

For once I put my family first and told Bob that I would be back in London within the week. "Alright Don," agreed Bob "I understand. I will try and stall him."

Arriving home, I received a note from Edwards telling me that the meeting was arranged for midday two days later at the Mirror's offices in Holborn Circus. Entering the building once more was like going home, having once worked there for some fourteen years.

But sentiment vanished when I came face to face with Maxwell. Maxwell had his own private lift but visitors were obliged to take the general staff lift up to his floor.

Stepping out of the lift, I found myself in a busy reception area which was already crowded with a throng of visitors all waiting for their audience with Maxwell. One of the receptionists gave me a cup of coffee and sat me down where I waited patiently to be summoned into the great man's kingdom situated in a vast office along the corridor. I waited for two hours before my name was called out in a manner that one might have likened to being a patient in a hospital waiting room.

Finally, I was ushered into his lavishly furnished suite. I saw a huge man sitting behind a huge polished desk. He bellowed: "Mr Short. I want you to take over our syndication. When can you start?" There was no handshake. No details discussed. He practically waved me away as though an agreement had been reached.

"I will get the lawyers to get a contract to you" he thundered. End of meeting. I could only think of Maxwell as a megalomaniac, but I believed I could manage his syndication if we could come to terms. I would wait for the contract to arrive.

I discussed the Maxwell approach with Sir David English to ensure that he would not view such a deal as a conflict of interest. But he was not concerned that our relationship would be compromised. He told me to take it.

Three days later I was having lunch at the Trattoria Terrazza in Soho, one of my favourite restaurants, when the manager came over saying I had an urgent call. I picked up the receiver and could not fail to recognise the stentorian voice. It was Maxwell.

"I want to see you right now!" screamed Maxwell down the phone.

"But I am just in the middle of lunch," I blustered.

"I'm sorry. But I want you here. Now!"

I apologised to my dining companion, my friend and publishing director Roger Houghton, leaving him to finish his meal alone and caught a cab straight back to Holborn Circus. Once more, I found myself in the reception area, again crowded with visitors and again Maxwell, having wanted to see me "immediately," kept me waiting for yet another hour.

I tried not to show my impatience when I was eventually ushered into his chamber.

"Ah," Maxwell greeted me, shuffling a wad of papers on his desk "Mr. Short, I am sorry. I have changed my mind. My son Kevin is going to take over the syndication department. So I do not need your services. Goodbye."

That was it. Fired before I had started! It was hard not to feel a little vexed. I had quit lunch on his command when he could easily have told me on his phone call that he no longer wanted to proceed with the syndication proposal.

Precious time wasted at the whim of a proprietor. He eventually overstretched his ego and resources. His life ended in tragedy when he fell from his yacht at sea.

The Daily Express newspaper group also called me to review their syndication arrangements, with the aim of Solo absorbing their operation, but we could not agree on terms. In many ways I was relieved as it would have meant taking on more staff.

Besides the Daily Mail was moving lock, stock and barrel to their new headquarters in Kensington and I had to find some suitable offices in close proximity. We viewed several locations before settling for a sufficiently quiet floor above Kensington market.

The operation continued uninterrupted and although we missed the atmosphere and magic of Fleet Street it was evident that all the major national newspapers were relocating into new territories. Fleet Street was never going to be the same.

We found Kensington an acceptable substitute and one of the Street's clubs Scribes moved across in close proximity to us, so we had not lost contact with a lot of our old friends.

Going Solo

I forged a deal with the Guinness Book of Records and created the internationally acclaimed Factfile strip cartoon adapted from the main book title. Artist Dick Millington drew fresh strips each day of remarkable record feats tabulated by Guinness and Factfile was published in the Daily Mail along with several other favourite strips including Fred Basset.

Strip cartoons were hot properties in syndication and Fred Basset was one of the most published strip cartoons in the world. I flew to America, Australia, South Africa and other countries to renew Fred Basset contracts with editors and of course our new Guinness Book of Records Factfile.

In the Autumn of 1997, it was again time to visit the Frankfurt Book Fair and I woke in my hotel room one morning to find a note that had been slipped under my door. It was from an American newspaper group executive who was anxious to meet me for breakfast. Would I be receptive to a takeover deal? His note asked. I met Kerry Slagle the following day. He was from South Carolina but headed a large corporate syndication service. He suggested that at sixty-seven years of age I must be considering retirement.

One year later, the Daily Mail hosted my farewell retirement party at Simpson's in the Strand. The merger had gone through.

1st January 1999 was a lonely day. My first day of retirement. A day of past memories rushed through my mind. A day of silent phones and bereft of office gossip. Of camaraderie lost.

My devoted and wonderful wife Wendy said I was insufferable for the first six months of being at home and I had to readjust my life, which gradually and happily I managed to achieve. But it was not easy.

Whenever I was invited back to lunch in town to meet with former colleagues now running the company I created, I felt awkward as stories of past times seemed repetitive and frayed.

They were naturally enthused by new deals, projects and fresh enterprises, in which I could not share. But I felt more than happy for them.

My own deal was over.

As I once wrote for Norah Docker. "The party's over. Bring on the next one."

Acknowledgements

My thanks to Jayne Fincher for sourcing pictures taken by her late father, my friend and acclaimed photographer Terry Fincher, who shared in so many assignments with me, and lasting gratitude to my dear departed Daily Mirror secretary Patsy Justice who kept scrapbooks of my cuttings without which these memoirs would probably have never been written. Finally, thanks to my Solo staff who assisted me in creating one of the world's leading syndication and editorial agencies.